Justice, Humanity, and
Social Toleration

Justice, Humanity, and Social Toleration

Xunwu Chen

LEXINGTON BOOKS

A division of
ROWMAN & LITTLEFIELD PUBLISHERS, INC.
Lanham • Boulder • New York • Toronto • Plymouth, UK

LEXINGTON BOOKS

A division of Rowman & Littlefield Publishers, Inc.
A wholly owned subsidiary of The Rowman & Littlefield Publishing Group, Inc.
4501 Forbes Boulevard, Suite 200
Lanham, MD 20706

Estover Road
Plymouth PL6 7PY
United Kingdom

British Library Cataloguing in Publication Information Available

Library of Congress Cataloging-in-Publication Data

Chen, Xunwu.
  Justice, humanity, and social toleration / Xunwu Chen.
    p. cm.
  Includes bibliographical references and index.
  ISBN-13: 978-0-7391-2243-3 (cloth : alk. paper)
  ISBN-10: 0-7391-2243-6 (cloth : alk. paper)
  ISBN-13: 978-0-7391-2244-0 (pbk. : alk. paper)
  ISBN-10: 0-7391-2244-4 (pbk. : alk. paper)
  1. Justice. 2. Humanity. 3. Toleration. 4. Interpersonal relations. I. Title.
  JC578.C468 2007
  303.3'72—dc22   2007028978

Printed in the United States of America

⊗ ™ The paper used in this publication meets the minimum requirements of
American National Standard for Information Sciences—Permanence of Paper for
Printed Library Materials, ANSI/NISO Z39.48–1992.

~

Contents

1   Justice: The Sum of All Moral Duty   1

2   Justice: East Meets West   21

3   Justice: Humankind's Duty and Path   49

4   Social Toleration: The Spirit of Justice in Our Time   93

5   Democracy: The Vehicle of Justice in Our Time   131

6   Justice: The Crowning Glory of Virtues   165

    Index   179

    About the Author   183

CHAPTER 1

~

Justice: The Sum of All Moral Duty

Ours is an age full of contradiction, asymmetry, and paradox. Perhaps never before in history has justice been so much a problem to humankind. Chasing after the fantasy of economic might and political powers, indulging in the world of desires and self-will, and enslaved in the iron cage of science and technology, humankind is heading for a divorce from justice. Falsity becomes "truth," and truth is buried by falsity. The real becomes unreal, and the fantastic becomes "real." Virtues become vices, and vices are considered virtues. The distinction between good and evil vanishes, but that between the powerful and the powerless becomes conspicuous and astounding. As a result, the world in which we live is "begot of nothing but vain fantasy, which is as thin of substance as the air, and more inconstant than the wind."[1] It becomes more and more "devoid of color, life, art, [and] humanity."[2]

Despite its rosy hues, ours is still a wrong-filled, absurdity-filled, and evil-filled world. Human love and compassion are brutally trashed by sadistic and bestial cruelty. Dreams of progress and a better life for a greater number of people in the world encounter the deplorable human self-destruction. Aspirations for liberty and autonomy retreat before occupation and domination. Calls for democracy and human rights are answered by the interests of the strong, hegemony, and imperialism. Globalization advances side by side with global exploitation. Barbaric terrorism is given the euphemism of "holy war" or "martyrdom." Justice, humankind's deeply wounded love, is bleeding and suffering.

1

The Nazi concentration camps and the Japanese "rape of Nanjing" are only a few decades behind us, and 9/11 and the genocides in Rwanda, Kosovo, Bosnia, and East Timor occur right under our noses, not to mention the glaring injustice and inhumanity in Darfur and the ongoing human destruction in the Middle East and elsewhere on Earth. "Why are times so dark, men know each other not at all?" asked the late medieval French poet Eustache Deschamps in the fourteenth century.[3] Should we not ask the same question today? In his *History of the Present*, Timothy Garton Ash observes, "Europe at the end of the twentieth century is quite as capable of barbarism as it was in the Holocaust of mid-century."[4] Away from the bosom of justice, "humanity" becomes a lost consciousness, struggling and agonizing. Without humanity, "justice" is a ghost of poverty, pale and dull.

Today, more than any other time, humankind needs justice—its beauty, its penetration, its truth, its wisdom, its healing power, its rational force, and its enlightenment. Today, more than ever before, we should recall a motto of the Holy Roman emperor Ferdinand I (1503–1564), "Fiat justitia, et pereat mundus" (Let justice be done, though the world perish).[5] Today, as at any other time, humankind must recover a sense of the duty of justice that is not a theatrical appearance or a mere costume to be put on and then discarded at will, but the permanent obligation of humankind and the principle of bond and hope of humankind. Today, as never before, humankind must emphasize the concept that justice is the sum of all duty for humankind. Today, no less than any other time, humankind must remind itself of these words of Edmund Burke: "Justice itself is the great standing policy of civil society; and any eminent departure from it, under any circumstances, lies under the suspicion of being no policy at all."[6]

What, then, is justice? What is the Zeitgeist (spirit of the time) of justice in our time? Ought we to demand justice be the first public duty and obligation of our basic social institutions? Is there such a thing as global justice? What is the relationship between justice and truth? What are the relationships between justice and those contemporary social values such as democracy, social toleration, and so on? Georg W. Hegel said that to philosophize is to think things over. We should think over various problems pertaining to human justice today, honoring the Socratic maxim to live an examined life and being philosophers in life.

Problems of Justice Are Human Problems

"It is because of justice that man is a god to man and not a wolf," said Francis Bacon in 1623.[7] Indeed, as Daniel Webster said in his speech at the funeral of

Supreme Court justice Joseph Story on September 12, 1845, "Justice is . . . the ligament which holds civilized beings and civilized nations together."[8] Justice is what Cicero called "the crowning glory of the virtues," or as a Latin proverb says, "Justitia virtutum regina" (Justice is the queen of virtues).[9] It is for humankind that justice is the sum of all moral duty. And unless humankind is just, there can be no true justice. In his characteristic style, Immanuel Kant said, "Out of the crooked timber of humanity no straight thing can ever be made."[10]

Today we often discuss justice as though humanity as a quality and humankind as a species were only of secondary or incidental importance to it. We entertain the seductive but false belief that we can have justice from the perspective of the universe, not merely human justice; that we can understand justice apart from our human perspective. Our wrong understanding of universal justice, objective justice, and natural justice becomes our Pandora's box. Not surprisingly, some asymmetries appear. The literature of justice thrives, but the calls for replacement of an ethics of justice by an ethics of care are also intensified. A terrible irony! The sleep of justice produces monsters. Simultaneously, there arises a dissonant contention: the dream of "justice" produces monsters, too. A serious paradox! Times and again, "justice" seems to turn from humankind's ideal lover into humanity's bitter foe. A heartbroken absurdity! We passionately condemn those crimes against humanity and gross violations of human rights around the globe, yet simultaneously we are misapprehending that the concept of global justice is a meaningful one. An obvious contradiction!

We must return to one simple, but often forgotten, truth: justice is exclusively of humankind and for humankind. The ideal of justice is exclusively, and will remain exclusively, a human ideal. Problems of justice are exclusively human problems, and will remain so. The standards of justice are established by humankind and applicable only to human institutions and human beings themselves. Besides God, human beings are the only beings in the universe for whom justice becomes an issue. Besides God, human beings are the only ones that ask questions about justice and search for it consciously. Other nonhuman species do not, and cannot do so. Besides God, only human beings understand, and can understand, justice. Nonhuman animals cannot, nor can stones, trees, mountains, rivers, or any lifeless beings.

Noticeably, human beings can understand justice only from the human perspective, not from any other perspectives, for example, not from the perspective of the universe, or of God, or of other nonhuman animals. Even when human beings raise questions about possible justice for other living species, such questions are still human questions. Human beings ask such questions only from a human perspective and only to human beings.

It is tempting, but unjustified, for us to speak of justice from the perspective of the universe. We are in no epistemic position to speak of such a kind of justice. We can speak only of justice from the human perspective. When we associate our perspective of justice with "the perspective of the universe" or "the perspective of God," these other perspectives that we speak of are only as we understand them—that is, from our human perspective—and the association that we make is essentially an association from our human perspective. While we do not need to exalt human solidarity over objectivity and universality, we must exalt the human perspective above the view from nowhere.

The term *universal* connotes universality to all human beings. We can still subscribe to realism and ground our concept of justice in our concepts of the cosmic order and natural laws. However, to make reference to the universe is one thing, while to speak as the voice and speaker of the universe is quite another. We should not enter into the impasse of a form of realism that claims justice to be a principle that is independent of and not mediated by human understanding. Paradigms of justice "must be within the human horizon. If they are not, then they are outside the human sphere."[11]

We should distinguish between justice in the universe (from our human perspective) and justice from the perspective of the universe. We can talk about justice in the universe, and in understanding justice, we also can make reference to the laws of nature from our human perspective. Still, to speak of justice of the universe from the perspective of the universe is another thing altogether. To define justice from our human perspective with reference to natural laws is one thing; to speak of justice per se from the perspective of the universe is quite another. There may be justice from the perspective of the universe. However, we are in no epistemic position to be the speaker of such a kind of justice. Whatever voice of universal justice we listen to, it is a human voice. Justice has truth and is grounded in truth, no question about that. However, the truths in which justice is grounded are mediated by human understanding.

Besides God, human beings are the only agents of justice. We cannot expect nonhuman animals, or stones or rivers or mountains, to be agents of justice. Justice is a norm exclusively for humankind, not for nonhuman beings. We cannot expect dogs, pigs, or trees to practice justice. While justice is the duty of basic human institutions, we are in no epistemic position to claim that it is the basic duty of any institutions of other beings. Moreover, human institutions, human practices, and human beings are the only possible objects of consideration of justice. Justice defines a human way of human existence, and this is a way for humankind only. Conversely, only the way of humankind can be judged to be just or unjust and is thus the object of consideration of justice. Nonhuman beings and their institutions, if they exist, cannot be the objects of concern of justice. This is true even of nonhuman beings or events that do great harm to humankind. For example, it makes no sense to call a tiger that bites its human trainer's hand unjust. Neither should we call a destructive hurricane unjust. Nor, if we were to discover some government in a group of wolves, would it make sense to talk about whether such a government is just or unjust.

Historically, the question of justice arose in the context of the making of humanity. For example, in the biblical tradition, the question of justice is part of the quest for cultivating humanity after the image of God and for standards of human conduct acceptable to God. In Islamic tradition, the question of justice is part of the quest for making human beings into believers of God and making them live up to God's standards. In the Confucian and Taoist traditions, the question of justice is about the standard both of humankind and of human government. In ancient Greek philosophy, questions of justice were about how humankind ought to exist. Morally, the questions of justice encompass the human questions of the way, *telo*, standards, and aspiration in existence and involve questions about the truth, good, and virtue of humankind and what a human world ought to be. They are part of the human question of the distinction between good and evil, right and wrong, humanity and bestiality.

It is also surprising that today we often speak of justice as though what we owe to each other as human beings and our human bonds were of only marginal or secondary importance. As a result, we often turn justice into the alienator of humankind, instead of seeing it as the ligament that holds together the human family. An absurd self-contradiction! Nevertheless, justice is the first public duty and obligation of humankind to humankind by virtue of the bonds in the family of humanity.

The duty of justice is a rise in humankind's particular obligation to humankind. Without a concept of our obligation to each other as human beings, any concept of justice would be inadequate and implausible. For example, without an understanding of our particular obligation to each other as human beings, the concept of justice in terms of John Stuart Mill's no-harm principle is implausible. And if justice implicates the no-harm principle, we must justify why harming other human beings or fellow citizens without cause is morally wrong and unacceptable. Furthermore, without a concept of our public obligation to each other, we cannot determine the scope of the requirements of justice in given contexts. For example, without such a concept, we cannot determine the scope of social toleration as a norm of justice in our times.

Correspondingly, only with a concept of our obligation to each other in the family of humanity does the concept of global justice become defensible and have compulsory force. This amounts to saying that we cannot defend a concept of global justice without some kind of cosmopolitan outlook. Today, when we are repelled by the genocides in Rwanda and Darfur, is there not a voice deep inside us that cries, "This is bestiality, and what we consider to be unspeakably sacred is being grossly violated"? When we condemn the Nazi concentration camps, is there not such a voice inside?

It is further surprising that today we often discuss justice as though the issue of what kind of person we ought to be were irrelevant. But justice would not be an issue to us as human beings if we did not care about what kind of persons we want to be. If there were no difference between being pigs and being men and women, why should we bother ourselves with the question of justice? Christine M. Korsgaard says profoundly, "Obligation makes us human."[12] Confucius and Mencius insisted that righteousness is an indispensable part of the substance of a human being in the full sense.

By and large, the duty of justice is as much a duty of moral virtue as it is of jurisprudence, as Kant would say. Being just is necessary for us to be what we ought to be. Conversely, that justice is a duty of moral virtue underscores the fact that the problems of justice are human problems. A pig has no duty to be just, because it has no duty of virtue. But human beings have such a duty. It makes no sense to talk about the moral virtues of nonhuman beings. The concept of morality is applicable only to humans.

Our practical interests may be incentives for us to abide by laws and do the right things in daily life. However, if our practical interests were all that mattered, there would always be other alternatives that were more effective than serving justice, as far as the pursuit of our practical interests was concerned. Justice matters to us not because we will be better off by serving justice than by practicing injustice, but because we want to be human beings, not pigs, not wolves. It is because we want to be loyal to our human identity, or, as Korsgaard indicates, we are so constituted to be normative.

In sum, the concern of justice is the concern of humanity, by humanity, and about humanity. The objects of concern of justice are human beings and their social institutions. The focus of justice is on human beings and human affairs. The problems of justice are human problems. The scope of justice is not beyond human activities. Our perspective of justice is a human perspective within the human horizon.

Understanding Justice: All Too Human

We have a view of justice only within the human horizon, and that horizon is built with the contributions of human cultures and theoretical constructions.

What Do Cultures Contribute?

That human beings have obligations, including the obligation to serve justice, is a striking fact. However, that obligations are human cultural artifacts is no small wonder. Obligations have a stable, coherent nature and structure; no question of that. Notwithstanding this, obligations, including our obligation to serve justice, are developed by humans. There should be a metaphysics of justice, but the metaphysics of justice is developed by humankind.

Friedrich Nietzsche nicely dubbed the human capacity to impose norms and obligations on human existences and institutions as humankind's "artistic cruelty." He said:

> Beware of thinking lightly of this phenomenon [the bad conscience], by reason of its initial painful ugliness. At bottom it is the same active force which is at work on a grandiose scale in those potent artists and organizers, and builds states. . . . Only the material, on which this force with all its constructive and tyrannous nature is let loose, is here man himself, his whole ancient animal self. . . . This secret self-tyranny, this cruelty of the artist, this delight in giving a form to one's self as a piece of difficult, refractory, and suffering material, in burning in a will . . . this wholly active bad conscience has finally (as one anticipates)—true fountainhead as it is of idealism and imagination—produced an abundance of novel and amazing beauty and affirmation.[13]

While obligation makes us human, it is our artistic cruelty—the ability to impose norms and structures on human existences—that brings home moral obligations for humankind through human cultures.[14] The duty of justice is not, and cannot be, created arbitrarily. Nonetheless, it is neither Albert Einstein's "closed watch" nor Isaac Newton's apple falling from above. Instead, it is the work of humankind's Leonian creativity and Aquarian vision and rationality in cultures.

There may be some independent, universal entity such as the Platonic form of justice. Nonetheless, our concept of justice is not a simple mirror or duplication of such a Platonic form. Though our concept may make reference to the universe, it is historically, culturally developed. It is a concept in which certain fundamental insights are defined and redefined historically and culturally as well as cross-culturally. A universal concept of justice exists because humankind has universally shared its insight into justice through collectively reflecting and examining the various cultural, historical experiences.

We must redefine *universality* here. Instead of conceiving it as transcending and remaining separate from space and time, we should define *universality* as existing and participating in all space and all times. In this light, universality and cultural immanence are not antithetical. The universal is immanent in the cultural. In order to understand the universal, we must understand its different cultural embodiments.

Different languages articulate the idea of justice differently. For example, in Greek, the word for *justice* connotes goodness. In English, *justice* is tantamount to reward and penalty as deserved. In French, it means acknowledgment and respect for the rights and dignity of every human being. In Latin and German, the words for *justice* connote lawfulness. In Chinese, *zhengyi* (正义) suggests setting righteousness to stand straight. It also signifies authentic truth and justified principle. In Arabic, the word is *adalah*, which means "balance."

Different linguistic articulations create diverse conceptual realities, meanings, temperaments, and obligatory forces of justice. For example, a conceptual reality of justice unfolds around individual rights in French and a different one around what is righteous in Chinese. The French word *justice* brings to mind the ideas of rights, liberty, and human dignity, while the Chinese *zhengyi* hammers home the ideas of fairness, reason, and standing straight (as standard). Also for example, in the Chinese language, idioms such as *yi bu rong ci* (义不容辞 "righteousness mandates one's service to it—righteousness") emphasize that the duty to justice—or the obligation to serve justice—is unconditionally mandated. In comparison, when in Greek and Latin, justice is called the "queen of virtues" or "crown of virtues," the obligatory force of the concept of justice is somehow different, though equal in dignity and power.

Different intellectual traditions diversify the ways of conceptualizing the general idea of justice and the substantial families of justice, grounding justice in different world outlooks. For example, the idea of justice with a cosmopolitan outlook differs from one with a political outlook. The different laws and governments of various human societies impart variety to the institutionalization of justice in their various cultures. In turn, diverse institutionalizations of justice produce diverse experiences and substantive understandings of justice.

In general, cultures contribute at least seven variances to justice:

1. perspective variance
2. meaning variance
3. value variance

4. obligatory force variance
5. historical temperament variance
6. rationality variance
7. horizon variance

Such cultural contributions are not properly appreciated.

The Value of Theoretical Construction
Metaphysics, metatheory, and theory have had bad press in philosophy and are the "usual suspects" to many philosophers today. Marginalization of the role of theoretical construction, especially metaphysical construction, in our understanding of justice becomes more and more a standard practice. Many philosophers discuss the understanding of justice as though it has to do only with cultures, not with theoretical construction. Under the pressure of the postmodern season, those philosophers who develop theories of justice today often rush to characterize their theories as "post-metaphysical" in order to profess their "innocence." However, without theoretical construction, our understanding of justice will be without an indispensable horizon and its ability to strive for the universal. In addition, without theoretical construction, we cannot answer the normative question about justice.

For some philosophers today, a necessary antagonism exists between theoretical construction and a historical approach today. However, a simple truth is that theoretical construction often draws heavily from historical understandings. Thus, for example, the Socratic theoretical construction of justice in an ideal republic does not lack reference to Greek cultural and historical experiences. As Richard Rorty rightly points out, John Rawls's theory of justice draws heavily from the American experience of more than two hundred years. Jürgen Habermas's critical theory of justice is embedded in the modern and contemporary German experience.

Conversely, historical approaches to justice cannot be without constructed theory. On the contrary, they all occur under specific theoretical horizons. For example, there could be no American historical approaches to justice without those Western philosophical theories, including natural right theory, liberalism, Platonic theory, Aristotelian theory, Kantian theory, and so on.

Noticeably, theoretical construction generally starts from some historical reflection. For example, Newtonian physics started from Newton's reflection on the event of an apple falling. Theoretical construction is generally stimulated by historical references and can be a synthetic reflection of historical experiences. From the epistemic point of view, universal principles of justice can be developed theoretically through generalizing the particular, historical experiences and references or through comparative studies of them.

Epistemically speaking, theoretical construction is the human way to ascend to a higher understanding and to reach a deeper understanding beyond historical references and experiences. Abstraction, conceptualization, and categorization constitute the crucial mediation through which we arrive at the universal and appreciate better and deeper the essence and substance of things. On this point, Hegel is profoundly right in pointing out that concepts bring us to a deeper level of the reality of things. Theoretical construction proffers to us a theoretical horizon and a set of analytical tools necessary for rational social and political criticism and a source of improvements of existing, historical justice. In Plato's *Republic*, Socrates was asked what the value of constructing an ideal republic in words was; he answered that such an ideal republic would serve as a reference by which we could see the defects of existing republics and know what was to be criticized and improved.

Furthermore, the normative question about the duty of justice is always a question of rationality, reason, and justification. Admittedly, cultural experiences, histories, and practices reveal insights into rationality, reason and justification of the duty of justice. However, without theoretical construction, cultural rationalities, reasons, and justification from experiences, histories, and practices remain fragmentary, incoherent, and merely particular to the circumstances. It is theoretical construction that provides the kind of synthesis, coherence, and unity of these cultural rationalities, reasons, and justifications. It is theoretical construction that lifts cultural rationality and reasons above the particular and local and connects them with the universal and transcendental.

Some philosophers argue that, in the absence of a disembodied, independent universal reason, any theoretical construction is, and can only be, constituted within a specific tradition; at the end of the day, the horizon that any theoretical construction provides is always that of a tradition within which the theoretical construction is made. Despite its attraction, this argument cannot stand. Human reason is embodied. Simultaneously, human reason can, and does, operate as a critical force that is both immanent and transcendent. That human reason is embodied in cultural rationalities and traditions is compatible with the fact that human reason can be and is simultaneously tradition transcending—that is, there can be intersubjectivity among particular traditions.

It is believed that theoretical construction alienates us from the truth that we encounter in the immediate experience and also dissects the truth. The belief is false. Fundamentally, instead of alienating us from truth, theoretical construction of perceptive understandings is necessary to synthesize these understandings. Admittedly, in theoretical construction, some concrete perceptions connecting us with the immediate experiences may give way to metaphysical reconstruction. But such a movement indicates progress in understanding: we move into a deeper understanding of the substance and essence of a cognitive object. Hegel correctly pointed out that conceptualization brings us into a deeper understanding of the essence and substance of things. As the fruit of the analysis and synthesis of perceptual cognitions, conceptualization brings progress to understanding by discarding the irrelevant and marginal and retaining the substantial and crucial, as well as going from the appearance to the fundamental.

Theoretical construction provides at least the following to our understanding of justice:

- a general world outlook, such as a cosmopolitan outlook or a political world outlook; a general world outlook provides a theoretical horizon
- theoretical analysis and synthesis
- conceptualization and schematization of thoughts
- theoretical justification
- abstraction and generalization
- general articulation of principles, norms, and maxims
- general articulation of standards and rules

Therefore, while engaging cultural traditions of understanding fuses our present horizon of justice with past ones, theoretical construction also integrates our present horizon with the future ones that are, to borrow the words of Victor Hugo, "Utopia today, blood and flesh tomorrow."[15]

Understanding of Justice as a Long River

Since human justice is mediated by human understanding, it follows that a good understanding of justice is a necessary condition for human justice to thrive. Then, how is a good human understanding of justice possible? What are the necessary conditions for us to acquire a good understanding?

Two of those necessary conditions are intellectual tolerance and toleration. Intellectual tolerance is the attitude of bearing with the other voices in the shared intellectual, moral, political, and practical discourses and inquiries. Intellectual toleration is the practice of allowing other voices to speak and including such voices in the shared discussions. Intellectual tolerance itself is a just humanistic attitude in understanding justice: being fair and reasonable to alternative approaches and ways of understanding. Intellectual toleration is a kind of humanistic practice.

Ours is a colorful age of cultural and intellectual diversity. It is a titillating age of wars on concepts, values, paradigms, institutions, and ideologies. In a democratic country or society, there can be various traditions of understanding justice. Around the globe, we encounter different civilizations that have different paradigms of justice. Diversity calls for tolerance and toleration. These, in turn, bring interaction and inclusion of different insights and lead to better understanding. With his characteristic style, Zhuangzi said, "Da zhi xian xian, xiao zhi jian jian" (大知闲闲, 小知间间 Great wisdom is inclusive and all embracing, while petty understanding is exclusive and discriminate), and, "Dao tong wei yi . . . wei da zhe zhi dao tong wei yi" (道通为一 . . . 唯 达者知道通为一 The *dao* synthesizes all into one . . . only he who is truly enlightened knows this truth).[16]

In the end, a good understanding of justice is akin to an endless river that consists of countless small streams. Each stream is expanded when it opens itself to other streams and joins them in a larger tributary. Each tributary is expanded when it joins others in a greater river and eventually joins the ocean. In other words, a good understanding of justice is a historically evolving consciousness in which fundamental ideas are defined and redefined in historical experiences and engagements of humanity.

What Is This Book About?

Brian Barry suggests, "A theory of justice may be characterized by its answers to three questions. First, what is the motive (are the motives) for behaving justly? Second, what is the criterion (are criteria) for a just set of rules? And thirdly, how are answers to the first two questions connected?"[17] The central task and primary focus of this book is to explore a new kind of justice: normative justice. It demonstrates that the principles of human rights, human goods (humanity as the end), and human bonds constitute a distinctive basis in their own right upon which a distinctive family of standards for evaluating basic social institutions ought to be established. It locates our sense of duty and commitment to our human identity as a distinctive source in its own right for our motive for behaving justly.

The book has six chapters, with chapter 1 as the introduction and chapter 6, the conclusion. Chapter 2 discusses the essence of justice, using as its guide the Chinese concept of justice as setting things right and erecting righteousness and truth. Its focus is on recovering the concept of formal justice. Philosophers today focus only on substantive justices such as political justice, legal justice, distributive justice, or corrective justice. Some even claim that we can sensibly talk *only* about substantive justices, not about formal justice.

The labels of *metaphysical realism* and *cognitivism* intimidate even philosophers such as Habermas.

Admittedly, we can easily defend a concept of substantive justice without loading ourselves down with the burden to define what formal justice is and to argue for the metaphysical reality of justice and its internal connection with good and truth. It is no wonder that philosophers like to label their concept of justice as a "political concept." However, doing so undermines significantly the value of justice. It damages the ontological and moral legitimacy of justice as the sum of the duty of humankind. Practicing bad faith on the issue of formal justice deprives us of the ability and possibility to talk about justice in a unified sense. The purpose of those who practice bad faith on this issue is to avoid the task of proving that justice has truth. However, that justice has the profoundest truth and is grounded in truth is something that we cannot afford to lose sight of.

"You must not give false testimony against your neighbor" is one of the most sacred rules of human conduct and may give us a glimpse of the unity of loyalty to justice and loyalty to truth. But the internal connection between justice and truth involves even more than that. Fundamentally, truth is justice's heart and blood, as reason is justice's head and eyes. The Chinese concept of *zhengyi* (正义 justice) drives home the idea that justice is true in essence and the substance that has truth—that it is not a mere contract for social cooperation and an umbrella for practical expedience, but a metaphysical and moral imperative of the duty and obligation of humanity. Unfortunately, the stocks of truth and reason are terribly undervalued in our time. But without truth, there can be no justice. Despite the rosy hues with which they clothe themselves, postmodern approaches to justice that deny the truth of justice are profoundly wrong. Their denials of universal truth in justice destroy the meaning and integrity of justice.

Justice finds no refuge in doubt, let alone falsity. The Chinese concept of *zhengyi* calls attention to this idea. According to *zhengyi*, in justice, truth stands straight, not crooked. Justice takes cultural forms and makes historical claims. It reveals its time spirit in every historical epoch. Amidst that, justice is grounded in universal truth; its substance is righteousness in truth and on truth.

A reasonable political concept of justice must ground itself in truth. Otherwise, its tenets for political practices and basic political institutions cannot be normative maxims, but only expedient rules of action; these tenets would not be the categorical imperatives of a moral "ought," but the hypothetical imperatives of a prudential judgment. Also, a reasonable political concept of justice must recognize the metaphysical unity of the truth of justice. It is not that a unified political concept of justice brings different metaphysical concepts of justice together. It is that a unified metaphysical and moral concept of justice leads different ideological doctrines of justice to a shared political concept of justice.

Chapter 3 is the heart of the book. It demonstrates that, in addition to *distributive justice* and *corrective justice*, there is the third family of justice, which I dub *normative justice*. It shows that the fundamental questions of justice include not only whether it should be the rule of reason or the reign of passion or force but also whether it should be the rule of humanity or the reign of bestiality. This chapter defines normative justice as setting human affairs right in terms of the principles of human rights, human goods (humanity as the end), and human bonds. It states that normative justice is a growth in humankind's commitment and loyalty to its human identity, implicating humankind's particular obligation to humankind. The concept of normative justice unites two concepts that are separated by some contemporary philosophers such as Habermas: justice and solidarity.

Naturally, the concept of normative justice would be pointless if its content, concern, objective, and focus could be included in either of the other two forms of justice. But each of the three families of justice has its own focused concern:

- Distributive justice focuses on fairness in distribution of resources, opportunities, burdens, powers, responsibility, and duty. Its main objects are the process, mechanism, and rules of distribution. It is about the allocation problem.
- Corrective justice focuses on correction of the wrong and rewarding of the right. Its main objects are the process, mechanism, and rules of punishment and reward. It is about the compensation and remedy problem.
- Normative justice focuses on the development of social structures and human associations as the basis of human rights, human goods (humanity as the end), and human bonds. Its objective is to erect humanity as a quality and a standard of regulating human affairs and evaluating social institutions. It is about the association problem.

Normative justice differs also from humanitarian morality. The duty of normative justice is unconditional, while the requirements of humanitarian morality are conditional. The former focuses on giving what is due and doing what is righteous, while the latter focuses on what is needed to release suffering and produce well-being and on doing what is compassionate and benevolent. Humanitarian morality has norms, too, but they do not have the kind of obligatory force that is compulsive in nature. Instead, the force of its norms is attraction and invitation of compassion.

The objects of concern of normative justice are basic social institutions. Nonetheless, normative justice is not identical to political justice. Normative justice is applicable to nonpolitical basic institutions such as marriage, religion, or education. For example, it commands us to erect righteousness in the institution of marriage. It dictates that marriage should be rectified in terms of rights, responsibility, humanity as the end, familial goods, and bonds; if marriage is merely a commercial contract, something is seriously wrong. Also, for example, normative justice dictates that religions must teach good and not preach evil; they must guide people to be good, not turn them into evil beings.

Ontologically, normative justice brings humankind's liberation from the bondage and causality of interests, desires, self-will, and force. It enables humankind to live freely in truth, good, beauty, and the sublime. Cognitively, it liberates humankind from the prison of falsity and unjustified beliefs, arriving at truth, substance, and reality. Morally, it obliges humankind to commit and be loyal to its human identity and to treat humanity as the end. Politically, it stipulates a family of standards of evaluating basic social institutions in terms of humanity. In short, normative justice exalts humanity above causality, falsity, instrumentality, and bestiality. Normative justice implicates a nonprudential "ought" in terms of truth, good, and exercise of the freedom of reason.

Global normative justice, which sets world human affairs in order in terms of human rights, human goods (humanity as the end), and human bonds, commands us to recognize our global obligation beyond distributive justice and corrective justice on the one hand and humanitarian morality on the other. It is the light to illuminate the darkness of our time wherein human beings know each other no more. It tears the masks off religious fascism and terrorism, ideological and cultural imperialism, and global economic and political exploitation and domination.

Chapter 4 explores social tolerance and toleration as the requirements of normative justice in our time. It makes evident that we cannot talk about social justice in a democratic society without emphasizing social tolerance and toleration; meanwhile, we cannot talk about true, stable social tolerance and toleration without emphasizing normative justice as their basis. Justice finds no refuge in doubt and unprincipledness, no question about that. Notwithstanding this, where there is the reign of terror and totalitarianism, there is the reign of injustice.

Admittedly, social tolerance and toleration are difficult. What should be tolerated and what the limits are of tolerance and toleration are not easy to define. As Bernard Williams puts it, toleration and tolerance seem to be at once necessary and impossible. Because they are difficult, social tolerance and toleration are challenging. They challenge us to do the right things for the sake of being right, even if we dislike it. They put our sense of justice, wisdom, and moral strength to the test.

The ideas of social tolerance and toleration would be easy to defend, but pointless, if we apply them only to things that are mutually compatible or have no serious consequences. They become important and our commitment to them will be challenged only when we apply them to that which threatens to cause consequences undesired by us. Social toleration becomes an issue when it is applied to fellow citizens and institutions that threaten to change our way of life and the course of human civilization in a direction we strongly oppose.

Philosophers such as Michael Walzer often talk about social toleration in terms of practical necessity, for example, the necessity for peace in a normal society. However, no practical necessity can force us to be tolerant and to practice toleration, even though they can be reasonable choices in given historical circumstances. Rawls appropriately argues that "[social] toleration is not derived from practical necessities or reasons of state."[18] No practical necessity can be the basis for a form of stable, sustainable social toleration, either. As Walzer notes, in history, different forms of toleration that were based upon practical necessity were notoriously unstable because necessity changed.

Global cultural toleration is a vehicle for global normative justice today. In global affairs, normative justice calls for recognition of the sovereignty and rights of nations and peoples and respect for and toleration of their ways of life. It impels us to recognize that "every human society, every people, indeed every age and civilization, possesses its own unique ideals, standards, way of living and thought and action."[19] Global normative justice calls for modernity and universal respect for human rights, human goods, and human bonds, but it also rejects global imperialism and colonization.

Global normative justice demands that nations and peoples live up to the spirit of our time. Notwithstanding, it indicates that "every nation has its own traditions, its own character, [and] its own face. Every nation has its own center of moral gravity, which differs from that of every other: there and only there its happiness lies."[20] Cultural, especially religious, intolerance is among the major avenues to global injustice and inhumanity. For example, the Al Qaeda terrorist movement today is an evil, criminal movement of cultural intolerance and terrorism. It is a mirror through which the truth that global humanity, peace, and stability call for global tolerance and toleration is reflected today.

Chapter 5 examines democracy as a possible instrument for realizing normative justice in our time. Like social toleration, democracy is difficult. If social toleration is justice's plum blossom standing in the snow, democracy may be justice's rose with thorns. If social toleration is the winter season that tests our endurance, democracy is the summertime trying our rational judgment. If social toleration means that we bear with our neighbors who loudly advocate what we just as passionately oppose, democracy may ask us to work with comrades whose intellectual competence cause us contempt, whose moral dispositions inspire no confidence, whose practical judgments scare us, and whose worldviews may bore us to death.

Nevertheless, democracy is the most desirable form of government and life today. It is a possible good candidate to resist the reigns of terror and totalitarianism in a normal society and state. It is a possible means of protecting rights and liberties, bringing home equality and reciprocity, and building common bridges everywhere. Democracy itself is not an intrinsic value. Like the Hindu god Shiva, it both inspires and threatens, liberates and destroys. It can be a good way to resist terror and totalitarianism, but simultaneously a tool of monstrous terror! It can be humankind's goldmine or its black hole. Never before have the allure and dangers of democracy been stronger than they are today.

Democracy will be valuable only if it is an instrument to realize justice. To do so, democracy must be wise. In history, democracy was the bête noire of many ancient and Enlightenment philosophers, who believed that democracy cannot be just because it cannot be wise; it cannot be wise because it is not ruled by reason, but by desires. All just forms of government are wise, as are all just forms of life. Democracy cannot be an exception. True democracy should be vigilant and rigorous, but also wise.

The book concludes with the statement of normative justice as setting human affairs right in terms of human rights, human goods (humanity as the end), and human bonds. It indicates that normative justice calls for reason, more reason, and always reason; humanity, more humanity, and always humanity; social harmony, more social harmony, and always social harmony. It asserts that the duty of justice is humankind's moral and ontological duty.

Albert Einstein once said:

Creating a new theory is not like destroying an old barn and erecting a skyscraper in its place. It is rather like climbing a mountain, gaining new and wider views, discovering unexpected connections between our starting point and its rich environment. But the point from which we started out still exists and can be seen, although it appears smaller and forms a tiny part of our broad view gained by the mastery of the obstacles on our adventurous way up.[21]

This is, at least, one way of stating the task of this book and the general philosophy of performing the task at hand.

Notes

1. William Shakespeare, *Romeo and Juliet*, in *William Shakespeare: The Complete Works*, the Oxford Shakespeare Edition (New York: Barnes & Noble, 1994), act 1, scene 4, lines 95–100.
2. Isaiah Berlin, *The Crooked Timber of Humanity* (Princeton, NJ: Princeton University Press, 1997), 46.
3. Cited in Eric and Mary Josephson, eds., *Man Alone* (New York: Dell, 1962), 17.
4. Timothy Garton Ash, *History of the Present: Eassys, Sketches and Dispatches from Europe in the 1990s* (London: Allen Lane, 1999), 368; cited in Peter Singer, "How Can We Prevent Crimes against Humanity?" in *Human Rights, Human Wrongs* (New York: Oxford University Press, 2003), 99.
5. H. L. Mencken, ed., *A New Dictionary of Quotations* (New York: Alfred A. Knopf, 1942), 626.
6. Edmund Burke, *Reflections on the French Revolution*, in *Edmund Burke* (New York: P. F. Collier & Son, 1937), 289.
7. Mencken, *New Dictionary of Quotations*, 626.
8. Ibid.
9. Ibid., 626, 627.
10. "Aus so krummem Holze, als woraus der Mensch gemacht ist, kann nichts ganz gerades gezimmert warden." Immanuel Kant, *Gesammelte Schriften* (Berlin: de Gruyter, 1923), vol. 8, p. 23; cited in Berlin, *Crooked Timber of Humanity*, v, xi.
11. Berlin, *Crooked Timber of Humanity*, 11.
12. Christine M. Korsgaard, *The Source of Normativity* (Cambridge: Cambridge University Press, 1996), 5.
13. Friedrich Nietzsche, *The Genealogy of Morals*, in *The Philosophy of Nietzsche* (New York: Random House, 1927), ii.18, 705; also cited in Korsgaard, *The Source of Normativity*, 1.
14. Korsgaard, *The Source of Normativity*, 5.
15. Victor Hugo, *Les Misérables* (New York: Modern Library, 1992), 561.
16. Laozi, *Dao De Jing*, in *Completed Works of Teachers* (*Zhu Zi Ji Cheng* 诸子集成), ed. Chingfan Guo (Beijing: Unity Publishing House, 1996), vol. 3, chap. 2.
17. Brian Barry, *Justice as Impartiality* (Oxford: Oxford University Press, 1995), 46.

18. John Rawls, *A Theory of Justice* (Cambridge, MA: Harvard University Press, 1971), 214.

19. Berlin, *Crooked Timber of Humanity*, 37.

20. Ibid.

21. Gary Zukav, *The Dancing Wu Li Masters* (New York: Bantam Books, 1980), 19.

CHAPTER 2

~

Justice: East Meets West

Let us start with the Socratic question "What is justice?" The question is about formal justice, that is, justice per se. It is about the Heideggeran *Being* of justice. It differs from a question about any substantive forms of justice such as distributive, corrective, economic, political, or global justice. For the most part, philosophers today have avoided the question about formal justice. It is alleged to be unanswerable, or dry and insignificant.

Running away from the question about justice per se is an example of Sartrean bad faith. Asking the question is not scratching where no itch exists, but getting to the root of the problem. To develop a metaphysics of justice is not to practice philosophical mischievousness, but to engage in one of the most important philosophical endeavors.

The question can be, and should be, answered. An answer to it has ontological and moral priority over answers to other questions pertaining to justice, including questions about substantive forms of justice. Admittedly, we cannot empirically verify our answer to the question about formal justice any more than we can hold the moonlight in our hand. However, just as the moonlight is real despite our inability to touch it, the question about justice is real and important even if we cannot empirically verify our answer to it.

To facilitate cross-cultural studies on the subject matter of justice simultaneously, I would like here to use a particular handle to pick up the Socratic question about justice, taking the Chinese concept of justice as the guide.

Justice: Righteousness Standing Straight

The Chinese counterpart of the English word *justice* is *zhengyi* (正义), consisting of two words: *zheng* (正) and *yi* (义). In some cases, *zheng* is an adjective modifying *yi*, and in others, *zheng* itself becomes the noun. For example, there is a Chinese saying: "Zheng xie bu liang li" (正邪不两立 Righteousness and injustice, good and evil, as well as orthodoxy and heresy cannot coexist). In this statement, *zheng*, which refers to *zheng yi* (justice), is a noun.

The word *yi* has two different but interrelated meanings. In one sense, it means "fitness," "righteousness," "propriety," "moral acceptability," and "reasonableness." Confucius said, "At the sign of profit, one must think of *yi* [righteousness]" and "A *junzi* [君子 a noble, authentic person] makes *yi* as his substance."[1] Mencius said: "*Ren* [仁 humanity] is a person's safe abode [home], and *yi* [righteousness], a person's correct path," and, "Chun qiu wu yi zhan" (春秋无义战 In the Spring and Autumn Period of ancient China, there were no righteous wars).[2] In both cases, Mencius spoke of *yi* as righteousness. Xunzi emphasized the dichotomy between *gongyi* (公义 universal righteousness) and *si yu* (私欲 personal desires). *Huai Nan Zi* reads, "Yi zhe, yi ye" (义者, 宜也 Righteousness means fitness); it also says, "A *junzi* thinks of *yi* [righteousness], not *li* [利 profit]. On the contrary, a *xiao ren* [小人 petty person] is greedy in acquiring *li* and does not care about *yi*."[3]

Zhuxi said, "*Yi* means the propriety of things"; "*Yi* means propriety in terms of *tianli* [the universal reason]"; and "*Yi* is the principle of the mind and connotes the propriety of things."[4] The *yi–li* (righteousness vs. personal gain) debate was a central drama of premodern Chinese philosophical discourses. Traditional Chinese moral discourses also vibrated with such vocabularies as *qing yi* (情义 the feeling of bond and sense of rightness), *ren yi* (仁义 fitness in terms of human bond and humanity), *li yi* (礼义 fitness in terms of rites), *xin yi* (信义 fitness in terms of trustworthiness), and others.

In another sense, *yi* means "the profound essence," "substance," "principle," and "truth." According to *Ci Yuan* (词源 *The Origin of Chinese Words*), *justice* is defined as "the justified, right, fair principle and truth."[5] In this sense, for example, we find such book titles as *Zhou Yi Zheng Yi* (周易正义 *The Essentials of the Book of Change*), *Kong Zi Zheng Yi* (孔子正义 *The Essence and Substance of the Teachings of Confucius*), *Meng Zi Zheng Yi* (孟子正义 *The Essence and Substance of the Teachings of Mencius*), *Chun Qiu Zheng Yi* (春秋正义 *The Truth of the Spring-Autumn Period*), *Wu Jing Zheng Yi* (五经正义 *The Essential Teachings of the Five Classics*), and *Shi Ji Zheng Yi* (史记正义 *The Essential Truths in the Records of History*). We also find such terms as *li zhi yi* (礼之义 the essence of rites) and *wen zhi yi* (文之义 the essence of text).

Mencius said, "He who lives on his physical strength to labor is ruled. He who lives on the mind [the rational] rules. . . . This is the *tong yi* [通义 universal truth]."[6] According to Mencius, the rational governs physical strength and passion; wisdom rules and physical strength is ruled. This is the *tong yi*. *Tong* (通) literally means "universal," and *yi* (义) means "truth" or "the essence of things."

Rejecting Zhuxi's view that we should search for the ultimate good through investigating external things, Wang Yangming argued, "Yu shi shi wu wu shang qiu zhi shan, que shi yi wai" (于事事物物上求至善, 却是义外 To search for the ultimate good in external things, we are outside the realm of *yi*, that is, we miss the essence and substance of the ultimate good).[7] Again, *yi* here refers to the profound truth or the essence of things. Thus, according to Wang, when we search for the ultimate good from things external to ourselves, we cannot find the truth. The ultimate good and its essence are within our mind.

The word *zheng* has two different but interrelated meanings, as well. In one sense, it connotes being rectified, justified, and standing straight, as contrasted to the wrong, the crooked, the unjustified, and the unacceptable. Confucius said, "To govern is to *zheng*."[8] That is, the duty of the government is to rectify the affairs of a normal society and set things right. Xunzi said, "Zheng yi er wei wei zhi xing" (正义而为谓之行 Morality is to set righteousness to stand straight).[9] Guanzi said, "Xing zhe, zheng zhi yi ye" (行者, 正之义也 Morality is to make righteousness to stand straight).[10] *Shen Jian* reads, "Zheng zhe, yi zhi yao ye" (正者, 义之要也 *Zheng* is the essence of righteousness).[11]

Dong Zhongshu of the Han dynasty said: "Zheng qi yi, bu bou qi li" (正其宜, 不谋其利 Erecting righteousness, not seeking profit and personal gain). Confucians talk about *zheng ming* (正名 rectifying names), *zheng ren* (正人 rectifying others), and *zheng ji* (正己 rectifying oneself). Chinese intellectual, moral, and political discourses are filled by such metaphors as *gong zheng* (公正 fairness), *zhong zheng* (中正 impartiality), and *zhong zheng* (忠正 loyalty and integrity).

In another sense, *zheng* signifies being authentic, pure, true, original, and legitimate, as contrasted to what is faked, unreal, peripheral, untrue, derivative, superficial, and illegitimate. In this sense, one talks about *zheng tong* (正统 the legitimate, authentic, or original tradition), *zheng zong* (正宗 the original, the authentic, the legitimate, or the pure), *zheng ben* (正本 the original or main copy), and *zheng dao* (正道 the correct path, pure truth).

Zhou Yi (周易 *The Book of Change*) reads: "Wen ming yi jian, zhong zheng er ying, junzi zheng ye" (文明以健, 中正而应, 君子正也 He should establish his personal strength by acquiring the virtue of civility and follow the principle of impartiality in order to be reflective, the way of a *junzi* is *zheng*).[12]

In this statement, the word *zheng* is used in two different senses: first, as the noun of *zhong zheng* (中正), connoting fairness, correctness, and being justified; and second, as an adjective describing a characteristic property of a *junzi*, connoting authenticity and truth.

In *Dao De Jing*, Laozi emphasized the distinctions between the real *dao* and the culturally defined "*dao*"—that is, between true humanity and culturally defined "humanity"—as well as real righteousness and culturally defined "righteousness."[13] For him, the distinctions are between the *zheng zong* (正宗 authentic) and the *fei zheng zong* (非正宗 inauthentic); the culturally established *dao*, humanity, and righteousness are faked, inauthentic, and untrue.

Mencius spoke of "hao ran zheng qi" (浩然正气 vast righteous energy), which he explained as follows:

> This energy is extremely vast and strong. If one nurtures it, not damages it, it will fill the whole universe. This energy is fueled by righteousness and the *dao*; without righteousness and the *dao*, this energy will have no *qi shi* [气势 momentum, powerful manner]. In addition, this energy imbibes the mother milk of righteousness days and nights, not formed by merely one single righteous act.[14]

In short, *zheng qi* (正气), in the Menciusian sense, is the kind of authentic, pure spiritual energy of righteousness.

Talking about *zheng qi* in the same sense, *Huai Nan Zi* declares: "A *junzi* [noble, authentic person] acts with *zheng qi* [the energy of righteousness]. A *xiao ren* [小人 petty person] acts with *xie qi* [邪气 the energy of evil, of wrong]."[15] It further states that *zheng qi* "is internally in harmony with the human nature, externally in harmony with propriety, and moves in accordance with reason."[16] For Confucians and neo-Confucians, a distinction exists between the orthodox and the heretical, as well as between the traditional and the antitraditional or nontraditional. This underscores the Chinese emphasis on the distinction between the authentic and inauthentic and between the legitimate and illegitimate. The orthodox is *zheng* (正 authentic, legitimate), while the heretic is *xie* (邪 crooked, impure, adulterated, and illegitimate).

Thus, in traditional Chinese thoughts, aspirations for *zhengyi* (正义) involve four concerns:

1. Rightness/fitness of things
2. Truth/essence of things
3. Authenticity of things
4. Legitimacy of the existence of things

Correspondingly, there are four distinctive Chinese concepts of *zhengyi* or justice.

In one concept, *zhengyi* means righteousness that stands straight, in contrast with both that which is crooked and cannot stand straight and that which is not righteous but stands out. The substance of justice is righteousness, and its characteristic is standing straight and being rectified. Here, standing straight has a moral connotation: it is the opposite of being crooked; it is fair from all perspectives and can face scrutiny of reason from all perspectives; and finally, what stands straight is a standard of conduct. Thus, *zhengyi* not only names the principles of *gong zheng* (公正 fairness and being straight), *gong ping* (公平 fairness and balance), *zhong zheng* (中正 mean and impartiality), *bu pian bu yi* (不偏不倚 impartiality), *li* (理 reason), and *i* (宜 rightness, fitness) but also implies that these principles stand straight, not crooked, as standards in a normal society.

Speaking of justice in this sense, Confucius said: "A *junzi* thinks of righteousness. A *xiao ren* thinks of profit."[17] In other words, a noble, authentic person sets righteousness to stand straight, but a petty person bends righteousness to advance personal interests. This is why a *junzi* is just and a *xiao ren* unjust. Confucius declared, "Wealth and social ranks that are acquired through an unrighteous (不义 *bu yi*) way are as meaningless as the passing cloud is to me."[18]

Mencius claimed: "He who mutilates humanity is a mutilator. He who cripples righteousness is a crippler. He who is both a mutilator and a crippler is an 'outcast.'"[19] For Mencius, whoever bends humanity and righteousness does not belong to a human community.

Xunzi also said: "We are all born with desires. To satisfy our desires, we pursue things. Because we pursue things without constraint and measurement, social conflicts arise. Conflicts bring chaos. The sage-kings dislike chaos. They therefore establish norms of propriety and righteousness to regulate us."[20] According to Xunzi, the sage-kings of ancient times established the norms of justice in order to prevent human conflicts. Elsewhere, Xunzi explicitly called the upstanding righteousness *zhengyi*.

In the above concept, *zhengyi* is moral righteousness that is in opposition to what is crooked for the sake of desires, power, passions, and practical expedience, bringing home normativity independent of such interests. It is a motivating principle that establishes standards and measurements of conduct.

We can appreciate the concept of *zhengyi* deeply by looking at its opposite, *bu yi* (不义 unrighteousness, absence of righteousness). The concept of *bu yi* encompasses what is wrong, crooked, unacceptable, blameworthy, and forbidden. Xunzi thus said, "Bao li qi yi wei zhi zhi zei" (保利弃义谓之至贼

Giving up righteousness for the sake of self-interest and advantage is an act of a bandit or a scoundrel).[21] That which is *bu yi* is wrong and bad, but not necessarily evil. For example, breaking a promise is *bu yi*, but not evil.

As for social institutions, the antithesis of *zhengyi* (正义 justice) is *fei zheng yi* (非正义 injustice). *Fei zheng yi* is not merely an absence of righteousness, but the presence of serious unrighteousness and evil. For example, some wars are *fei zheng yi* in the sense that they are unjust. At times, *fei zheng yi* and *bu yi* are interchangeable in meaning, but the concept of *bu yi* emphasizes the absence of righteousness, while *fei zheng yi* focuses on the presence of evil and unrighteousness. *Bu yi* connotes wrong in terms of failure to meet established standards of social conducts. *Fei zheng yi* connotes both wrong and evil, a violation of both established norms of social practice and the truths and laws of human history.

In another concept, *zhengyi* means authentic, great, original, unadulterated, or pure righteousness. It names the great, profound righteousness, not some petty, insignificant, or superficial rightness. *Zhengyi* brings out a stock of metaphors, including *daoyi* (道义 righteousness in terms of the *dao* (道), *gongyi* (公义 universal righteousness), *dayi* (大义 great righteousness), and *gongli* (公理 universal reason). Zhuxi thus said, "Social institutions must be . . . fair, impartial, right and moral" (*gong ping zheng da* 公平正大).[22] Also in this sense, one says, "Tie jian dan dao yi" (铁肩担道义 Having an iron shoulder to shoulder righteousness in terms of the *dao*) or "Da yi mie qing" (大义灭亲 Great justice overcomes love and affection).

The concept of *daoyi* brings home the idea of the sublime, inviolable, universal, and supreme righteousness. It ushers in both normativity and sublimity. Confucius urged us "xing yi yu da dao" (行义以达道 to practice righteousness to arrive at the *dao*).[23] One should work to set righteousness standing straight and therefore to bring *dao* to the society.

Xunzi claimed, "Dao yi zhong zhe qing wang gong" (道义重则轻王公 When one cares about righteousness in terms of the *dao*, one will consider social ranks and prestige to be secondary).[24] When one commits oneself to *daoyi*, rank and prestige are no long important in one's eye. Instead, in one's moral consideration, "Gongyi sheng si yu" (公义胜私欲 Universal righteousness overcomes personal desires).[25] Accordingly, one "xing yi yi zheng" (行义以正 practices righteousness and sets things straight) and "gong zheng wu si" (公正无私 being fair, not selfish).[26]

Cheng I said: "The way of a ruler to bring people to him is to treat them with tolerance, to give them a government of humanity, and to be beneficial to them. If he does so, who will not come to him? If a ruler gives only *xiao ren* [小仁 petty kindness], but violates *daoyi* for undeserved fame . . . why should people love him and come to him?"[27] Here, *zhengyi* is *daoyi*. And *daoyi* is not some small kindness, but righteousness that is of great importance. *Zhengyi* is not petty correctness, but the fundamental righteousness standing straight.

When *zhengyi* is understood in the two senses above, it is opposed not only to *bu yi* and *fei zheng yi* but also to *xiewu* (邪恶 crooked evil). *Xie* (邪 crooked, not standing straight) is opposed to *zheng* (正 standing straight) and is wrong, perverting, and satanic; for example, a *xienian* (邪念 a crooked, perverted idea) is an evil idea, well beyond an idea that is *bu yi*. *Wu* (恶) is evil, bad, and totally unacceptable. *Xiewu* is therefore a condition or substance of great evil, something that destroys the integrity, happiness, and welfare of a normal society. *Xiewu* attacks the humanity of a normal society. It perverts the normal human relations in a society and corrupts human consciences. For example, violent crimes such as murder, rape, and various forms of random destruction of life are *xiewu*, rather than *bu yi*.

Speaking of standards of righteousness, Mencius said:

> When one has no moral sensibility and norms of conduct, one will indulge in one's *xie chi* [邪侈 evil desires]. As a result, one will do all sorts of evil. To punish them after they do wrong would be akin to invite them to throw themselves into the net—that is, let them freely be criminals and then catch them.[28]

Here, *xie*, which perverts one's desires and interests, is an abstract substance of evil that brings perversion, illness, corruption, and degradation. Speaking of *xie chi*, Mencius cited as examples those individuals' or rulers' perverted desire for powers and wealth and acts of aggression and transgression in order to gratify individual lusts.

Xunzi also warned us to "fang xie pi er jin zhong zheng" (防邪僻而近中正 avoid crooked evil and be associated with fairness and rightness).[29] For Xunzi, *xie pi* (邪僻) brought perversion, illness, and degradation to a person, a people, and a society.

When *zhengyi* is antithetical to *bu yi*, the dichotomy is between right and wrong, fit and unfit, and acceptable and unacceptable. When *zhengyi* is opposed to *xiewu*, the antithesis is not only between good and evil, but between great good and great evil. Justice is great good. Injustice is great evil. Here, the concept of evil is broader than the concept of injustice, just as the concept of good is broader concept than that of justice. Injustice is a particular kind of evil, a great evil. It not only is evil in terms of being crooked, vicious, and satanic but also produces great perversion and damage. Conversely, justice is a particular kind of good, a great righteousness.

In addition, *zhengyi* is not *xiaoyi* (小义 petty righteousness) and *xiao ren* (小仁 petty kindness). The distinction between great righteousness and petty rightness, as well as that between great humanity and petty kindness, is qualitative, not quantitative. *Xiaoyi* and *xiao ren* are not injustice, but they are not good enough to be counted as just either. An act of *xiao yi xiao ren* (小义小仁) is not necessarily bad, but to call it a just act is to apply the word *justice* to the wrong object. In many cases, the phrase *xiao yi xiao ren* connotes something negative—that is, something the speaker is critical of. There are two kinds of *xiao yi xiao ren* acts:

1. Those in which the good produced is small and the righteousness embodied is insignificant
2. Those in which the actor is not sincere about doing good; therefore the good that the act produces is inadequate to the requirements of the context, and the rightness that it has is too trivial in terms of both the standards of justice and the contexts in which the act occurs

In a further another sense, *zhengyi* connotes the rectified, justified, or verified truth, principle, and substance. Confucius emphasized the importance of *zhengmin* (正名 rectifying names/institutions) to *zhengyi*. *Zhengmin* is crucial to *zhengyi* because it rectifies the substance of institutions, setting each institution to stand for its substance. Whereas *zhengyi* names the rectified principles of institutions, *zhengmin* rectifies the principles. Therefore, as Xunzi said: "*Dao* refers to the principle of government. The mind recognizes the *dao* through correct argumentation, reasoning, and *zhengmin*."[30]

Zhengyi in this sense has both metaphysical and epistemic dimensions. Metaphysically, *zhengyi* is the authentic substance and true essence of a thing to which a justified epistemic claim corresponds. Cognitively, it is the essential insight into the profoundly real. Thus, *zhengyi* brings home the correct teaching. Its opposite is *yi duan xie jiao* (异端邪教 a heretical view and evil teaching). *Yi duan xie jiao* preaches falsity, evil, perverted desires, and cunning.

When *zhengyi* is opposed to *xieyi* (邪异 crookedness, heresy, and abnormality), the dichotomy is between legitimate and illegitimate, true and false, right and wrong. For example, when Mencius was criticized for being too critical and argumentative, he defended himself by saying that, in doing what he did, his purpose was to "*zheng* [set straight] the mind of people, to put *xie shuo* [邪说 evil, crooked teaching] away, to reject wrong conduct and send excessively vulgar talk to exile."[31] The *xie shuo* to which Mencius referred brought perversion, aversion, and subversion to a normal society and social progress.

Shen Jian states, "Xie shuo luan zheng du" (邪说乱正度 The crooked, evil teachings destroy righteous standards and measurements) and "Fang xie shuo, qu yun zhi, yi baijia, chong sheng dian, ze dao yi ding yi" (放邪说, 去

淫智, 抑百家, 崇圣典, 则道义定矣 If we put evil teachings away, abandon perverting "wisdom," constrain hundreds of schools of thinking, and respect the classics of the sage, justice or righteousness of the *dao* can be firmly established).[32] *Xie shuo* here refers to that which brings perversion, aversion, and subversion to a normal society.

Finally, *zhengyi* signifies the great, authentic, original, or pure truth, essence, and substance. To have justice with regard to something is to understand the true, original, and unadulterated essence, substance, and meaning of that thing. That is, *zhengyi* is the true substance and essence of things and the truth and reason of things. *Zhengyi* in this sense emphasizes the universal truth and righteousness, not truth or righteousness as defined culturally and conventionally.

A passage in *Dao De Jing* reads:

When the *Dao* is lost, the doctrine of virtue arises.
When virtue is lost, the doctrine of humanity arises.
When humanity is lost, the doctrine of righteousness arises.
When righteousness is lost, the doctrine of propriety arises.
Propriety is the superficial expression of loyalty and faithfulness,
And the beginning of disorder.[33]

According to Laozi, when the authentic truths of the *dao*, virtue, humanity, and righteousness are lost, conventional doctrines or beliefs of virtue, humanity, righteousness, and propriety thrive. When these authentic truths are lost, the *zhengyi* of the *dao*, virtue, humanity, and righteousness are lost.

The four Chinese concepts of justice above collectively explicate the idea of justice as setting things right and setting righteousness to stand straight. They hammer home the ideas that justice is righteousness standing straight as the standard; that justice is grounded in truth; that justice is the original, authentic, profound, and good substance of things; and that justice brings about the acceptability and legitimacy of social practices, institutions, or a person's conduct. Therefore, we can define the Chinese concept of justice as follows:

Justice is the condition in which the true, authentic, and great righteousness stands straight in social life; it is the propriety or fitness of things that stands straight and embodies the good *par excellence*; it stipulates standards that define what is acceptable and what is unacceptable and by which things are set right.

This definition is of formal, not substantive, justice. It is about the essence of justice per se, the essence that all substantive forms of justice embody.

In the definition above, the qualifier "true, authentic, and great" signifies that:

1. in justice, righteousness is real, not artificial
2. in justice, righteousness is universal and original
3. in justice, righteousness is significant and profound, not petty and trivial

The qualifier indicates that justice is something fundamental. Violation of it threatens to cause fundamental harm to a normal society and public good and to totally betray the universal truth and good.

The qualifier "stands straight" indicates, first, that in justice, righteousness is unadulterated and not crooked, and second, that in justice, righteousness stands as a reasonable and acceptable standard. Justice is not anything that is adulterated, compromised, or bent, even in a slight degree. It is originally authentic, but also stands straight, not bowing to anything. Its sublimity, authority, and sovereignty cannot be transgressed and violated. Its dignity is not secondary to anything. Its posture cannot be anything less than standard. Here, standing straight is not merely standing out.

As a potentiality, what is righteous can stand straight. As an actuality, only righteousness that stands straight is called justice. When righteousness is contradicted, twisted, or compromised, it becomes injustice. Great injustice is *xiewu* (crooked evil). Injustice or *xiewu* is not only a privation of justice but also a perversion of justice. *Xiewu* can stand out, but not straight. Justice not only exalts good above evil and righteousness over unfitness but also standing straight over standing out.

The Chinese concept of justice gives us a clue: Justice means setting things right; it means that righteousness stands straight. In addition, *zhengyi* has both righteousness and the quality of *zheng* (being rectified, standing straight). Therefore, justice is the necessary and sufficient reason to act or to abstain from action; it establishes standards and normativity.

The Voice of Human Reason in Justice

The Chinese concept of justice brings us back to what we, for the most part, lose perspective of in a postmodern season: Justice means the rule of reason. It establishes rational standards of evaluating human conduct and basic social institutions. Justice exalts not only good over evil but also truth over falsity and reason over desire, passion, or practical expedience. Justice rejects the reign of terror. The metaphors of *dao* (道 the way), *li* (理 reason, principle), *gongli* (公

理 public reason, universal reason), *gong dao* (公道 fairness, public way), and *tianli* (天理 the reason of the universe) all convey one enduring idea: the voice of justice is the voice of human reason. To appreciate this, let us take a look at the voice of reason that has so fascinated Chinese philosophers.

Laozi pioneered the Chinese tradition of associating justice with reason. According to him, justice names the human way of government and has the voice of the *dao*, the universal way. He pinpointed the fact that a wise king "yi zheng zhi guo" (以正治国 governs the state with justice);[34] *zheng* (正) refers to *zhengyi* (正义). In addition, governing the state with justice means "yi dao li tian xia" (以道莅天下 to govern the empire by the *dao*).[35] For Laozi, the opposite of governing by justice is governing by desires. This is why a wise king is "qing xin gua yu" (清心寡欲 clear in mind and having few desires). A wise king is level-headed and follows reason only. Laozi put a set of questions to anyone who wants to be a true king: "Can you keep the spirit and embrace the One without departing from them? . . . Can you clean and purify your profound insight so it will be spotless?"[36]

Laozi rejected cultural standards of justice because, for him, cultural standards are not the rational, true, authentic standards of the *dao*. For him, "Shi ren er hou yi" (失仁而后义 When [true] humanity is lost, the doctrine of righteousness arises).[37] The rise of cultural standards signifies the eclipse of the real, rational standards of justice. He emphasized, "ren fa di, di fa tian, tian fa dao, dao fa zi ran" (人法地, 地法天, 天法道, 道法自然 Humankind models its rules after the Earth; Earth, after heaven; heaven, after the *dao*; and the *dao* is natural).[38] So far as justice is concerned, while justice means following the voice of reason, the only true voice of reason is the voice of the *dao*.

Laozi's rejection of cultural standards of justice creates vagueness and indeterminacy of justice. To see this, we can compare his view with Plato's. Both philosophers insisted that justice is essentially rational and reasonable; the precept of justice is a precept of the cosmic order or rationality. But Laozi's *dao* of justice is undefined and indeterminate; Plato's form of justice is a fixed form and determinate.

Reflecting Laozi's problem, Confucius adopted the opposite strategy—defining justice culturally. For Confucius, justice is the way of reason, no question about that. This is why we ought to "xing yi yu da dao" (行义以达道 practice righteousness in order to arrive at the *dao*).[39] However, for him, while justice means setting things right, the standards of justice by which things are set right are developed by human reason in culture, in accordance with the human understanding of the *dao*. Justice establishes a class of standards *par* human reason, and these standards embody the *dao* but are definite and specified. In this context, reason and justice entail each other. Human reason not only establishes the standards of justice in a normal society but also administers interpretation and understanding of the standards of justice.

For example, political justice mandates that a just government must conduct itself by the principles of trust, rightness (independent of practical interests and desires), *zhong* (中 impartiality), and *gong* (公 fairness). That is, while political justice means setting political affairs right in terms of the *dao*, it also obliges a government to follow reason and conduct itself by the rational norms of trust, fairness, and impartiality. Confucius declared:

> When a ruler is prudent in establishing the measurements and standards of the government and careful in establishing good laws and codes and dismisses incompetent ministers, he sets things right. . . . A ruler will enjoy public support if he is tolerant. A ruler will enjoy public trust if he is trustworthy. A ruler will enjoy success if he is wise. A ruler will make his people happy if he is fair.[40]

That is, for Confucius, the four rational principles of guardianship are tolerance, trustworthiness, wisdom, and fairness. When a ruler governs an empire by these four principles, the ruler follows the *dao* and righteousness stands straight.

Mencius traced the origin of human justice to the rational human nature, associating justice with moral rationality. He asked: "Xin zhi shuo tong ran zhe he ye? Wei li ye yi ye. . . . Gu li yi zhi yue wo xin, you chu huan zhi yue wo kou" (心之所同然者何也? 谓理也义也. . . . 故理义之悦我心, 犹刍豢之悦我口 What is common of all human minds? It is reason. It is righteousness. . . . Reason and righteousness please our mind as meats please our palate).[41] For Mencius, not only is our sensibility of justice inherent in our rational human nature, but reason and justice are also inseparable. That is, justice entails reason, and reason leads to justice; reason claims justice and justice is a principle of reason. Noteworthy in Mencius's statement above is that he explicitly used the concept of *li* (理 reason, principle), associating it with justice. Elsewhere, Mencius argued: "Bu yi gui ju, bu neng cheng fang yua. . . . Bu yi liu lü, bun neng zheng wu yin" (不以规矩, 不能成方圆. . . . 不以六律, 不能正五音 Without rules, one cannot draw square and circle. . . . Without the six rules [of music], one cannot set the five tunes right).[42] Therefore, justice presupposes the rule of reason.

Xunzi also insisted that justice is characteristically reasonable and rational; this is why justice has the transforming force vis-à-vis humankind. Xunzi argued that the original human nature is evil, chaotic, and irrational, needing to be transformed into good and rational. For him, the purpose of justice is to transform humankind rationally, and the force of justice is its ability to do so. In his words: "The human nature is bad. . . . Therefore, there is the need for civilizing influences of teachers and laws and guidance of propriety and righteousness."[43]

For Xunzi, justice rationalizes and civilizes humankind; justice means the rule of reason: "Cheng xin xing yi ze li, li ze min, min ze tung yi" (诚心行义则理, 理则明, 明则能变矣 If we practice righteousness sincerely, we become reasonable; becoming reasonable, we become enlightened; becoming enlightened, we transform ourselves).[44] In other words, when we follow righteousness, we follow reason, and in doing so, we transform ourselves for the better. Xunzi thus claimed, "Yi, li ye, gu xing" (义, 理也, 故行 Righteousness is reason; this is why it is the rule of morality).[45]

The book *Guanzi* reads:

> Righteousness is the fitness of everything in everywhere. Ritual propriety is fitness in terms of human feeling and the truth of righteousness. Reason is that which defines righteousness and stipulates ritual propriety. In short, while ritual propriety comes from righteousness, righteousness comes from reason, and reason defines fitness.[46]

Like Xunzi, Guanzi emphasized the importance of social institutions to a society. Equally crucial, like Xunzi, Guanzi insisted that righteousness and reason bring about each another; righteousness means the rule of reason.

Huai Nan Zi reads, "Yi zhe, xun li er xing yi ye" (义者, 循理而行宜也 Righteousness means acting with fitness in accordance with reason [principle] in social life).[47] In other words, righteousness is propriety *par* reason in action. *Huai Nan Zi* further states, "Yi yi xing li, ming lie er bu zhui" (以义行理, 名立而不坠 If we follow reason and practice righteousness, we can establish ourselves in social life without falling).[48] Elsewhere, it explicitly speaks of justice as *li* (理 reason, principle), indicating that the *dao* has *li* and one of its *li* is righteousness.

For Zhuxi, righteousness is a precept of the universal reason, or *tianli* (天理 the reason of the Heaven). He said, "*Tianli* is the general name for humanity, righteousness, propriety, and wisdom," and went on to explain that "*tianli* is a general name. Its precepts are humanity, righteousness, propriety, and wisdom."[49] Justice is ontologically a part of the universal reason and inherent in human reason. Zhuxi further argued, "The distinction between the human moral mind [reason] and human desires is the distinction between *gong* [公 fairness, impartiality) and *si* [私 partiality], and *zheng* [正 the right] and *xie* [邪 the crooked or evil]."[50]

In connection with the above, Zhuxi associated the principles of justice and humanity. In his words, "Gong, ren de dao li" (公, 仁的道理 Fairness is the principle of humanity).[51] He argued, "Where humanity [as a value] exists, *gong* [as a norm] exists."[52] Elsewhere, he insisted: "Humanity exists only when *gong* [as a norm of public life] exists. When *si* prevails in public life, humanity [as a value] disappears."[53] According to Zhuxi, justice as fairness (*gongdao* 公道) is essential for humankind to flourish as humankind. In justice, humankind exists in reason, embodying the quality of humanity.

Another point is this: While justice implies the rule of reason, following the voice of reason is not identical to following instrumental rationality. Righteousness that stands straight is independent of the calculation of interests and benefits. Justice is the most reasonable not because it is the most rational as far as the means–end relationship is concerned, but because it is right in terms of *he qing he li* (合情合理 confirmation to and approval by both our moral feeling and human reason). From the point of view of the instrumental reason, the rule of interests is not necessarily irrational; that is, one can turn the rule of desire into the instruction of calculative, instrumental reason.

To examine further the relation between justice and reason, let us leave formal justice to focus particularly on political justice for a moment. Many Chinese philosophers explicitly reject *bao zheng* (暴政 government by violence and repression), *nude zheng* (虐政 abusive, oppressive, and repressive government), and *yin zheng* (淫政 government by excessive desires and violence). *Bao zheng* here refers not to a military dictatorship, but to a government that employs excessive force and violence and whose governmental measures such as taxes and laws are extremely coercive and beyond reason. *Nude zheng* has all the flaws of *bao zheng* and, in addition, under a *nude zheng*, abuse becomes an institutionalized practice. *Yin zheng* is a kind of government in which everything is excessive: the rules and ministers pursue excessive personal desires; governmental measures are excessive, as are governmental activities.

According to *Kong Zi Jia Yu*, Confucius said:

> When executive orders are not given on time and governmental rules are vague, this is called *zei* [贼 wickedness]. To tax people all times and excessively, this is called *bao* [暴 violence, oppression, repression]. Criticizing first and not allowing people to have a chance to make corrections before punishing people [for their failures], this is called *nude* [虐 abusing]. Only when these three evils are absent in governmental measures, should governmental measures be allowed.[54]

Here, Confucius explicitly rejects governments of *zei*, *bao*, and *nude*. A government of *zei* is incompetent and irresponsible. A government of *bao* exploits its own people with oppression. A government of *nude* oppresses its own people excessively and is in effect a criminal government. A government of any of the three is a government of desires or forces, not of reason, and as a result, is unjust.

Mencius also cited governments of *bao zheng* (暴政), *nude zheng* (虐政) and *yin zheng* (淫政) as paradigms of unjust government. He put forth the following argument:

> Confucius said, "There are but two ways (of government) to follow: that of humanity and that of inhumanity." When a ruler *bao* (暴 oppressing, repressing and exploiting) his people to the extremity, he will lose both his kingdom and life. When he *bao* (暴) his people not to the extremity, his kingdom still will be weakened and his life still will be endangered. Such a ruler of *bao*(暴) will be called King "You" (幽, King You was a king of Chinese Zhou dynasty who was an extremely wicked king and ruled with extremely oppressive and repressive measures and forces) and King "Li"(厉, King Li is another king of Chinese Zhou dynasty who was extremely wicked and stupid). ... *Shi* (<<诗>> the book of Poetry) reads: "The mirror of Yan (殷) dynasty (Yan Shang dynasty) was not far away. It was in the time of Xia (夏) dynasty (whose last wicked and abusive king was overthrown by the founder of *Yan Shang* dynasty).[55]

According to Mencius, one who lives by the sword, dies by the sword. A government of and by oppression will be overthrown violently. For him, it is a people's right and duty to overthrow a *bao jun* (暴君 tyrant) and to discard a *bao zheng*. Governments of *bao zheng*, *nude zheng*, and *yin zheng* are governments of irrationality and injustice.

The dichotomy between a just government, as a government of reason, and an unjust government such as a *bao zheng*, *nude zheng*, or *yin zheng*—governments of desires and force—is at the core of both the Confucian and Taoist political philosophies, with a difference in emphasis. For Confucians, a *bao*, *nude*, or *yin* government is unreasonable because it is inhuman, anti-humanity, or humanly insensitive and extremely irrational. In the eyes of Taoist masters, such a government is unreasonable because it is unnatural, it does not follow the laws of nature. Instead, such a form of government is self-willed and acts on subjective will and desires.

The Chinese concept of just government accords well with Plato's concept in *The Republic*: a just government is a government of wisdom, not of desires or force. Meanwhile, for Chinese philosophers, justice as the rule of reason implies the idea of justice as the rule of humanity. The rule of reason involves the rule of humanity as a standard. Humanity (仁), righteousness (义), and reason (理) are inseparable. Just social institutions embody them all together. Just, reasonable institutions are humanly judgment-sensitive institutions.

In short, in traditional Chinese thoughts, justice means the rule of reason and rejects the rule of terror or the rule of desires and passions. Justice brings home the *dao*, *gongli* (公理 universal reason), and *tianli* (天理 the reason of the universe). It is reason's answer to the sabotage of powers, forces, desires, practical expedience, and material interests. It is reason's answer to tyranny, oppression, *bao zheng*, *nude zheng*, and *yin zheng* in government as well as *huang* (荒 wasting), *yin* (淫 excessiveness), and *luan* (乱 disorder) in social life. Human justice is humankind's universal way in terms of human reason.

Flexibility in Understanding and Practicing Justice

A main challenge to the concept of formal justice is the argument that no concept of formal justice can account for the fitness of all things in all diverse situations. However, this argument can be rejected by the Chinese concepts of *li yi fen shu* (理一分殊 the principle is one, but its embodiments are many) and *quan* (权 flexibility in understanding and practicing) in justice.

Formal justice is one, but its embodiment can be many—that is, in different contexts and situations, its embodiments vary. This one-to-many relation is *li yi fen shu*. Formal justice is the *li* (理 principle) and the *yi* (一 one), and the *fen* (分 embodiments) of formal justice are *shu* (殊 different, particular). The concept of formal justice presupposes the existence of substantial, particular justices. Formal justice is formal because it can account for all forms of particular justice but is not reducible or restricted to any one of them. Context matters importantly to justice. First, contexts are the concrete, substantive conditions under which the formal justice articulates itself. Second, they are the conditions under which the whole of truth of a particular instance of justice is formed.

Zhuxi used a beautiful metaphor to illustrate the idea of *li yi fen shu*: there is only one moon in the sky, but its rays are countless. The concept of *li yi fen shu* explains the idea that formal justice is one, but substantive families of justice can be diverse. The essence of justice is setting things right and setting righteousness to stand straight. But in diverse contexts, things are set right differently. In various contexts, righteousness may take different forms and have different emphases.

Thus, the concept of *li yi fen shu* highlights the idea of diversity of substantive justice and diversity of contextual interpretations of justice. There is formal justice, by which we account for what makes persons, institutions, practices, and social conducts just. Simultaneously, formal justice is embodied in different kinds of particular, substantive justices in particular contexts. While justice means setting things right, things are set right in context. At times, the requirements of setting things right and the content and meanings of righteousness diverge. In different ages, justice has different time-spirits.

This amounts to saying that there should be—and there is—consistency and integrity in all true interpretations of righteousness in different contexts; simultaneously, the same principle of justice must be interpreted in a flexible way so that it responds to the contexts in which justice lives. The diverse substantializations of justice do not indicate that formal justice loses its unity, any more than the countless moonbeams have not disintegrated the moon. Instead, it is that justice has different embodiments, the same as the same moon having countless moonbeams. True understanding of justice demands creativity and a judgment-sensitive attitude.

The concept of *li yi fen shu* brings to the foreground the concepts of *jing* (经) and *quan* (权). *Jing* refers to basic tenets and doctrines, and the orthodox teachings embodied in the canonical texts. *Quan* means flexibility, making adjustment to contexts in interpreting and applying principles in given contexts. The concept of *jing* teaches unity in basic beliefs, and the concept of *quan* teaches creativity and being responsive to context. For many Chinese philosophers, without *quan*, one becomes dogmatic in understanding righteousness, and a dogmatic view on righteousness is not only one-sided but also wrong. Therefore, traditional Chinese philosophers emphasize both formal justice as "one" and particular justices as "many" and, accordingly, the importance of the ability of *quan* in connecting the many and the one.

Mencius gave the following example to illustrate the indispensability of *quan* in interpreting righteousness. Asked whether a man should rescue his sister-in-law by giving her his hand when she was drowning in water and whether he would violate propriety if he gave her his hand, Mencius answered: "The principle of propriety indeed requires that a man and a woman, who are not a married couple, should not touch each other physically. However, a man will be a wolf if he does not give his hand to his drowning sister-in-law."[56] The metaphor of a wolf connotes evil. In the example, a man giving a hand to his drowning sister-in-law does not violate the rules of propriety, but rather practices *quan*. His act of *quan* does not compromise righteousness in the given context, but sets righteousness standing straight.

In light of the above, *quan* enables us to read righteousness properly in context. Only if we recognize righteousness in context can we have justice. Justice involves having the authentic truth and essence of things, which presupposes interpreting properly the truth, meaning, and value of things. To have proper interpretation of the truth and what is right, we must interpret them contextually.

In *The Analects*, Confucius was worried that his students, who might be with him as far as following the basic teachings and tenets of the *dao* was concerned, could not follow him when it came to *quan*.[57] He taught his disciples to avoid four vices: *i* (意 = 臆 arbitrariness), *bi* (必 being dogmatic), *gu* (固 closed-mindedness), and *wuo* (我 being self-centered or subjective). Arbitrariness leads one to interpret the truth according to one's own will. Dogmatism leads one to be blind to contexts in which the truth lives. Closed-mindedness imprisons one in prejudices and biases. And self-centeredness leads one to distort the truth to meet one's own interests. The four vices prevent a person from having the truths of things and properly seeing their fitness.

Quan is indispensable for applying appropriate standards of righteousness in context. Guanzi said: "Qian li zhi lu, bu ke fu yi sheng; wan jia zhi du, bu ke ping yi zhun. Yan da ren zhi xing, bu ke yi xian chang, yi li zhi wei xian" (千里之路, 不可扶以绳; 万家之都, 不可平以准. 言大人之行, 不可以先常, 义立之为贤 One should not try to make a road of a thousand miles be exactly the same all the way like a rope. One should not try to model ten thousand houses to be exactly the same. A great person focuses on righteousness in context, not on invariance of the precedence. Thus, only the wise can establish righteousness).[58]

Any attempt to make a thousand-mile road be exactly the same all the way is unreasonable. Conditions on the road will be diverse. Likewise, attempting to make ten thousand houses be exactly the same will make them unusable and unlivable. Holding to the rule and not knowing how to be flexible in a given context, one perverts the *dao* and loses righteousness. Therefore, Guanzi further explained: "Dao ye zhe, tong hu wu shang, xiang hu wu qiong, yun hu zhu sheng" (道也者, 通乎无上, 详乎无穷, 运乎诸生 The *dao* has no ceiling above and no exhaust in details and produces millions of things in movement).[59] Mencius characterized a person incapable of being *quan* in application of the norm of *zhong* (中 impartiality) in context as practicing the bandit's way.[60]

Neo-Confucian philosophers who emphasized the universality of righteousness also stressed most seriously the importance of *quan* to justice. Cheng I and Cheng Hao said:

The standard that was used in Spring and Autumn Period [of ancient China] to draw distinctions between right and wrong is *zhongyoung* [中庸 impartiality]. To understand properly the principle of *zhongyoung*, we must have the ability of *quan*. *Zhong* [中 impartiality] means being proper in terms of contexts. Thus, if we dogmatically understand *zhong* as the median between sage-king Yu's eagerness to serve the world and Yen Hui's staying at home, we do not understand the essence of *zhong*. In some contexts, being eager to serve the world is *zhong*. In other contexts, staying at home when it is necessary is also *zhong*. . . . *Quan* is crucial to *yi* [righteousness].[61]

According to the Cheng brothers, only if we practice *quan* can we really understand *yi* properly. If we dogmatically interpret impartiality as the middle point between two extremes, we do not really understand the meaning of impartiality. Impartiality is to give each its due in context.

Wang Yangming argued: "*Zhong* is a precept of *Tianli* [天理 the reason of the universe] and its meanings vary in different contexts. Accordingly, we should interpret it contextually. . . . We should interpret *zhong* in the manner of *in shi zhi yi* [因时制宜 setting standards proper to contexts]. We should see that the meaning of *zhong* is not *a priori*."[62] According to Wang, while righteousness implicates the norm of impartiality, meanings of impartiality vary from situation to situation. To recognize that righteousness is impartiality is to recognize what formal justice is. To interpret what is impartial in particular contexts is to interpret what is substantial justice or the concrete embodiment of justice in given contexts. *Quan* is indispensable for us to recognize the "many" of justice.

The concept of *quan* should not be understood as bending or compromising the rules for the sake of practical interests and expedience, however. In *quan*, the rule or principle is not abandoned or compromised for the sake of personal interests, but is interpreted contextually. To appreciate this, we can compare Mencius's example that a man should give his hand to his drowning sister-in-law to rescue her with the two biblical examples: Abraham's false assertion that his wife was his sister, and Lot having children with his daughters.[63]

In the first case, Abraham made the false claim to protect his life. His act was a tactical act of doing what was best for himself in a given circumstance, not a flexible or creative interpretation of a principle—that is, the rule that one should tell the truth. It was not an act of contextual interpretation of truth, but an act of telling a lie for practical expedience. The essence of the matter here is that Abraham's statement that his wife was his sister had no truth. Abraham himself did not see his own act as interpreting contextually the principle that one should always tell the truth, nor did he see it as an act of properly interpreting righteousness in a given context. He therefore accepted Pharaoh's rightful reproach: "What is this you have done to me? Why did you not tell me that she is your wife? Why did you say, 'She is my sister,' so that I took her for my wife?"[64]

In Mencius's example, the act of giving one's drowning sister-in-law a hand is not an act of abandoning or bending the rule of propriety, but an act of contextual interpretation of the rule. A man would have acted immorally had he had physical contact with his sister-in-law under normal circumstances, especially for the sake of having physical pleasure. However, the act of giving a hand to one's drowning sister-in-law to rescue her is not having physical contact with her for physical pleasure, but rescuing her from danger and harm. Here is the difference. In Abraham's case, it is not that Sarah is Abraham's wife in one context and his sister in another context; in Mencius's case, having physical contact with one's sister-in-law to have physical pleasure is one thing, but rescuing her by giving her one's hand is quite another.

Mencius's example differs from the case of Lot's having sexual relations with his daughters, too. When Lot's two daughters made him drunk in order to make him sleep with them so that they could beget his children to continue the family line, they did not interpret contextually the moral taboo that prohibited father–daughter sexual intercourse, but simply abandoned it, feeling they had justified reasons. Their reasoning was:

1. Their father was old and, in their circumstance, no woman could come to him;
2. Given their circumstance, no man on Earth would come to them, either;
3. Therefore, if they wanted to have offspring, they could only have them through sleeping with their father.[65]

In the cases of both Abraham and Lot, what is practiced is not *quan*—that is, interpreting truth and principle contextually—but practical expedience. What is chosen is not how to apply a moral principle flexibly and creatively in a given context, but abandonment of a moral principle for the sake of practical expedience and advantage in a given context. In short, in both cases, the intent is not to set righteousness standing straight contextually, but abandoning righteousness for practical expedience.

The concept of *quan* again reinforces the idea that the key to justice is to listen to the voice of human reason. Human reason is crucial to appreciate the concept of *li yi fen shu* of justice and to exercise the ability of *quan*. Our case now boils down to this: Justice as setting things right and setting righteousness to stand straight requires us to interpret righteousness in context and therefore to grasp the universal truth of justice in context; setting the truth to stand straight means setting both the universal and particular truths upright in context. To do so, what voice should we listen to—reason, passion, desire, or power? The answer is reason. Only reason, not desires or dreams of power, can lead us to set things right.

The concept of *quan* also teaches us to be creative in articulating the spirit of justice in given historical contexts. Similarly, the concepts of *li yi fen shu* and *quan* remind us of the fact that true human reason is not, and need not be, totalitarian. Here, we should recall Jürgen Habermas's criticism of Enlightenment reason. According to Habermas, Enlightenment reason

> failed to keep the unforced force of reason from both the *totalitarian* characteristics of an instrumental reason that objectifies everything around it, itself included, and from the *totalizing* characteristics of an inclusive reason that incorporates everything and, as unity, ultimately triumphs over every distinction.[66]

Enlightenment reason seeks to oppress every difference and claim of context. As a result, it loses the "unforced force of reason." In light of this, practice of *quan* is not disloyal to reason, but renders the unforced force of reason evident.

As a result, the concept of *quan* indicates the importance of social tolerance and toleration. It returns us back to the reality of *li yi fen shu* (the principle is one, but its embodiments are many). The concept of *li yi fen shu* demands intellectual and moral creativity in different times and places, while indicating the possible diversity of paradigms of justice. Not only may different peoples approach the same justice from different avenues, but they also have rights and are entitled to do so—though, in the end, all should be united together under truth and reason, just as all roads lead to Rome and all stars shine under the same sky. The concept of *quan* teaches that the proper response to intellectual and moral diversity is neither oppression or repression of difference nor polarization of difference, but creative toleration and engagement.

Justice: The Symmetry of Truth, Good, and Duty

The preceding discussions provide us with sufficient grounds to defend the metaphysics of formal justice, which in turn sustains the concepts of universal justice and global justice. There is universally recognized justice amid diverse cultural contexts and different time-spirits (Zeitgeist) of justice. There is also global justice that implicates the norms of the obligation of humankind to humankind in global human affairs. There are universal justice, truth, and reason. There is global justice in terms of universal reason and truth in global affairs.

Admittedly, cultural diversity is the color of our age. Still, we do better when we do not lose perspective of the universal amid diversity. It remains essential that we see *li yi fen shu* of justice today. Thus, for example, we should not be igno-rant of the differences among the Chinese concept of *zhengyi*, the Judeo-Chris-tian concept of justice, the Hindu and Buddhist concepts of *dharma*, and the Islamic concept of *adalah*. However, we will be better off and do the right thing when we have a perspective of the common point among these different views on justice. For example, all of them indicate that justice means setting things right and having righteousness stand straight. We do better if we remember that so far as justice is concerned, all correct avenues lead to Plato's "the sun above."

We must not underestimate the differences among the approaches to jus-tice from realism, critical theory, and pragmatism. But the Chinese concept of justice offers us a strategy to sort out the differences: appreciating *li yi fen shu* and being able to *quan* allows us to defend the concept of formal and objective justice with realism without its hard edge, to accommodate the concept of historically self-trial justices without abandoning the concept of formal justice, and to appreciate the contribution of practices and contexts to justice in line with pragmatism without throwing away the baby of formal justice with objective truth when we throw out the bathwater of totalitarian-ism, repression, oppression, exclusion of difference, and absolutism.

The concept of formal justice would be pointless if there were no universal truth or if justice were not grounded in truth. Habermas rightly points out that there is a difference between the *acceptance* of a concept of justice and the *acceptability* of such a concept. Formal justice must have universal ac-ceptability, but it cannot if there is no universal truth in which formal justice is grounded and which constitutes universal justifiability of formal justice. Thus, at the end of the day, justice, good, and truth, while differing from one another, nevertheless entail one another.

Justice focuses on righteousness. Good focuses on value, worthiness, praiseworthiness, and desirability. Truth indicates reality.

Justice imposes norms of obligation. Good radiates attractiveness and at-traction. Truth brings enlightenment.

Simultaneously, justice, good, and truth are internally connected. Justice is good and has truth. What is right has truth and must be good. If what is right had no truth, it would not be truly right, making the concept of rightness meaningless and unintelligible. Likewise, if what is right were bad, it would not be truly right, in turn rendering the concept of rightness worthless.

The concept of *zhengyi* brings home the internal connection of justice and truth, rejecting the view that a reasonable political concept of justice can be freestanding, that is, not grounded in truth. Justice is metaphysically real, cognitively justified and reasonable, morally desirable and praiseworthy, and normatively right. *Zhengyi* has not only truth, but the profoundest truth.

The relationship between truth and justice continues to be heatedly debated. The Rawls–Habermas debate is a highlight of the disagreements. For John Rawls, a reasonable political concept of justice is freestanding. That is, a political concept of justice presents itself not as a concept of justice that has truth and is true, but as a reasonable one that can serve as the basis for social cooperation among free and equal citizens. Elsewhere, Rawls clarifies his position by saying that in a political concept of justice, the idea of truth is not rejected but left to comprehensive doctrines to use or deny. Thus, the core of Rawls's strategy of being "political" is to avoid the justification problem. In essence, this strategy recommends the Sartrean "bad faith." With it, we pretend not to have the justification problem.

As a form of bad faith, being merely political is the limit of Rawls's political concept of justice, not its strength. It reduces the meaning, value, and normativity of justice. The problem is not only that a true concept of justice is a better candidate for the "reasonable" to us but also that the essence of justice is setting things right, but we cannot set things right without setting them right on the ground of truth. Moreover, even with being merely political and staying in the Sartrean bad faith—that is, delaying the difficult decision and avoiding facing the hard truth and choice now—we still have the burden of justification.

Rejecting Rawls's claim, Habermas insists that a reasonable concept of justice *must* be grounded in truth. Habermas properly asks: "We have reason to ask why Rawls does not think his theory admits of truth and *in what sense* he here uses the predicate 'reasonable' in the place of the predicate 'true.'"[67] He rightly insists that a reasonable political concept of justice "must furnish the premises that we and others recognize as true, or reasonable" and must demonstrate reasonable acceptability.[68] However, Habermas yields to the pressure of postmodernity and therefore refuses to recognize any metaphysical truths of justice, labeling his concept of truth in justice as postmetaphysical.

As a kind of Sartrean bad faith, being postmetaphysical handicaps Habermas's concept of justice, though clothing it with some fashionable dress. Such a bad faith reduces the substance and value of justice. The problem is that postmetaphysical truth cannot be freestanding without falling into self-contradiction or turning into something else. The postmetaphysical strategy may lead us to a temporary shelter of bad faith, but not a true home of justification.

As a timely remedy, the Chinese concept of *zhengyi* brings us back to what we, for the most part, try to avoid: Justice has truth. Justice is metaphysically, morally, and politically real. There are distinctions between true justice and false justice and between true justice and true injustice, as well as between true injustice and false injustice. Metaphysical truth, like air, is something we will truly appreciate it only when it is there no more. In addition, there is a distinction between a true *concept of* justice and a false one; the former imposes a true norm of moral obligation, while the latter cannot give rise to true moral obligation.

The metaphysical, cognitive, and moral unity of the truth of justice can accommodate the substantial and historical diversity of the truths of justice. There is *li yi fen shu*. Here, it is not that a unified political concept of justice brings different metaphysical and moral concepts of justice together, but rather that a unified metaphysical and moral concept of justice leads different ideological concepts or doctrines of justice to arrive at a shared political concept of justice. The difference between a concept of justice that has truth and one that has no truth exists between the true duty and obligation of justice and the false one. Only a concept of justice that has truth gives rise to the true duty and obligation of justice. For example, if a concept of fairness is false, then either the norm of obligation that it imposes has no claim to validity or it imposes no norm of obligation.

In light of the above, we can reject relativist and postmodernist approaches to justice. The problem is not that relativist approaches emphasize the relativity of justice and that postmodern approaches emphasize the cognitive value of local experience and contexts in understanding justice. Instead, the problem is that both relativist and postmodern approaches presuppose incredulity to any metanarratives of human history and humanity. They reject the unity of the truth of justice, the unity of the truth of humanity, and the unity of the truth of human experiences, and they therefore destroy the integrity of the concept of justice. They bring us to a slippery slope where we have no way to draw a distinction between justice and injustice.

An artist cannot create a great painting in ignorance or with the wrong or bad instruments. A novelist cannot write a great novel with a wrong understanding and ignorance. A poet cannot write great poem with ignorance and stupidity. And we cannot set basic social institutions right with a false concept of justice. A normal society cannot have justice without standards and normativity that are essentially just.

Justice is an intrinsic good. Being righteous is praiseworthy and valuable in its own right and also has dignity in its own right. In the same way, the original truth of things is praiseworthy and valuable and has dignity in its own right. Justice certainly makes individual person, social institutions, and a normal society virtuous. Nonetheless, it is not that justice is good because it makes individual persons, basic social institutions, and a normal society virtuous. Rather, it is that, being good, justice makes, and can make, individual persons, basic social institutions, and a normal society virtuous.

Being an intrinsic good, justice implicates duty and obligation on humankind. Moreover, the duty of justice is the most transparent duty and the sum of all duties of humankind for the following reasons. First, it is a duty of virtue. As an intrinsic good, justice brings us human character, ethical substance, moral truth, and human realization. Second, it is a social duty and obligation. As an intrinsic good, justice not only brings rationalization and humanization to the world in which we live but also makes the world reasonable. Third, it is an ontological duty. Humankind has an undeniable, ontological duty to do the right things—to follow the *dao*, as Chinese philosophers put it.

The duty of justice is the first public duty and obligation of a human being, more than something virtuous to do. Thus, some Western philosophers list the duty of justice as a universal human duty. Chinese philosophers say, "Yi bu rong ci" (义不容辞 It is not allowable to avoid serving justice). In a different way, Thomas Nagel and others' suspicion and skepticism of the possibility of global justice reveals an insight into its nature: Global justice imposes an obligation that cannot be identical to the requirements of global humanitarian morality in terms of virtue and compassion. In other words, global justice, if it exists, imposes an obligation; it doesn't merely issue requirements of virtue and compassion. Global justice defends global humanity, but is not identical to universal benevolence and compassion in global affairs.

Overall, justice gives rise to duty and obligation in terms of reason, truth, and good. Indeed, for humankind and basic human institutions such as government and law, justice is the sum of all duties. Justice is the way, reason, and duty to act or abstain from action. It is the way, reason, and duty of humankind to organize their lives, and it is the way, reason, and duty for basic human institutions such as government and law to be organized.

In conclusion, ever since time immemorial, two roads have diverged in front of humankind. One is the road of justice; the other, the road of injustice. The road of justice is the road of truth, good, and duty. The road of injustice is the road of falsity, evil, and perversion. Justice or injustice—like "To be or not to be"—that is the question for humankind yesterday, today, tomorrow, and ever after!

Notes

1. Confucius, *The Essence and Substance of the Analects* (*Lun Yu Zheng Yi* 论语正义), ed. Liu Bao Nan, in *Completed Works of Teachers* (*Zhu Zi Ji Cheng* 诸子集成), vol. 1 (Beijing: Unity Publishing House, 1996), 14.12, 15.18.

2. Mencius, *The Essence and Substance of Mencius* (*Mengzi Zheng Yi* 孟子正义), ed. Jiao Shun, in *Completed Works of Teachers*, vol. 1, 4A10, 7B3.

3. Liu An, *Huai Nan Zi* (淮南子), ed. Gao Shiu, in *Completed Works of Teachers*, 7:169, 7:159.

4. Tang Kailin and Zhang Younghuai, eds., *Becoming a Man and Becoming a Sage* (Changsha, China: Hunan University Press, 1999), 176.

5. *Qi Yuan* (Beijing: Commercial Publishing House, 1980), 2:1665.

6. Mencius, *Essence and Substance of Mencius*, 3A4.

7. Wang Yangming, *Practical Learning* (Guangzhou, China: Flower City Publishing House, 1998), 8.

8. Confucius, *Essence and Substance of the Analects*, 12.17.

9. Xunzi, *Xunzi* (荀子), ed. Wang Xianqian, in *Completed Works of Teachers*, 2:313.

10. Guanzi, *Guanzi Xiao Zheng* (管子校正), ed. Liu Xiang and Dai Wang, in *Completed Works of Teachers*, 5:685.

11. Xun Yue, *Shen Jian* (申鉴), ed. Wu Dao Chuan, in *Completed Works of Teachers*, 7:745.

12. *Zhou Yi* (周易), ed. and trans. Fang Fei (U Lu Mu Qi, China: Xinjiang Youth Publishing House, 1999), 97.

13. Laozi, *Dao De Jing* (道德经), ed. Wei Yuan, in *Completed Works of Teachers*, vol. 3, chap. 38.

14. Mencius, *Essence and Substance of Mencius*, 2A2.

15. Liu, *Huai Nan Zi*, 221.

16. Ibid.

17. Confucius, *Essence and Substance of the Analects*, 4.16.

18. Ibid., 7.16.

19. Mencius, *Essence and Substance of Mencius*, 1B8.

20. Xunzi, *Xunzi*, 271.

21. Ibid., 61.

22. Zhuxi and Lü Zhuqian, *Words of Reflection on Things at Hand* (*Jin Si Lu* 近思录), ed. Lü Zhuqian (Guangzhou, China: Flower Publishing House, 1998), 463.

23. Confucius, *Essence and Substance of the Analects*, 16.11.

24. Xunzi, *Xunzi*, 18.

25. Ibid., 68.

26. Ibid., 351, 356.

27. Zhuxi and Lü Zhuqian, *Words of Reflection*, 199.

28. Mencius, *Essence and Substance of Mencius*, 3A3.

29. Xunzi, *Xunzi*, 49.

30. Ibid., 406.

31. Mencius, *Essence and Substance of Mencius*, 3B9.

32. Xun Yue, *Shen Jian*, 744, 748.

33. Laozi, *Dao De Jing*, chap. 38.

34. Ibid., chap. 57.

35. Ibid., chap. 60.

36. Ibid., chap. 10.

37. Ibid., chap. 38.

38. Ibid., chap. 21.

39. Confucius, *Essence and Substance of the Analects*, 16.11.

40. Ibid., 20.1.

41. Mencius, *Essence and Substance of Mencius*, 6A7.

42. Ibid., 4A1.

43. Xunzi, *Xunzi*, 327.

44. Ibid., 75.

45. Ibid., 363.

46. Guanzi, *Guanzi Xiao Zheng*, 684.

47. Liu, *Huai Nan Zi*, 169.

48. Ibid., 71.

49. Zhuxi, *The Recorded Words*, ed. Wing-Tsit Chan (Taipei, Taiwan: Giliu Books, 1993), vol. 6.

50. Zhuxi and Lü Zhuqian, *Words of Reflection*, 467.

51. Zhuxi, *Recorded Words*, vol. 1.

52. Ibid.

53. Ibid., vol. 6.

54. Wang Su (王肃), *Kong Zi Jia Yu* (孔子家语 *Confucius's Family Teaching*), in *Zi Bu Jing Yao* (子部精要 *The Essential of the Volume of Teachers*), *Si Ku Quan Shu* (四库全书 *The Complete Works of Four Storehouses*) (Tianjin, China: Tianjin Classics Publishing House, 1998), 1–8, 2.

55. Mencius, *Essence and Substance of Mencius*, 4A2.

56. Ibid., 4A17.

57. Confucius, *Essence and Substance of the Analects*, 9.30.

58. Guanzi, *Guanzi Xiao Zheng*, 515.

59. Ibid.

60. Mencius, *Essence and Substance of Mencius*, 7A26.

61. Zhuxi and Lü Zhuqian, *Words of Reflection*, 106.

62. Wang Yangming, *Practical Learning*, footnoted by Deng Yang (Guangzhou, China: Flower Publishing House, 1998), 85.

63. Gen. 12 and Gen. 19, respectively.

64. Gen. 12:18–19.

65. Gen. 19:31–32.

66. Jürgen Habermas, *The Philosophical Discourse of Modernity* (Cambridge, MA: MIT Press, 1987), 341.

67. Jürgen Habermas, "Reconciliation through the Public Use of Reason: Remarks on John Rawls' Political Liberalism," *Journal of Philosophy* 92, no. 3 (March 1995): 122.

68. Ibid.

CHAPTER 3

~

Justice: Humankind's Duty and Path

Since Aristotle, philosophers in West have taken for granted that there are only two general families of justice: *distributive justice* and *corrective justice*. Notwithstanding this, justice has three general families. The missed third family of justice is what this chapter will discuss. I call this family of justice *normative justice* and define it as "setting human affairs right in accordance with the principles of human rights, human goods (humanity as the end), and human bonds." This family of justice differs from both distributive justice and corrective justice in substance, focus, and scope.

Normative justice covers a family of particular concerns of justice—the concerns of human rights, human goods, humanity as the end, human bonds, and the profoundest truth and substance of basic humanity. It dictates a class of maxims corresponding to these concerns as the righteous reasons to act or abstain from action and the righteous reasons that have priority and compulsory force in moral and political consideration. Conspicuously, this family of justice defines a genus of humankind's obligation to humankind and a genotype of the social obligations of basic human institutions. Accordingly, it stipulates a set of standards for evaluating basic social institutions and human conduct.

Admittedly, while fairness in the distribution of economic goods and political offices provides a standard paradigm for distributive justice, and punishment of a murderer for the crime that he has committed is a model of corrective justice, it is not easy for us to locate an archetype case for normative justice. This may create a wrong impression that normative justice

49

encompasses distributive justice and corrective justice, or alternatively that it is included in one of them. This underscores the challenge for us to define the content, focus, object, problem, and scope of normative justice.

Still, it is time for us to bring home the long-missed third family of justice. An adequate concept of it is indispensable for a complete understanding of the nature and scope of justice in general and a better perspective of global justice in particular. It proffers a new view of basic social institutions.

Justification of Normative Justice

It surely should strike us as self-evident that justice sets human affairs right for humankind. Otherwise, justice would not be the right thing for humankind to practice. Fundamentally, the questions of justice are palpably and exclusively human questions—that is, they are the questions of, for, and by human beings. Equally crucial, the objects of concern of justice are exclusively human. Moreover, justice implicates norms of obligation that put constraints only on the discretion of human beings to act or to abstain from action. It is no wonder that humankind is both the author and receiver of justice.

What is the implication of all of the above? It indicates that the consideration of human rights, human goods, humanity as the end, and human bonds is, and ought to be, a particular concern of justice in its own right. If justice ought to set things right for humankind, then humankind's entitlement, human goods, humanity as the end, and human bonds in the human family ought to have their due claims in justice. If justice sets human affairs right and is the right thing for humankind to practice, then justice must be an intrinsic human good, or it must be the case that in justice, an intrinsic human good is realized. If so, humankind has the obligation of justice and such an obligation is beyond prudence. If the questions of justice are exclusively questions of, for, and by humankind, the human questions from the perspective of human rights, human goods, humanity as the end, and human bonds must be among the core questions of justice. If justice implicates the norms of the obligation of humankind to humankind, then human bonds must constitute a justification for such an imposition. If humankind is both the author and receiver of justice, then the basic principles of justice are human principles and reflect the most fundamental human concerns, among them human rights, human goods, humanity as the end, and human bonds.

Fundamentally, the most authentic, profoundest truths of humankind are that human beings have rights, that the quality of humanity has intrinsic worth and is the end for humankind, that there are universal human values, and that universal human bonds exist. Human affairs cannot be set straight if humanity is crooked, and when human rights, human goods (humanity as the end), and human bonds do not stand straight in human affairs, humanity is crooked. Correspondingly, basic human institutions can be just if and only if they are grounded in these truths and are up to standards based on the principles of human rights, human goods (humanity as the end), and human bonds.

Further arguments are as follows. Justice sets a standard of how human beings should be treated: a human being should be treated as an end. As Immanuel Kant argues, in the duty of justice, one treats one's own humanity as the end and humankind as the end. Kant thus says, "It is in itself a duty of every man to make mankind in general his end."[1] In addition, justice sets another related standard of how human beings should be treated: the dignity and rights of a human being should be respected and honored. In terms of the above, the consideration of human rights, human goods (humanity as the end), and human bonds should be a particular consideration of justice itself. At any rate, a distinctive and independent concern of justice is to define the standard by which human beings ought to be treated by other humans. Justice is the affirmation to the rule of humanity and the rejection of the reign of bestiality.

Justice makes human beings think, act, and feel as humans. This is the reason why justice is not only a necessary virtue of humankind but also a universal duty. Justice arises in the commitment and obligation to humanity to be away from bestiality. The ideas of justice as an obligation or duty of humankind and as a virtue of humankind differ from one another, though they are interrelated. As Christine Korsgaard points out:

> Obligation differs from excellence in an important way. When we seek excellence, the force that value exerts upon us is attractive; when we are obligated, it is compulsive. For obligation is the imposition of value on a reluctant, recalcitrant, resistant matter. Obligation is the compulsive power of form.[2]

In connection with this, the requirements of virtue are conditional. In comparison, the requirements of obligation are unconditional. All the same, the fact that justice is both a virtue and an obligation of humankind indicates that a distinctive and independent concern of justice is how human beings ought to be and what human beings ought to do. And such an "ought" is not a prudential "ought," but a moral one independent of prudential concern. In turn, the question of how human beings ought to be necessarily brings home the centrality of the principles of human rights, human goods (humanity as the end), and human bonds.

The concept that the obligation of justice is a public one presupposes that we have legitimate claims on each other in terms of human rights, human goods (humanity as the end), and human bonds and that we owe it to each other to honor such claims. Had we no rights, we would have no legitimate claims on one another, and then there would be no public obligation. Were there no common human goods, there would be no justifiable claims of us on others. Were there no common human bonds, there would be no claims of obligation, let alone public obligation.

Of course, the idea of normative justice as an independent family of justice would be pointless if it could be included in either distributive or corrective justice. Conspicuously, the consideration of human rights, human goods, humanity as the end, and human bonds is irreducible to the consideration of fairness either in distribution of resources, power, opportunities, burdens, public offices, and responsibilities or in correcting wrongs. Accordingly, normative justice differs from both distributive justice and corrective justice in substance, focus, objective, problem, and scope.

With regard to the focus, normative justice does not look merely at fairness and impartiality in distribution of basic liberty, duties, resources, burdens, and the like. Instead, its gaze falls on how, in the distribution of these things, each person is treated as a human being and as the end and how, accordingly, human values and bonds are promoted. The objective of distributive justice is to set the procedure of distribution right. Normative justice's is to set human relations right. It is concerned with putting human affairs right, to the extent that human rights and dignity are respected and emphasized, human goods and values stand straight, and human bonds are enhanced. Normative justice promotes humanity as a quality and standard of life and humankind as a unique species that has intrinsic moral values and inherent moral dignity.

In scope, distributive justice is applied only to the area of distribution, that is, procedures and rules for distribution. Normative justice is applied to areas where truth and substance of humanity, basic human rights, human goods, humanity as the end, and human bonds are in question. Consider normative justice as making a government be a government, a piece of law be a piece of law, or a marriage be a marriage. Justice here is not concerned with distribution, but with making each institution to be what it is meant to be. In other words, normative justice erects the substance of each institution. Not surprisingly, when a statute taxes a married couple who have children but subsidizes two persons who have children together but do not get married, we can reject such a piece of law as unjust. The injustice here is not unfairness of distribution of resource and duties, but destruction of human bonds and the human family. The injustice is that such a piece of law promotes human irresponsibility.

In terms of problems, distributive justice is about distribution problems, while normative justice is about family association problems—that is, how human beings associate with one another as a family—as well as problems of truth and substance. Distributive justice stipulates a set of standards for evaluating the procedures, mechanisms, and processes of distribution; it implicates a family of norms governing such procedures, structures, and processes. Similarly, normative justice establishes a set of standards for evaluating the institutions, structures, and practices through which human members associate with one another in a normal society and the correspondence between symbols of social institutions and the reality and substance of those institutions; it implicates a family of norms governing institutions, structures, and practices.

There are cases that raise questions about both distributive justice and normative justice and in which these two kinds of justice may need some coordination. One example would be legislation about gay marriage—that is, the "marriage" between two persons of the same sex. An article of law, whether it legalizes or bans gay marriage, will face on the one hand questions about the rights to resources and benefits—that is, questions of distributive justice—and on the other hand questions about making an institution to stand for its substance—that is, a question of normative justice. It will face allocation problems, which are concerns of distributive justice, and human bond problems as well as problems of privacy rights, which belong to the province of normative justice.

Eminently, normative justice also differs from corrective justice in content, focus, objective, problems, and scope. As far as content is concerned, normative justice is about getting human rights, human goods, humanity as the end, and human bonds to stand straight, whereas corrective justice is about correcting any wrongs and making proportional compensation. In focus, normative justice does not examine how punishment and reward should be proportional and as merited; instead, it focuses on how, in punishing the wrong and rewarding the right, we promote human rights, goods, and bonds and emphasize humanity as the end and human beings as agents who have moral and social responsibility. The objective of corrective justice implies to some extent a return to the former status quo (before the wrong is committed); normative justice neither implies nor is concerned with this. Corrective justice presupposes that some wrong has been committed; normative justice has no such presupposition.

Noticeably, corrective justice is applied to any area where wrongs occur. The scope of normative justice is only in areas where human rights, human goods (humanity as the end), and human bonds need to be set straight. Thus, for example, repaying a standing debt is an act of corrective justice, as are punishments of past or ongoing crimes against humanity such as ethnic cleansing—murdering, enslaving, or forcibly driving out any civilian population. The development of laws and institutions to protect human rights, prevent any such crimes in the future, and erect humanity as the end in human affairs belongs to the category of normative justice. Reconstructing basic international institutions, including laws to make such crimes impossible, is the task of global normative justice.

In terms of problems, evidentially, corrective justice is about compensation and remedy problems. Normative justice is about association problems as well as problems of the truth and substance of basic social institutions. Corrective justice stipulates standards of evaluating the procedures, rules, and mechanisms of compensation and remedy; normative justice establishes standards of evaluating social institutions and social practices as well as the correspondence between the symbols of institutions and the reality of them.

Conversely, normative justice is not the general family of justice that includes distributive justice and corrective justice as two subfamilies. The considerations of distributive justice and corrective justice are independent concerns in their own right and are not reducible to or included in the considerations of normative justice. At the end of the day, distributive justice, corrective justice, and normative justice are three parallel families of justice, not families of justice in two different orders or levels.

The objects of concern of normative justice are basic social institutions. However, we should not confuse normative justice with political justice. Normative justice is concerned with political institutions such as governments, but it is also concerned with other basic, nonpolitical institutions such as marriage, religion, or education. For example, righteousness should stand straight in marriage, which means that marriage should be rectified in terms of rights, responsibility, humanity as the end, familial values, and bonds; it need to be the institution of family, not an institution of commerce or politics. It also makes perfect sense to insist that religions must teach goods, not preach evils—that they make people be good, not turn them into evil beings. Furthermore, normative justice is not identical to political justice because the former has moral and metaphysical dimensions. For example, in normative justice, the obligation of humankind to humankind is moral and ontological, not merely political.

Fundamentally, normative justice differs from minimal humanitarian morality in essence and substance. Normative justice gives what is due; it is essentially proportional—that is, it cannot be excessive or insufficient. By contrast, humanitarian morality cares about the well-being and suffering of others. It need not be proportional—it *can* be excessive or insufficient. For example, a society should honor a citizen's right to vote in accordance with the constitution of the society. But a person who is in a position to be a Good Samaritan to another needy person can be a Good Samaritan or a Decent Samaritan or a reluctant and grudging helper to that person.[3]

Normative justice erects righteousness in human affairs. Minimal humanitarian morality brings benevolence and compassion to the suffering and needy. Normative justice implicates the norms of obligation among the equal members of the human family. Minimal humanitarian morality sets requirements for those who are in a position to give, in situations in which there are others in need. The objective of normative justice is to set human affairs right. The objective of minimal humanitarian morality is to release human suffering and assist the needed, not aggravate suffering.

What becomes evident is that the fundamental question of justice involves both the question of whether there should be the rule of reason or the reign of passion or force and the question of whether it should be the rule of humanity or the reign of bestiality. In such a context, human rights, human goods (humanity as the end), and human bonds together establish a distinctive, independent family of norms of obligation and standards of evaluating basic social institutions and practices. While the greatest principle for humankind is justice, humanity is a distinctive concern of justice. While justice is the norm for humankind, humanity is a core principle of justice, and serving humankind is the purpose of justice. Therefore, social justice has three general families: distributive, corrective, and normative.

The Contemporary Debate

The justification offered above for a concept of normative justice as an independent family of justice can be appreciated more in light of some contemporary debates on justice, including global justice. Thomas Nagel distinguishes between the norm of justice and the norm of minimal humanitarian morality in global affairs, while agreeing that crimes against humanity should be condemned and stopped. He correctly suggests that there should be a distinction between global justice and global humanitarian morality. Notwithstanding this, his position has a slippery part. For him, the concerns of justice and of humanity are totally separated, independent of each other, and in global affairs, the concern of humanity does not go beyond compassion and humanitarian care for human suffering and need. Nagel's view thus raises a question here: Is there a concern of humanity beyond the concern of benevolence?

Contrary to Nagel, Korsgaard dances with the concept that our humanity identity imposes moral obligation on us. She points out that our concept of our own humanity is "the source of all reasons and values."[4] Her view is instructive. If humanity is the source of all reasons and values for human action, it should be the source of the duty and obligation of justice. In her argument, Korsgaard actually brings back what many philosophers today, for the most part, set aside: the idea of human bond. Rooted in the recognition of the humanity among all human beings, the idea of human bond is a key to appreciating normative justice in general and global justice in particular.

Korsgaard's view accords well with the idea that the duty of justice is to treat humanity as the end; human beings and basic social institutions have the obligation to serve humanity. Indeed, her view actually implies an argument for justice in terms of humanity: if our humanity identity is the source of normativity of our conduct, then it is the source, or at least a source, of justice. According to Korsgaard, "We must treat our humanity identity as a form of practical, normative identity."[5] Where this will lead us? When we treat our humanity identity as a normative identity, we owe it to each other as human beings to treat each other as human beings, which in turn obliges us to be just to each other and develop social institutions that will set things right among us; we recognize each others' human rights, the shared human goods and humanity as an intrinsic value, and the common human bonds.

In Korsgaard's view, our commitment to our humanity as the normative identity is loyalty to humanity. As Bernard Williams points out, "Humanity is, of course, a name not merely for a species but for a quality."[6] Our commitment to humanity is our loyalty to both humankind and the quality of humanity. Thus, for example, out of this loyalty, we think that the international community ought to prevent crimes against humanity such as those in Rwanda, Bosnia, Kosovo, and East Timor and should punish those who commit them.

Thomas Scanlon differs from Korsgaard noticeably. According to him, the source of our moral motivation is "the desire to be able to justify one's actions to others on the grounds they could not reasonably reject."[7] By this token, our motivation to be just is rooted deeply in such a desire. Our desire to justify our action on grounds that other fellow citizens or fellow human beings in a human community cannot reasonably reject is a desire to be loyal to our identity as a citizen of a particular human community. Scanlon does not talk about universal human bonds or advocate the idea of loyalty to our humanity identity. Perhaps, this is the main reason he cannot answer the question of why "lacking this desire is a particularly serious fault" for a person.[8]

An argument to defend Scanlon's view would be that we have the desire he talks about because, as Korsgaard indicates, we are constituted as norma-tive beings—that is, we are constituted as human beings; pigs, dogs, and wolves do not desire to be reasonable or to justify their acts rationally, but human beings do. An argument could be that we have such a desire also because we do not want to do anything or live in a way that is disloyal to our humanity identity—that is, being less a human being. Indeed, if it did not matter whether we would act as human beings or dogs or pigs, we would not bother ourselves with the questions about justification and the justice of our action.

Amid all this, the concept of normative justice still generally eludes phi-losophers today. Despite their differences so far as division of justice is con-cerned, contemporary philosophers follow the Aristotelian division of justice between distributive justice and corrective justice. None of them recognize normative justice as a distinctive kind of justice.

Philosophers of political liberalism recognize the association of justice with human rights and basic liberties, but their approaches to justice have three conspicuous shortcomings. First, the norm of honoring basic human rights is considered to be a suffix to a political, contractual act, not an *a priori* norm of moral obligation in terms of humanity. Second, a clear asymmetry exists between the emphasis on justice as the first virtue of social institutions and the lack of emphasis on justice as a crucial social obligation of basic social institutions. Third, not surprisingly, the idea of humanization of basic social institutions is totally absent, and thus the idea that, in justice, human-ity is a universal value, identity, and moral bond for humankind vanishes from the picture.

Communitarian philosophers do not fare any better. They recognize the association of justice and communal good. Their approaches preserve an an-cient insight: the fundamentals of justice are that no one shall suffer wrong and that the public good be served. Amidst this, communitarian views also have three problems. First, noticeably, the internal connection of justice to human rights is absent. Second, their concepts of public good are too com-munal-interest laden, not common humanity based; accordingly, in the com-munitarian concepts of public good, humanity as the end goal and universal human bonds are not emphasized. Third, the idea that an individual person should be just for the sake of his or her humanity is absent. Thus, the concept that justice should be a substance of a human being and a human community is also absent.

Utilitarianism appreciates justice no more adequately than either political liberalism or communitarianism does. According to utilitarianism, justice brings greater happiness to a greater number of people, and correspondingly, justice is defined in terms of the happiness that it brings to a normal society. At most in utilitarianism, the principle of justice is in essence a principle of prudence. No wonder the utilitarian concept of justice raises some eyebrows. Utilitarianism cannot reject the kind of unjust practices or institutions that sacrifice the well-being of a smaller number of people—a minority in a society—to promote the well-being of a greater number of people. Neither can it reject the kinds of political practices that use a small number of humans as tools for the happiness of a greater number of people. However, as John Rawls rightly argues, "Justice denies that loss of freedom for some is made right by a greater good shared by others."[9] Utilitarianism also cannot account for serving justice as a public obligation to us except as something reasonable to do.

In comparison, contractualism has the first two shortcomings of political liberalism and, in addition, inadequacy regarding the social obligation of justice. Seeing the norms of justice as the products of social contracts, contractualist philosophers explain that justice is the reasonable principle for social cooperation, but cannot justify the obligation of justice adequately. For example, in what sense do we have contract with the peoples of Rwanda or Kosovo such that we are obliged to denounce the crimes against humanity there? Here, contractualism cannot provide us with a viable concept of global justice. Again, Nagel's misgiving about the possibility of global justice being beyond the boundary of a state is rooted in the assumption that we do not have the kind of relationship with citizens of other countries as we have with citizens of our own.

Neopragmatist philosophers correctly suggest that our sense of justice is associated with our loyalty to our particular human ties—for example, familial and communal bonds. However, for many neopragmatist philosophers, universal humanity is nothing more than an outdated metaphor. In neopragmatism, the idea of justice as loyalty to the universal human bond is rejected as useless. American idealist philosophers such as Josiah Royce do indicate that justice is a fidelity to humanity. Royce's insight needs to be rescued with the Kantian idea that justice recognizes humanity as the end; justice demands treating all human beings as the ends, not merely means to other ends.

The debates over global justice today give us a titillating glimpse of the present lacuna in the ongoing discussions of justice, too. Taking Nagel's view as the guide, he rightly indicates that "social justice is a rise in exclusive obligation"; however, he wrongly suggests that such an exclusive obligation does not go beyond the boundary of a state or a people.[10] He lists three reasons for caution. First, beyond the border of the state, we have no relationship with others that gives rise to the obligation of justice. Second, beyond the border of the state, we cannot be both the authors and the receivers of justice. Third, beyond the border of the state, there is no institutional force to sanction or punish violation of alleged global justice. Therefore, he concludes that the concern of humanity in the global affairs belongs to the province of "minimal humanitarian morality," not justice.

Nagel's skepticism about global socioeconomic justice is shared by a great number of philosophers today. Kai Nielsen observes that, according to those skeptics of global justice,

> we cannot speak of justice for the world community as a whole. . . . Justice is only possible, the claim goes, where there are common bonds of reciprocity. There are no such bonds between a Taude of Highland New Guinea and a farmer in Manitoba. In general there are no such bonds between people at great distances from each other and with cultural ties, so given what justice is, we cannot correctly speak of global justice.[11]

Thomas Pogge, Joshua Cohen, Charles Sabel, A. J. Julius, and others defend the concept of global justice. But their approaches seem to show excessive bravado, not convincing arguments. They do not answer the Nagelian doubt: Where is the exclusive obligation that gives rise to global justice beyond state borders? What is the basis for such a kind of obligation of justice? They have failed to address the Nagelian problem: Where is the common bond of reciprocity that gives rise to global justice?

Pogge evokes the concept of cosmopolitan responsibilities.[12] However, he conflates the problems of normative justice and those of distributive justice and would not be able to address the misgiving of Nagel. To a great extent, he also does not distinguish between "wanting" and "ought." Simon Caney, in his discussion of justice beyond borders, defends a kind of cosmopolitan outlook on justice,[13] but he is handicapped by his lack of a concept of normative justice.

In addition to the above, philosophers today do not usually emphasize that justice is the duty and obligation of basic social institutions. They recognize that justice is the first virtue of basic social institutions such as laws and the government, but not their first social duty and obligation. These philosophers do not appreciate the fully obligatory force of justice, as expressed beautifully in the motto "Fiat justitia, et pereat mundus" (Let justice be done, though the world perish) of Holy Roman emperor Ferdinand I and as expressed beautifully in the line of Alexander Hamilton in 1788, "Justice is the end of government. It is the end of civic society."[14] As a result, they

ultimately do not conceive the duty of justice as a moral "ought" and obligation, but in terms of aspiration for virtue.

The Historically Opened Road

The lacuna in contemporary discourse on justice leaves us some challenges
here, which in turn leads us to see a path opened but not taken at the crucial
junctures in the history of Western philosophies. At one such juncture, Immanuel Kant came close to dividing justice among the three families that I
argue for in this chapter. And Royce almost took the untaken path. Views
of Rawls, Jürgen Habermas, and others also imply some leads to a concept of
normative justice.

In *Metaphysical Elements of Justice*, Kant outlines three principles of justice:

1. "Maintaining in relation to others one's own worth as a human being.
   This duty is expressed in the proposition: 'Do not make yourself into a
   mere means for others, but be at the same time an end for them.'"
2. "Do[ing] no one an injustice"; that is, doing no wrong to others
3. Giving a person what is his or her due[15]

In substance, Kant's first principle of justice is a principle of normative
justice that I defend here. The second principle reminds us of corrective
justice, while the third is at home with distributive justice. In essence, Kant's
three principles collectively point to the direction of justice as setting human
affairs right in terms of humanity. Essential to Kant's view here is the suggestion that justice is centered on humanity and implicates maxims for how
human beings should be treated.

Kant also contributes the idea of a republican cosmopolitan order in
which there is solidarity of humankind and in which a violation of justice
at one place on the Earth is felt at all other places. He further bequeaths us
these celebrated words: "Out of the crooked timber of humanity no straight
thing can ever be made."[16] If justice is setting things right, nothing can be
set right when humankind itself—which is tasked to establish justice—is
crooked!

Royce wanders around the starting point of the path opened but not taken.
He argues: "Justice means, in general, fidelity to human ties in so far as they
are ties. Justice thus concerns itself with what may be called the mere forms
in which loyalty expresses itself. Justice, therefore, is simply one aspect of loyalty—the mere formal and abstract side of loyal life."[17] For Royce, justice is
loyalty to human ties that include our concrete, communal ties and, in addi-

tion, formal human ties of humankind. To say that our sense of justice is part of our loyalty to the universal ties among human beings amounts to saying that our concept of justice is mediated by our concept of universal humanity. Noticeably, for Royce, true human ties themselves are of intrinsic value, and our loyalty to these ties creates our obligation to justice independent of our concerns of practical interests. Equally crucial, our common human ties are compatible with and embodied in our concrete human ties.

Amid Rawls's insistence on the separation of a reasonable political concept of justice and a metaphysical concept of the human person, his political concept of justice presupposes a Western concept of humanity. Rawls's first principle of justice is: "Each person is to have an equal right to the most extensive basic liberty compatible with a similar liberty for others."[18] In the principle, the Western vision of the human being as a free, autonomous being is claimed. Otherwise, if a person were not autonomous and had no rights, justice would not prescribe that each person is to have an equal right to the most extensive basic liberties compatible with those that others enjoy.

Moreover, according to Rawls, "Each person possesses an inviolability founded on justice that even the welfare of society as a whole cannot override. For this reason justice denies that the loss of freedom for some is made right by a greater good shared by others."[19] To say that justice recognizes the inviolability of each person is to say that justice presupposes as its counterpart a particular concept of humanity. Otherwise, why would there be such a thing as the "inviolability" of a person? Admittedly, Rawls never evokes the Kantian concept of humanity as the end. Still, he clearly defends the belief that each person has inviolability by virtue of being a human being and should not be used as a tool to the welfare of a society as a whole or to some alleged goods.

This leads us to Habermas. He draws a distinction between justice and solidarity: justice is concerned with individuals' rights, while solidarity is concerned with the communal web in which humans socialize. In such a distinction, justice emphasizes "the inviolability of the individual by postulating equal respect for the dignity of each individual," while solidarity "protects the web of intersubjective relation of mutual recognition by which these individuals survive as members of community."[20] Justice "postulates equal respect and equal rights for the individual," whereas solidarity "postulates empathy and concern for the well-being of one's neighbor." Of greater importance, "both principles have one and the same root: the specific vulnerability of the human species."[21] Like Rawls, Habermas has not arrived at a concept of normative justice. Unlike Rawls, he insists on the association of a reasonable political concept of justice and a universally recognized concept of the human person.

This notwithstanding, the philosophers mentioned above bring us to a path opened but not taken: the path to the family of normative justice. Their measured approaches reveal that there is a family of justice whose concern, focus, objective, problem, content, and scope differ from those of distributive justice and corrective justice. For example, treating humanity as the end, honoring the inviolability of a human being, and maintaining loyalty to the human bond are not distributive problems or compensation problems, but rather association problems and the problems of correspondence between symbol and reality—that is, doing justice to the name of humanity.

Contrasted to the Western philosophers mentioned above, traditional Chinese philosophers have actually taken the new path, though have not reached its end. In Confucian and neo-Confucian philosophies, humanity, righteousness, propriety, wisdom, and trust are five standing norms of human conduct and basic social institutions; and among them, the norm of humanity is the leader: "Ren tong si de" (仁统四德 Humanity leads the four virtues).

Confucius spearheaded the Confucian approach. For him, setting human bonds right and erecting ren (仁 humanity) are the core concerns of justice. In The Analects, ren is the quality that a person and basic political institutions such as government must embody. "Yi ren wei ji ren" (以仁为己任 Make realization of humanity one's mission) is a maxim for both individuals and governments. According to Confucius, "[We should] overcome ourselves and return to propriety in order to realize humanity. The day when all in the world overcome themselves is also the day that the world in which the ideal of humanity is realized."[22] To overcome oneself and return to propriety is to establish and realize humanity within oneself and in society, which in turn is the core task of setting human affairs right.

Since justice puts human bonds right and erects humanity, it is internally associated with zhengmin (正名 rectifying names), and a just government is a government of xinyi (信义 righteousness in terms of trust). Zhengmin refers to making the substance of social roles, human relations, and basic social institutions fit their names. For example, a king must be a true king, a minister must be a true minister, a father must be a true father, and a son must be a true son. In The Analects, when asked by his disciples what would be his priority if he were asked to govern, Confucius answered, "Zhengmin." He argued, "To govern is to zheng [正 erect righteousness]."[23] Governance should erect righteousness in human affairs, which in turn implies setting basic human relations right by making them embody the reality and substance that their names connote.

In connection with the above, one standard of evaluating basic social institutions, particularly the government, is xinyi. The xinyi of a government implies:

1. The relationship between a government and the people is set straight and reliable;
2. There is a true correspondence between the name and the substance of a government;
3. A government has a praiseworthy character of humanity.

The *xinyi* of a government shows that its relationship with and commitment to the people is rectified and the name of a government designates a true substance. The substance of a government should deserve its name. So should the substance of other basic social institutions, including the family, the law, and education.

With a different emphasis, Confucius further said prophetically, "When one sets one's mind on humanity, one will be free of evil."[24] Evil is great injustice. When one sets one's mind on humanity, one knows what is right and wrong, good and evil, as well as righteous and unrighteous. When one sets one's mind on humanity, one knows what is required of a human being and what one's human identity requires of oneself. When one sets one's mind on humanity, one knows what human goods and human bonds are. As a result, one is free of unjust acts and of evil against humanity.

Confucius also claimed, "Only a person of humanity knows whom to love and whom to hate."[25] That is, only a person of humanity knows the just way to love and hate. Only such a person *could* know who is righteous and should be loved, and conversely who is *bu yi* (不义 unrighteous, evil) and should be hated. By the same token, only a government of humanity is free of evil and injustice. Unless a government has its standards of humanity and thus is guided by the ideas of the human goods and bonds, it will not be free of evil and unjust acts and policies.

This brings us to Mencius, a Confucian master of the Socratic style. For Mencius, a just person embodies basic human qualities such as trustworthiness, righteousness, tolerance, and wisdom; a just government embodies the basic principles of humanity, righteousness, wisdom, and trustworthiness. Mencius was the first Chinese philosopher to insist explicitly that a particular concern of justice should be to defend human dignity, the first Chinese philosopher to reject abuses of human dignity as unjust, and the first to use the term *ren zheng* (仁政 government of humanity), as contrasted to *bao zheng* (暴政 government of oppression and repression), *nude zheng* (虐政 abusive, oppressive, and repressive government), and *yin zheng* (淫政 government by excessive desires and violence), claiming that *ren zheng* is forever invincible.

Mencius distinguished between a just government and an unjust one.[26] For him, a just government respects the human dignity of individual persons and the dignity of the people of a community, cares for the welfare of the people, and facilitates the growth of human ties such as the relationships between the ruler and the ruled, parents and children, husbands and wives, siblings, and friends, as well as communal ties. Admittedly, Mencius has no explicit concept of human rights. However, he made extensive reference to the inviolability of a person's human dignity and talked explicitly about a person's entitlement to be treated as a human being. Equally crucial, for him, was the idea that treating a person with dignity is a component of social justice. Indeed, for Mencius, justice obliges us to respect human dignity.

Mencius gave the following example to illustrate the centrality of honoring a person's human dignity in justice:

> Here is a basketful of rice and a bowl full of soup. Getting them will mean life; not getting them will mean death. When they are given with abuse, even a wayfarer would not accept them; when these are given after being trampled upon, even a beggar would not accept them.[27]

In this example, Mencius indicated that one standard of justice was respect for a person's human dignity and that an act violating human dignity was always a great injustice.

Elsewhere, Mencius insisted that our senses of humanity and justice are integral parts of our moral reason and, in addition, that our sense of righteousness is rooted in our feeling of shame.[28] Shame is the emotion of self-reproach we feel when we live in a way or perform an act that is below the standards of our human selves. For example, we should feel ashamed if we submit ourselves to abuse in order to get a bowl of rice. Mencius also insisted that only a person of humanity is free of evil; only a person of humanity knows what is required of a person and would not do evil against his or her own humanity or the humanity of others.

Mencius further stated: "If we cannot establish humanity, we cannot establish righteousness. Humanity is a person's safe abode; righteousness, a person's right path."[29] In the statement, righteousness as a path is built around humanity as the house; righteousness is centered on humanity. By the same token, the concern of humanity is the central concern of justice. For Mencius, the concerns of humanity include the concerns of human dignity, the truth and substance of humanity, and the human bonds embodied in familial and communal bonds.

Admittedly, from time to time, Mencius spoke of *ren* as the quality of commiseration for the suffering of fellow countrymen. Still, it remains the case that more often Mencius used the term *ren* to signify a general human quality and indicated that the concern of humanity was a comprehensive concern of the truth, substance, bonds, and dignity of a human person. Mencius is the first Chinese philosopher to associate the concept of *ren* explicitly with the concept of human dignity. He insisted that, from the point of *ren*, there are enduring standards of *yi* (义 righteousness) and that human beings should be treated with a measure of dignity. In the example of a hungry beggar refusing a bowl of rice that is given with abuse and the metaphor that humanity is the home and righteousness is the path, we can see that, for Mencius, humanity is a quality that gives a person the human dignity, the sense of shame, and moral character.

Neo-Confucian philosophers, for the most part, follow Mencius's footsteps in their approaches to justice. For them, a primary concern of justice is to set human relationships right in a normal society. Zhou Dunyi said:

> The ancient sage-kings established rites of propriety and laws to regulate, enlighten, educate and transform people, to set the three headropes [纲 key relations]—the relations between the ruler and the ministers, between father and son as well as between husband and wife—right, and put all human relationships in their proper places. As a result, people live in happiness and peace and everything is in harmony. . . . The world is transformed into a world of *zhong zheng* [中正 justice] and order and peace reach their highest points.[30]

For Zhou, setting human relations right—starting by setting the three key human relations right—is a distinctive and central concern of justice; in addition, justice must attune human nature properly so that the quality of humanity thrives within a person and in the society; accordingly, the function of just laws is to cultivate the quality of humanity in order to transform people for the better.

Cheng I said:

> The way of the sage-kings of Yao and Shun is the just way in the universe. This just way in the universe develops human relations to their best. The way of the five dictators of the Spring and Autumn Period is to follow their selfish interests and to act in a way that contradicts humanity and righteousness. . . . The way of the kings takes human persons as the foundation.[31]

For Cheng I, as well, setting human relations right is a distinctive and crucial concern of justice, as is treating humankind as the foundation or the end, not a means to other ends.

Admittedly, a concept of human rights is absent in traditional Chinese philosophies. Accordingly, no concepts of normative justice have been developed in traditional Chinese philosophies. However, traditional Chinese philosophies develop three distinctive ideas:

1. A central task and concern of justice is to defend human dignity.
2. Justice is meant to set human affairs right in terms of human values; it has a central obligation to set human relationships right in a normal society.
3. Justice erects the idea of humanity and setting human bonds right.

Therefore, Chinese philosophies lead us into the road to normative justice, though not through to the end.

In summation, in history, Western and Eastern philosophical approaches to justice have pointed to a road opened but not taken to normative justice. It is this road that we should take now.

Normative Justice and Humankind's Sensibility of Normativity

A definition and elaboration of normative justice itself is in order now. Normative justice is defined as setting human affairs right in terms of human rights, human goods (humanity as the end), and human bonds. This new, third family of justice exalts humanity as the end, as a quality to stand straight in our lives, and as the basis for a set of standards of evaluating basic social institutions; it makes the authentic truth and essence of humanity shine in the world.

The focus of normative justice falls on the obligation of humankind to humankind. One of its basic tenets is beautifully embodied in the preamble of the United Nations' 1948 Universal Declaration of Human Rights, which reads, "Recognition of the inherent dignity and of equal and inalienable rights of all members of the human family is the foundation of freedom, justice and peace in the world." "Inalienable rights," "inherent dignity," and "the human family" are among the watchwords of the principles of human rights, human goods (humanity as the end), human bonds; they are the watchwords of normative justice itself.

The elements of the definition of normative justice are:

- *The principle of human rights:* Human rights exist and are inviolable; the consideration of them is distinctive and central in social justice. The principle prescribes that "a human right . . . is a reason to treat persons in certain ways."[32] It dictates that justice gives what is due to a person in terms of his or her rights. Inscribed in justice is the inviolability of each person's human dignity and basic liberties, compatible with the same liberties of other members of the family of humankind. The principle stipulates that it is morally wrong and disallowed to deny what is entitled to a person and to treat a human person without dignity.

- *The principle of human goods:* Humanity has intrinsic value and is the end in the human existence. Universal human values exist. The considerations of humanity as the end and of universal human values are distinctive and central in justice. The principle stipulates that a person should maintain in relation to others his or her own worth as a human being. A duty prescribed by this principle is not to make oneself into a mere means for others, but to be at the same time an end for them. The principle dictates that basic social institutions must treat humanity as an end in itself, not merely as a means to an end, and must promote fundamental human values. It commands that it is morally wrong and impermissible to treat, whether intentionally or unintentionally, a human person merely as a means to an end and not to respect fundamental human values.
- *The principle of human bonds:* Universal human bonds exist and are of intrinsic value; the consideration of them is distinctive and central in justice. Formal human ties among all human beings impose a moral obligation on each person to treat other persons as human beings. The principle dictates that local human bonds such as familial and communal bonds also have intrinsic value and that the consideration of them is central in justice. It further stipulates that it is morally wrong and disallowed to act if performance of the act will damage human bonds; it is morally wrong and forbidden for any human institutions to pervert humanity and fundamental human bonds.

Normative justice is a rise in humankind's exclusive commitment and loyalty to its own humanity identity. This includes several aspects:

- the commitment to be a human being in the full sense, rising above bestiality and nonhuman animal existence
- loyalty to the idea of human integrity and unity, not to a half-human, half-beast existence
- commitment to preserve what is essential for humanity and humankind

Normative justice singles out a distinctive family of humankind's obligation to humankind. It establishes a particular family of standards of evaluating how human beings associate with one another in a normal society and in the family of humankind in the world. It expounds a set of standards for evaluating basic social institutions in terms of their commitment to humanity and basic human values.

Loyalty to our humanity identity requires being just to ourselves and vice versa. Our humanity identity is our most transparent normative identity. We are not angels or beasts, and we should not try to be either of them. Blaise Pascal said prophetically, "Man must not think he is on a level with either beasts or angels, and he must not be ignorant of those levels, but should know both."[33] If we are not loyal to our humanity, we do not give our humanity identity its due. Nor do we recognize and set straight the basic truth of us as human beings. Loyalty to our humanity identity entails loyalty to the humanity identity of our fellow human beings. The humanity identity is a universal normative identity of all people. When we are loyal to one, we are loyal to all. Conversely, when we are disloyal to one, we are disloyal to all. Admittedly, in addition to our normative identity—that is, our humanity identity—we have also other practical identities such as our cultural identity and communal identity that demand due loyalty, too. Nonetheless, the fact that we have various kinds of loyalty and commitments does not alter the fact that loyalty to our humanity identity gives rise to a distinctive class of social obligation.

Normative justice is a rise in the recognition of and loyalty to our humanity identity. This, in turn, leads to a distinctive family of social obligations in terms of human rights, human goods (humanity as the end), and human bonds and therefore a particular basis for a set of standards for evaluating basic social institutions. Loyalty to our own humanity makes us recognize our human rights, inherent dignity, and intrinsic worth as humans. And in recognizing these, we also recognize fellow human beings' same rights, dignity, and worth. In this way, we see the universal bonds among all human beings and appreciate the concept of universal human values—that is, what is valuable to all human beings.

In short, normative justice comes from our loyalty to our and others' humanity and arrives at humankind's exclusive duty to itself. It brings to light a family of wrong, evil, and injustice and addresses the concerns of human dignity, freedom, rights, and responsibility. It dictates a class of public obligations for humankind and basic human institutions amid the consequences, burdens, and self-sacrifice of the obligations, as well as their imposition and restriction, which normally will be sufficient to reduce the amount of happiness and pleasure of individual persons.

Now, our obligations to humankind in terms of human rights, human goods, humanity as the end, and human bonds are not extendable to nonhuman animals. What we owe to fellow human beings, we do not owe to other animals. We owe to fellow human beings recognition of their rights, dignity, and intrinsic worth, as well as our common human bonds and common human values. But we do not owe nonhuman animals recognition of any of alleged "rights," any more than we do for stones, mountains, or rivers.

Korsgaard notes, "Obligation is a reflective rejection of a threat to your identity."[34] A refusal to recognize and honor human rights, humanity as the end, and human bonds threatens our identity. But a refusal to recognize nonhuman animals' rights, values, and bonds does not. Indeed, the concepts of animal rights and an obligation to animals to respect their rights are unintelligible, paradoxical, and absurd. They actually pose a threat to the value of human rights. The animal rights movement, which allegedly teaches us human compassion, in effect undermines our concept of humanity. The concept of animal rights degrades the distinction between human beings and nonhuman beings.

Obligations, including the obligation of justice, presuppose reciprocity. All obligations, including our obligations to fellow human beings, are mutual. For example, the fact that we are obliged to recognize fellow human brings' rights presupposes that fellow human beings are also obliged to recognize our rights. Conversely, if fellow human beings do not recognize our rights, their act of nonrecognition cancels our obligation to recognize theirs. But there can be no mutual obligations between human beings and nonhumans. As Habermas explains:

> "Obligation" presupposes the intersubjective recognition of moral norms or customary practices that lay down for a community in a convincing manner what actors are obliged to do and what they can expect from one another. 'In a convincing manner' means that the members of a moral community appeal to these norms whenever the coordination of action breaks down.[35]

No intersubjective recognition of moral norms and obligation exists between humans and animals. As Korsgaard points out, the idea that nonhuman animals have obligations to us is "absurd."[36] Human beings and animals do not form a community of mutual obligations, moral or legal.

A distinction between normative justice and humanitarian morality is in order. They differ in focus, content, problems, and scope. To start with, normative justice focuses on setting human affairs right. By contrast, humanitarian morality focuses on easing human suffering. The substance of normative justice is rectified and erected righteousness; the substance of humanitarian morality is full kindness, benevolence, and generosity. Gross and systematic violation of human rights, human values, humanity as the end, and human bonds represents not merely the failure to prevent avoidable human suffering but also the fundamental wrong and evil in terms of failing to meet or contradicting the standards of acceptability of human institutions and conduct. Lack of sympathy for human suffering should be subject to moral criticism, but not punishment in the name of justice. Normative justice is applied to areas where human rights, human goods, humanity as the end, and human bonds are at issue, while humanitarian morality is applied to areas where there is a call for easing human suffering and assistance to human need. The force of normative justice is obligatory; the force of humanitarian morality is attraction of virtue.

The essential distinction between normative justice and humanitarian morality is between justice and compassion. Justice is a proportional response to what is due and entitled; it cannot be a disproportional or undue response, either excessive or insufficient. By contrast, compassion or benevolence can be an excessive—that is, disproportional—response to what a person is entitled to. Compassion is about suffering. Justice is about whether a burden is due or undue, and suffering may not be an undue burden. Looking at it the other way, an undue burden does not necessarily bring unhappiness and suffering. In addition, justice is an act of reciprocity between two equals. On the contrary, compassion or benevolence is a paternal act of kindness that a party in a stronger position gives to someone in a weaker position. Justice presupposes reciprocity, while benevolence has no such presupposition. Justice is about right and wrong, good and evil, acceptable and unacceptable. Benevolence or compassion is concerned with happiness and suffering, interests and harm. Justice is the norm among the equals; benevolence is the stronger's norm of virtue toward the weaker.

Our sense of justice is internally connected with our feeling of shame—that is, the feeling of self-reproach for being below given human standards—which internalizes our concept of normative justice. The force of the feeling of shame lies in one's unwillingness to fall below the standards of oneself and basic humanity. Our sense of benevolence is associated with the feeling of commiseration, and the force of commiseration lies in one's unwillingness to see others continuously suffering.

Habermas indicates that the feeling of being obliged has three elements:

1. From a third-person perspective, transgression arouses the feelings of "abhorrence, indignation and contempt."
2. From the perspective of those affected, transgression brings the feelings of "violations and resentment toward second persons."
3. From a first-person perspective, transgression arouses feelings of shame and guilt.[37]

By this reckoning, the feeling of shame is the emotion that makes us feel obliged to be just from our human point of view. Our duty to humankind and fellow human beings imposes such a feeling of obligation on us.

In light of the above, we can interpret the obligatory force of normative justice beyond that of humanitarian morality as follows:

1. From a third-person perspective, transgression of human rights, human goods (humanity as the end), and human bonds arouses the feelings of abhorrence, indignation, and repugnance.
2. From the perspective of those affected, transgression of human rights, human goods (humanity as the end), and human bonds produces the feelings of violation, harm, subjugation, impairment, wrong, and evil.
3. From a first-person perspective, transgression of human rights, human goods (humanity as the end), and human bonds arouses feelings of shame, dislike, self-rejection, and guilt.

In comparison, benevolence or compassion, although lack of it leaves human suffering unattended, is incapable of producing the feelings described above.

The Call of the Human Conscience

"How great a burden mankind is for man," wrote Hannah Arendt.[38] Neglect of humanity is an evil; marginalization of humanity is a greater evil; and perversion of humanity is the greatest evil. Impairment of humanity is an injustice; violation of humanity is a greater injustice; and crimes against humanity belong in the category of the greatest injustice. "Impairment of humanity" here means harm for humanity as a value and humankind as a species in the world. "Violation of humanity" connotes abuse of human rights, universal human values, and human bonds. The archetypes of crimes against humanity include murdering, enslaving, or deporting any civilian population or persecuting them on political, racial, or religious grounds.[39]

Michael Walzer puts forth a concept of universal, thin morality "consisting of prohibitions against 'the grossest injustice' like 'murder, deception, betrayal, gross cruelty' and 'torture, oppression and tyranny.'"[40] Noticeably, a distinction exists between a universal morality in terms of the universal duty of justice and a universal humanitarian morality. The Walzeran universal, thin morality belongs more to the provinces of universal morality in terms of normative justice and corrective justice. True distinction between right and wrong is first of all the distinction between humanity and inhumanity. Justice is humanity standing straight; injustice is inhumanity, or humanity crooked. If justice exists, then humanity exists and stands straight; conversely, if humanity does not exist or is not standing straight, there is no justice. There is injustice wherein there is inhumanity as *xie wu* (crooked evil) or injustice as a perversion of justice.

The concept of antihuman justice is absurd. Institutions that are against humanity or lead to either violation or marginalization of humanity are unjust and evil. Individual conduct that marginalizes or violates humanity is unjust and evil. We can disagree on what *antihumanity* is. Some may believe that communism is antihumanity; others believe that capitalism is. Still, we should have no disagreement that what is antihumanity is unjust and evil. As a matter of fact, it makes no sense to claim anything against humanity to be just. Instead, we ought to identify that which is antihumanity as perfectly unjust. Anything that is against humanity damages and perverts humanity and therefore is something humankind should reject. That which is antihumanity is not good to humanity; it cannot be reasonable, fair, and justified to human beings, and it will not be a virtue to human beings. Therefore, antihumanity is an intrinsic evil.

Some may argue that some states of affairs or events such as natural disasters damage humankind, but it would be unreasonable to characterize them as unjust; by the same token, not all of what is antihumanity is unjust. This argument is a bad one. Natural disasters are amoral and not the objects of the concern of justice. They cannot be judged to be just or unjust. They cannot be the objects of concern of justice precisely because we cannot apply the qualifier of being "antihumanity" to them. They may be harmful to humankind, but are not antihumanity. Can we claim that a river or mountain is for humanity because it is beneficial to the lives of the members of a human community? If not, how can we claim that a volcano is antihumanity because it is damaging to the lives of a human community?

It makes no sense for us to talk about justice that is irrelevant to humanity. If humans as a species were irrelevant to justice, justice would not be a problem to humankind. If justice were irrelevant to humankind, to talk about justice would make no difference to humankind.

If humankind were irrelevant to justice, the following two claims would be true. First, humankind is not an object of concern of justice; that is, human beings and institutions could not be judged just or unjust. But this claim is absurd. To the contrary, setting God aside, human beings and institutions are the *only* possible objects of concern of justice. We cannot apply the concept of justice to nonhuman beings. Stones and trees are neither just nor unjust, and there is no justice of dogs or pigs. And if human conduct and institutions are objects to which the concept of justice is exclusively applied, then humanity is not—cannot be—irrelevant to justice. Furthermore, humans are the only beings asking questions about justice, reflecting their experience in terms of the concept of justice, and aspiring to be just. Apart from God, the problems of justice remain exclusively human problems. Besides God, humans are the only agents and subjects of justice.

The second claim that would be true if humankind were irrelevant to justice is that an act or institution which violates humankind—for example, an act that violates human rights, values, bonds, and the idea of humanity as the end—cannot be judged to be just or unjust. This claim, too, is absurd. To the contrary, violation of humanity is great injustice for several reasons: it is a great evil, it is a great wrong, and it perverts things. Violation of humanity is a great evil because it distorts and destroys humanity. Violation of humanity perverts things because it corrupts and subverts the natural way of the existence of things in the world.

Justice erects humanity for humankind. First, justice implicates the duty of humanity on humankind. Second, it makes excellent human institutions that are indispensable for the members of the human family to extend their lives together. Third, it makes human beings excellent; for example, justice makes human beings reasonable, dutiful, and good. Fourth, humanity as a quality and humankind as a species are the exclusive objects that justice can affect. Justice cannot change a stone, nor can it change a dog or a pig.

Can humanity as a quality be irrelevant to justice? The answer is no. Otherwise, human conduct or an institution that violates humanity as a value would be irrelevant to justice and could not be judged unjust. If this were true, we could not call it unjust. But we are justified in calling a government that deprives its people of human rights, dignity, and human bonds unjust and evil. We are justified to do the same to other basic social institutions. An important reason that we want justice is to defend human dignity, integrity, goods, rights, and bonds. In reality, justice in the human world means that humanity triumphs over bestiality; the rule of humanity overcomes the reign of bestiality or inhumanity. Justice in the human world dictates that crimes against humanity are great injustice and evil. "Crime against humanity signifies 'a level of callousness that embodies the very essence of evil itself.'"[41]

A clarification is in order. In some contexts, some acts that appear to "harm" humanity actually serve it. Taking capital punishment as an example. Despite its appearance, capital punishment is not an act of antihumanity. The act of executing a criminal who deserves death reaffirms the concepts of human agency and social responsibility. For this reason,

Philosophers, such as Immanuel Kant and G. W. F. Hegel, have insisted that, when deserved, execution, far from degrading the executed convict, affirms his humanity by affirming his rationality and his responsibility for his actions. They thought that execution, when deserved, is required for the sake of the convict's dignity.[42]

The principle of justice is also not the principle of prudence. In real life, some may be motivated to practice justice by the prudential reason for self-protection. But from the point of view of self-protection, it may also be justifiable to practice injustice. For example, we might practice domination and repression to protect our interests and the interests of those we care about. If we ought to subscribe to the idea of justice in order to protect all human beings, we must justify why we need to protect the interests of all human beings. Without a concept of human bonds, the idea of protection of all human beings loses its normative force. If we ought to subscribe to justice because it is the most reasonable thing to do, then why does being reasonable matter to the extent that it is obligatory?

Furthermore, if humanity as a value were irrelevant, there would be no difference between humans and pigs or dogs or machines, and as a result it would be pointless of talking about justice at all. In other words, we want to be just because we want to be a being of humanity in the full sense; we want to be just because humanity as our normative identity and as a value is of the greatest importance. Justice would have no significance to us if we did not mind being like dogs, pigs, wolves, or other beasts, or even like stones or pieces of wood. Thus, the idea that humanity as a value is irrelevant to justice is paradoxical. The truth is the opposite.

At any rate, justice is internally connected with the value of humanity. For this reason, justice rejects subjectification, objectification, social alienation, and subjugation—in short, any forms of perversion of humanity. It rejects any forms of dehumanization, repression, enslavement, and exploitation of humankind. It rejects any dehumanized ideologies and antihumanity social forces that we call evil, whether it is in the form of Nazism, racism, sexism, ethnic cleansing, religious discrimination, sexual subjectification or objectification, social subjugation, or political-economic exploitation.

In connection with the above, normative justice rejects ingratitude, impiety, disloyalty, betrayal, and indifference as injustices. Though these are not crimes against humanity, they are evils that pervert humanity. They are the insinuating serpents in the garden that are evil and that sow the seeds of evil. They twist righteousness—for example, humanity as the end, universal human values, human nature, and human bonds. They bend the truth and substance of humanity.

Ingratitude is an injustice in terms of being irresponsive to the communal matrix from which we are benefited. "Wang en fu yi" (忘恩负义 Ingratitude violates justice), we are told by traditional Chinese philosophies; that is, *wang en* (忘恩 ingratitude or forgetting gratitude) is *fu yi* (负义 a violation of righteousness). Ingratitude violates justice or is an injustice because it does not give what is due and is not fair, it is indifferent to human goods and human bonds, and it makes a person fall below common human standards.

Impiety is an injustice in terms of being forgetful of the communal source to which one is indebted. Disloyalty is nonappreciation of the communal relationships into which one enters. Impiety and disloyalty are unjust because they both trash human goods and human bonds and also do not give back what is due. While justice is a rise in the obligation of reciprocity, impiety and disloyalty betray directly and contradict the obligation of reciprocity.

Indifference is the failure to respond humanely to the communal experience in which one extends one's existence. Indifference is unjust because it disregards human goods and bonds and treats human beings as things and means to some other ends.

True, in comparison to crimes against humanity, impiety, disloyalty, and indifference may be less in degree and not of great magnitude. However, they are unjust because in them righteousness and humanity do not stand straight.

In sum, normative justice asserts that all forms of inhumanity violate the standards of justice and betray humankind's obligation to humankind. Any turning of human beings into things, commodity, and mere tools in the world is profoundly unjust and evil. All forms of crimes against humanity are forms of great injustice. Therefore, normative justice turns a world in which humanity fades into a world in which humanity thrives.

Justice and Partiality to Humankind

Obviously, the concept of normative justice as discussed above is not applicable to nonhuman beings. It not only gives priority to humanity as a quality and humankind as a species in its concern, but also is ontologically and morally partial to humankind because it belongs exclusively to humankind. Indeed, all three families of justice—distributive, corrective, and normative—have partiality toward humans; they implicate humankind's exclusive public duty and obligation exclusively of and toward humankind. Justice is partiality to humanity, and partiality to humanity is justice.

Richard Rorty gives as an example the case in which we kill crows and other animals carrying disease to ensure human safety:

Suppose that the crows, or the kangaroos, turn out to be carriers of a newly mutated virus, though harmless to them, is invariably fatal to humans. I suspect that we would then shrug off of the accusation of "specieism" and participate in the necessary massacre. The idea of justice between species will suddenly become irrelevant. . . . Loyalty to our own species must come first.[43]

Evidentially, Rorty's claim is justified. Human beings have the right of self-defense. However, while we feel justified in killing animals that carry viruses, we are not similarly justified in killing humans who carry deadly diseases. Otherwise, we can be rightly accused of murder or crimes against humanity.

We recognize human rights, but do not acknowledge nonhuman animals' alleged rights. Our discretion can be justified by the fact that we cannot consistently both deny fellow human beings' rights and claim our own human rights; but we can consistently both claim our human rights and deny nonhuman animals' alleged rights; our denial of animal rights only makes our defense of human rights more consistent. If we deny fellow human beings' human rights, we cannot be loyal to our humanity identity. However, we can be loyal to our humanity identity while denying rights to nonhuman animals; indeed, our denial of nonhuman animals' rights only makes our defense of our humanity more consistent.

We can talk about justice only from our human perspective of human justice, not from the perspective of the universe. The qualification "from our human perspective" is crucial here. As Bernard Williams indicates, to claim that human beings are the most valuable beings to us is one thing, but to claim that we are the most valuable beings in the universe is quite another.[44] To conflate these two claims is to confuse the point of view of the universe with the point of view of human beings. We can claim that humanity is a central value to us and that human beings are the most valuable beings and unique substances from our human point of view. However, we would be unreasonable to claim that humanity is the central value of the universe beyond human perspective, that human beings are the most valuable beings in the universe from the point of view of the universe. Therefore, we can claim that, from our human point of view, human beings and other nonhuman beings are not equal, even though, as Zhuangzi would argue, in the eyes of the *dao*, human and nonhuman beings are equal.

In normative justice, the value of humanity has priority over other values. If there are "values" that are incompatible to the value of humanity, we are justified in rejecting them. When some values that are compatible with the value of humanity in general are in conflict with the value of humanity in a given circumstance, we are also justified in rejecting them in that circumstance. For example, at some point of a biomedical experiment that uses human subjects, a conflict may exist between the desire to have knowledge and the consideration of the welfare of the involved human subjects. Justice dictates that the value of humanity has the priority over the value of knowledge in such a context.

For the same reasons, in some circumstances, normative justice rejects some violent practices that are destructive to human lives and seriously damage human rights, dignity, and bonds in a given circumstance, even if these practices aim at promoting values that may be instrumental to promote some goods. For example, normative justice rejects offensive wars to advance democracy—say, the invasion of another country whose government is totalitarian and oppressive. Normative justice also rejects such practices as extremist religious *jihad* that uses violence in the name of God to force people to change their beliefs and even endorses terrorism in the name of religion.

Simultaneously, normative justice demands equal respect for the human rights and dignity of all human beings. While emphasizing the importance of humankind over nonhuman beings, normative justice does not privilege one group of people over other groups. Normative justice insists on differentiation and discrimination between humankind and nonhumans, but rejects discriminations among human beings. Here, a fine line exists between giving just loyalty to our familial, communal relations and unjustly, selfishly privileging our own group of people. We are just in being loyal to our familial, communal relations; our formal bonds to humanity are consistent with our particular bonds to our community and are embodied in such particular bonds. However, loyalty to our communal bonds does not command us to privilege our own group of people over other groups of people in our common community. Just loyalty does not oblige us to hide our relatives who commit crimes from police. Justice sets right our relations with our familial members and the members of our community. However, right relations do not include becoming accomplices in a crime.

Therefore, normative justice has a Janus face. It rejects all forms of discrimination within the human family, be it racist, sexist, or cultural discrimination. Simultaneously, it involves a loyalty to the great human family.

Humanity, Metaphysics, and Other Problems

Admittedly, the discussions and arguments thus far have taken for granted the concept of humanity in itself. But one is not unreasonable to be unsettled with a metaphysical concept of humanity per se. What humanity per se is has been heatedly debated throughout history. As a matter of fact, today, an asymmetry exists in Western philosophies: the steady shining of the idea of human rights and human dignity goes hand in hand with a steady eclipse of all metaphysical concepts of humanity; humanity is necessary, but not metaphysical—a serious paradox. Many philosophers choose to avoid the burden of proof of metaphysical humanity by labeling their views on justice as political or postmetaphysical, but such bad faith weakens their stances on justice.

Is there humanity in itself? If there is, what is wrong with the strategies that philosophers hitherto have adopted to define humanity? My answer is as follows: humanity in itself exists, though humanity per se is not a homeless, disembodied soul. There is a universal substance called humanity that is embodied, at least that can be embodied, in all human beings. And humanity as such is a substance that should not be identified with its attributes. Previous strategies to define humanity in itself fail the task because they all attempt to define humanity in terms of its attributes, attempting to locating humanity—the substance—in this or that of its attributes. A better strategy can consist of three arguments: the transcendental, the empirical, and the pragmatic.

The transcendental argument goes like this: It strikes us as self-evident that various human attributes and characters exist and are intelligible. Therefore, humanity as the substance must exist. Otherwise, these human attributes and characters cannot exist, let alone be intelligible.

The empirical argument says that empirically humankind is a species of its own, differing from nonhuman animals such as dogs, cats, and tigers as well as from lifeless beings such as mountains, trees, stones, and metals. Therefore, humanity as a unified concept exists. Humanity as a unified concept is not empty but has reality and empirical content; it follows that humanity can be metaphysically argued for and defended through generation and abstraction.

The pragmatic argument declares that we are better off believing in a united, metaphysical concept of humanity. In other words, the belief in a metaphysical concept of humanity has contributed significantly to improving our human lives and existences. Therefore, we ought to believe in a metaphysical concept of humanity, or at least we should believe in a metaphysical concept of humanity as a Pascalian wager.

The three arguments above—the transcendental, the empirical, and the pragmatic—provide the good and sufficient reasons for us to subscribe to a metaphysical concept of humanity. But it is the affirmation of human rights, human goods, and human bonds that brings concrete currency to the concept of universal humanity. Many of us may still disagree on what the exact components of human rights, human goods, and human bonds are, but there is less controversy about the general ideas of them—for example, human rights connote some general entitlements; human bonds, some internal connections among human beings.

Amid the above, the concept of universal humanity is challenged by tribalism, postmodernism, and provincialism, which reject the concepts of universal human rights, human goods, and human bonds. In "Human Rights: A Bill of Worries," Henry Rosemount writes:

> My own skepticism is directed not toward any particular moral or political theory in which rights play a role, but toward the more fundamental view of human beings as free, autonomous individuals on which all such theories more or less rest. . . . The concept of human rights and related concepts clustered around it, like liberty, the individual, property, autonomy, freedom, reason, choice, and so on, do not capture what it is we believe to be the inherent sociality of human beings.[45]

Herbert Fingarette also says:

> I am quite prepared to attack the doctrine of individual rights—attack it at least to the extent of arguing that it is not so purely beneficent a doctrine as we tend to assume today. Along with its benefits, it has profound potential as a socially disruptive and anti-human force. It is against the background of a Confucian vision of human life that this corrosive effect of rights-based morality comes clearly in focus.[46]

To various challenges, including the above, my basic response is this: The transcendental, empirical, and pragmatic arguments provide us good and sufficient reason to subscribe to a unified concept of humanity; a unified concept of humanity suggests that human rights exist; human goods exist and human bonds exist; as a result, we have good and sufficient reason to believe that documents such as the French Declaration of the Rights of Man and of the Citizen (1789) and the United Nations' Universal Declaration of Human Rights (1948) have profound truths.[47]

On a different front, a rivalry exists between a cosmopolitan outlook and a political outlook on justice. The great challenge from a political outlook is that universal human bonds do not exist, or even if they do exist, they do not give rise to the obligation of justice. In a political outlook, human rights are the political and legal rights established by laws and states rather than inherent natural rights—the Kantian concept of humanity as the end is set aside. Nagel and others' skepticism of global justice is a direct outcome of such a political outlook. However, the concept of normative justice has a cosmopolitan outlook that can be well defended by the transcendental, empirical, and pragmatic arguments above.

Global Justice and Its Problems

The discussions above have paved the way for us to bring home a new family of global justice: global normative justice as setting global human affairs right in terms of human rights, human goods (humanity as the end), and human bonds. This family of global justice differs from global distributive justice and corrective justice in substance, focus, objective, problem, and scope.

Nagel suggests: "We do not live in a just world. . . . But it is much less clear what, if anything, justice on a world scale might mean."[48] Nagel is concerned with global socioeconomic justice, about which he has misgivings.

> In a broad sense of the term, international requirements of justice include standards governing the justification and conduct of war and standards that define the most basic human rights. Some standards of these two kinds have achieved a measure of international recognition over the past half-century. They define certain types of criminal conducts.[49]

However, Nagel observes, "The normative force of the most basic human rights against violence, enslavement, and coercion and of the basic humanitarian duties of rescue from immediate danger depends only on our capacity to put ourselves in other peoples' shoes."[50] Thus, the normative force of basic human rights is that of minimal humanitarian morality.

As mentioned earlier, Nagel gives three reasons for his misgivings about global justice:

1. No human relationships beyond state borders give rise to the obligation of justice.
2. Beyond the border of the state, we cannot be both the authors and receivers of justice.
3. There is no institutional force to act as an auxiliary force for justice.

However, Nagel's three reasons cannot stand. First, universal human bonds do exist. They give rise to the global obligations of justice, such as the obligation to treat other human beings and to meet certain standards of treating human beings as human beings. It may be the case that such an obligation does not include a requirement for the rich to give to the poor. Still, our obligations of justice to other human beings beyond the state border do exist. Second, while we are the receivers of global justice or injustice, we can be the authors or coauthors of them by articulating or contributing to articulating them, or practicing or coding them through a democratic process. Third, Nagel's final reason is more about the challenge for the implementation of global justice than about whether global justice exists.

With regard particularly to global socioeconomic justice, Nagel's main problems are his political, not cosmopolitan, outlook and his assumption that justice divides into only two kinds: distributive and corrective. With a political outlook, Nagel sees no universal basis in terms of relationships for global socioeconomic justice and no global institutional sanctioning force to implement global justice; that is, no relationship beyond the state borders can impose the obligation of justice on us and no legitimate institutional sanctioning force can implement any alleged global justice. "Justice is something we owe through our shared institutions only to those with whom we stand in a strong political relation. It is . . . an associative obligation."[51] Thus, for Nagel, if socioeconomic justice is about fair and equal distribution of resources and wealth and socioeconomic equality, no relationship beyond one's own borders can give rise to the global obligation of justice.

Many philosophers today often talk about global justice as global distributive justice, too. Lars Ericsson's claim, "To formulate a theory of global justice is to lay conditions for a fair distribution of the world's goods and resources among its population," summarizes the trend.[52] Other philosophers differ, indicating that global justice is some kind of corrective justice—that is, justice to correct wrongs such as stopping crimes against humanity and violation of human rights and punishing wrongdoers in the world today.[53]

Therefore, to put things in perspective, the gloomy scene is that for the most part, philosophers today more or less see global justice as dividing between global distributive justice and global corrective justice. In the sense of the former, philosophers talk about fair distribution of resources, power, burdens, opportunities, and responsibility among East, West, North, and South. Nielsen suggests that global justice "requires an extensive redistribution between North and South."[54] In the sense of global corrective justice, on the other hand, we talk about international intervention in areas and countries where there are serious human rights violations and crimes against humanity. Writings of Walzer and Habermas provide us with insights into global corrective justice.

Identifying global justice exclusively with global distributive justice, Nielsen falls into despair about the prospect of what can be accomplished in terms of global justice. He feels ambivalently that "it is indecent to talk about global justice. . . . Talk about it—setting out normative accounts of global justice—is at worst hypocritical or self-deceptive and at best empty

and ideological."[55] For him, this feeling of ambivalence involves two conflicting aspects:

1. "Our very humanity—our sense of common human decency—impels
   us to try to see this matter through to the end: to come to see that there
   are requirements of global justice."
2. "When we face, or try to face, the question, 'What is to be done?'
   lapsing into despair and coming to think such talk of global justice is
   self-indulgent prattle is very seductive."[56]

Nielsen recognizes the existence of "inhumanity" in the globe and per-
ceives the connection between global inhumanity and "global injustice."
Nonetheless, he fails to see that the limit of global distributive justice is not
the limit of global justice itself; the limit of what we can accomplish through
global distributive justice is not the limit of what we can accomplish through
global justice in general. Nagel, Nielsen, and others tacitly recognize global
corrective justice. What they should recognize is another family of global
justice: global normative justice.

Joshua Cohen and Charles Sabel defend the concept of global socioeconomic justice. They insist, "Conceptions of global justice offer accounts of
human rights, standards of fair government, and norms of fair distributions
(including access to such basic goods as health and education)."[57] But what
they advocate is inadequate. They are concerned only with the distributive
aspect of global socioeconomic justice. Though they rightly insist on norms
of justice in international affairs, they conceive such norms merely from the
perspective of distributive justice. The same is true of others such as A. J.
Julius.[58]

Two other distinctions also contribute to muddying the water. One is
Nagel's distinction between the obligation of justice and what he dubs "basic
humanitarian duties" and his claim that the obligation of justice does not
include "an obligation to live in a just society with everyone" and to live
in a just world with everyone. Another is some philosophers' distinction
between global justice and international justice—the former dealing with
individual human beings and the latter with relations among nations and
peoples. This is also the distinction between globalism and internationalism
on global justice.

The way for us to sort out the confusions above is to see that, in addition
to global distributive justice and corrective justice, there is a third family of
global justice: global normative justice. Global justice includes global distributive justice, which is concerned with distribution of resources, power,

responsibilities, burdens, opportunities, and tasks in the global human family. Simultaneously, global justice is also concerned with establishing a global order in which humanity as the end and value stands straight, in which human rights are protected, and in which universal human bonds grow and thrive.[59] It is concerned with humankind's basic obligation to humankind.[60]

For example, global justice calls for a fair global socioeconomic order in which there can be fair distribution of resources around the globe. But it also implicates the norms of obligation to respect national sovereignty, the rights of a nation or people to autonomy, and norms of obligations to each other among nations and peoples, as well as the norms and obligations of nations and peoples to live up to the ideals of human rights, human goods, and human bonds. Global justice demands fair and humanistic global institutions in economic globalization, but also global development of democracy, democratization of global human institutions, and global inclusion.

Global justice includes but is not limited to corrective justice, too. Terrorism, genocide, and other forms of human rights abuse and human destruction are global evils and paradigms of global injustice. Overcoming them and establishing global justice are urgent tasks of our time. At the same time, global justice involves more than correcting the wrong. The concern of global justice is not limited to the problems of compensation and remedy. Global justice has a distinctive concern of global humanity—protection of human rights, promotion of human goods, and development of human bonds on the Earth. It has a distinctive imperative to reject any identification of globalization with Western hegemony in our time. It is concerned with democracy and inclusion in global politics, socioeconomic lives, and intellectual dialogues.

Even in its answer to crimes against humanity, violation of humanity, and various social evils around the world, global justice is concerned not only with compensation and remedy problems but also with the problems of reconstructing human relations and human institutions in terms of basic human principles and human values. The Confucian classic *Great Learning* suggests three objectives of global justice: making the brightest virtues of the universe shine, renovating the people, and being in union with the ultimate good.[61] The suggestion is instructive.

Global justice calls for international intervention when human rights are grossly violated or crimes against humanity occur in a country or society. But what international intervention should bring about in the subject countries is not only corrective justice but also normative justice—that is, not only stopping the existing crimes but also introducing basic infrastructures and institutions that will prevent such crimes in future and that will protect human rights, human goods (humanity as the end), and human bonds. We must pay attention to when and in what contexts there should be international intervention, as well as what the international intervention should accomplish. My contention is that the objective of international intervention is not to return a country to the status quo ante but to establish something more fundamental—that is, to set human affairs right in terms of human rights, human goods (humanity as the end), and human bonds. In other words, the objective of international intervention is to bring about not merely corrective justice but also normative justice.

The former status quo may leave much to be desired as far as respect for human rights and the dignity and protection of human goods and bonds are concerned. It is likely, too, that the present status quo—in which human rights are violated, human goods are marginalized, and human bonds are abandoned—is itself a continuity of the former situation. We must also bear in mind that without an emphasis on realization of normative justice as the objective of international intervention, such interventions can easily result in new colonization, domination, and imperialism. International intervention can take different forms. Some are humanitarian in nature; others are interventions of justice to restore human rights, humanity as the end, and universal human bonds—in short, to eliminate inhumanity and restore humanity.

National bonds constitute one kind of real human bonds. Accordingly, the national bond of a people has its due claim under global justice. Thus, global normative justice demands mutual recognition and respect among nations and peoples. Meanwhile, nations and peoples have the obligation of justice to be loyal to basic humanity. Such loyalty must not be undercut by a nation's loyalty to its history, experience, and independence. Global normative justice implicates standards of evaluating government policies and global institutions in terms of global humanity.

Global normative justice calls for democratic inclusion and cultural toleration in global political and economic lives. It mandates standards of managing, regulating, and resolving international conflicts and calls for international democratization. However, its focus is not on the redistribution of power but on the establishment of humanity as the quality and the end of human existence. It recognizes globalization as a profound movement.

In short, global normative justice means setting global human affairs right in terms of human rights, human goods, humanity as the end, and human bonds. It has its distinctive focus, concerns, content, problems, objectives, and scope, interspersed with those of global distributive justice and global corrective justice, neither of which is included in the other. Global normative justice implicates the obligations of humankind to humankind in the globe. It singles out a distinctive family of standards for evaluating policies of governments pertaining to global affairs and international and transnational institutions. It defines a distinctive family of objectives of what we want in the domain of global institutions and in the policies that are in a position to affect the global order.

The distinction between global justice and international justice, which philosophers dance around today, needs to be clarified here. The Ericsson distinction is significantly flawed. In this version,

> international justice . . . is basically a relation that holds two or more independent nations, states or societies. Global justice, in contrast, is basically a relation that holds between human or sentient beings within something called the global society. To formulate a theory of international justice is to lay down conditions for laws of nations. To formulate a theory of global justice is to lay conditions for a just distribution of the world's goods and resources among its population.[62]

The distinction is suggestive but significantly flawed and does not offer us a useful map of global justice.

On the one hand, global justice is not limited to global distributive justice. On the other hand, international justice does have its distributive dimension. The distinction between international justice and global justice is not even a distinction between global political justice and global socio-economic justice. Global justice is also concerned with international affairs such as war and peace.

Global justice is concerned not only with individual human beings but also with nations. It deals with relationships among nations, setting relationships among nations and peoples right in terms of human rights, human goods, humanity as the end, and human bonds. It dictates respect for the rights and sovereignty of a nation or people, including cultural rights. It calls for global cultural toleration and inclusion and for democratization of international organizations that deal with global human affairs, whether it is a world financial or health care organization. My contention is therefore that the distinction between international justice and global justice is a distinction between part (international justice) and whole (global justice), not between two kinds of justice.

A distinction between global normative justice and global humanitarian morality is also in order. They differ in essence, substance, focus, scope, and objective. Global normative justice is obligatory and imposes norms that are compulsory in nature; global humanitarian morality is not obligatory and has requirements that are attractive but not compulsory in nature. The distinctions between them include at least the following six factors.

First, global normative justice recognizes and emphasizes universal human bonds and, in terms of these bonds, imposes the obligation of humankind to humankind and establishes a set of standards for evaluating human institutions and conduct. Global humanitarian morality does not presuppose universal human bonds. Global normative justice has a cosmopolitan outlook, while global humanitarian morality can have merely a political outlook.

Second, global normative justice is the mutual obligation among equals and presupposes reciprocity among them, whereas global humanitarian morality is a policy of the stronger toward the weaker and emphasizes the strong's benevolence toward the weak. Thus, while global normative justice is from all human beings to all human beings, global humanitarian morality is from ones who can give to the ones who need to receive. Global normative justice is a function of humankind's exclusive obligation to humankind; global humanitarian morality encompasses humankind's benevolence toward all sentient beings, including nonhuman animals.

Third, global normative justice sets humanity as the end that must stand straight in global human affairs. Global humanitarian morality, on the other hand, focuses on the well-being and needs of the needy and the task of easing suffering. Global normative justice is called for when humanity is lost, global humanitarian morality when there is human need for assistance of provision to exist or other conditions to live.

Fourth, global normative justice is proportional—that is, it gives what is due to human beings in the world, focusing on:

- redeeming the due claims of human rights, not on paternal protection of the weaker in front of the stronger
- the due claim of humanity as the end and human goods, not compassionate love that can be boundless
- the due claim of human bonds, not exclusive affection of relations

It is the Aristotelian call for giving proportionally what is due, not Buddha's call for love and compassion indiscriminately and limitlessly.

Fifth, there are areas of concern that belong to global normative justice but not to global humanitarian morality and vice versa. For example, regulating wars and conflicts between nations or peoples and bringing world peace are the concerns of global normative justice, but not of minimal humanitarian morality. Meanwhile, the idea that a rich nation should try to provide particular provisions—say, a certain amount of foods and medicine—to its neighbor nations and peoples in poverty belongs to the concern of global humanitarian morality, but is not the concern of global normative justice.

Sixth, global normative justice can enlist the support of legally sanctionable forces and institutional forces such as international laws and tribunals. Global humanitarian morality relies exclusively on our human science and must never appeal to the support of force.

In sum, there is global justice, and there is global normative justice by humanity as a distinctive family of global justice. The realization of global justice is a central task of globalization today.

A Humanist Concept of Justice: The Unfinished Painting

In conclusion, I would like to highlight seven concepts that I have developed in this chapter.

First, there is a distinctive family of justice, one of the three families, that focuses on setting human affairs right in terms of human rights, human goods (humanity as the end), and human bonds. Justice means that righteousness stands straight. While justice brings us the most authentic truth of life, one class of the most authentic truth is that human affairs ought to be set right in terms of human rights, human goods (humanity as the end), and human bonds; humanity ought to stand straight, and out of crooked humanity, nothing can stand straight.

Second, normative justice is humankind's exclusive commitment and loyalty to humankind's humanity identity. It implicates a distinctive family of obligation and establishes a family of standards for evaluating basic human institutions. It has its focus, consideration, ideal, content, and scope. It is parallel to distributive justice and corrective justice. This family of justice is not Shakespeare's Juliet who was "still strange to the world," but the Hindu *dharma* and Taoist *dao* existing together with humankind since the immortal time. At the dawn of the creation of humankind, the seed of justice was sowed.

Third, the obligation of humankind to justice is the first social, public obligation of humankind and of basic human institutions. Conversely, the first duty of justice is justice for humanity, in terms of humanity, and by humanity. Justice boundless as sea and sky is not an illusion, but humankind's universal obligation and norm. Facing the seduction of interests, desires, passions, and cravings, we must remember the bond of humanity by our common essence and substance.

Fourth, justice is the righteous reason for humankind to act or abstain from action. It is the righteous human reason for human institutions to structuralize human practice. Global justice is the righteous human reason for human beings to act or abstain from action in global affairs; it is the righteous reason for global human institutions to structuralize human practice in global affairs.

Fifth, human justice is the only kind of justice in the universe that can be intelligible to human beings, within the human horizon and sphere. The most important sources of the normativity of human justice are human reason, human values, and human beings' humanity identity. Human justice may be a precept of natural law. However, justice is a principle that is for humankind and developed by humankind. Justice is not some immortal flower of Fairland, but the shining rose of the human world. We are in no epistemic position to know if justice is some eternal principle of the universe or of God, but we know that justice is the eternal principle of humanity and humankind.

Sixth, humankind humanizes justice, and justice civilizes and rectifies humankind. Humankind expands justice. Justice enlightens humankind. Not as moonlight mirrored in the water or flowers reflected in a glass, justice is the morning sun, the spring wind, and the midautumn moon.

Seventh, human justice is both universal and particular, absolute and historical. It is both Taoist eternal *dao* and an extended and extending poetry, novel, and painting in which basic ideals and ideas are defined and redefined in Zeitgeist, articulated in timely human idioms.

Justice is the way of being human, a way in which there is, to borrow a line from Margaret Mitchell, "a glamour to it—a perfection, a symmetry like Grecian art."[63]

Notes

1. Immanuel Kant, preface to *The Metaphysical Elements of Ethics*, in *Kant* (London: William Benton, 1952), 42:373.

2. Christine M. Korsgaard, *The Source of Normativity* (Cambridge: Cambridge University Press, 1996), 4.

3. With regard to the concept of a Good Samaritan, I benefit from reading Judith Jarvis Thomas's "A Defense of Abortion," *Philosophy and Public Affairs* 1, no. 1 (1971): 47–66.

4. Korsgaard, *Source of Normativity*, 122.

5. Ibid., 132.

6. Bernard Williams, *Making Sense of Humanities* (Cambridge: Cambridge University Press, 1995), 88.

7. Thomas Scanlon, *The Difficulty of Tolerance* (Cambridge: Cambridge University Press, 2003), 138.

8. Thomas Scanlon, *What We Owe to Each Other* (Cambridge, MA: Harvard University Press, 1998), 7.

9. John Rawls, *A Theory of Justice* (Cambridge, MA: Harvard University Press, 1971), 3–4.

10. Thomas Nagel, "The Problem of Global Justice," *Philosophy and Public Affairs* 33, no. 2 (2005): 113–47, quote on 132.

11. Kai Nielsen, *Globalization and Global Justice* (New York: Humanity Books, 2003), 226.

12. Thomas Pogge, *World Poverty and Human Rights: Cosmopolitan Responsibilities* (Cambridge: Polity, 2002).

13. Simon Caney, *Justice beyond Borders: A Global Political Theory* (Oxford: Oxford University Press, 2006).

14. H. L. Mencken, ed., *A New Dictionary of Quotations* (New York: Alfred A. Knopf, 1942), 627.

15. Immanuel Kant, *Metaphysical Elements of Justice*, trans. John Ladd (Indianapolis, IN: Hackett, 1999), 37; see also Kant, "Introduction to the Science of Right," in *Kant*, 401.

16. "Aus so krummem Holze, als woraus der Mensch gemacht ist, kann nichts ganz gerades gezimmert warden." Immanuel Kant, *Gesammelte Schriften* (Berlin: de Gruyter, 1923), vol. 8, p. 23, cited in Isaiah Berlin, *The Crooked Timber of Humanity* (Princeton, NJ: Princeton University Press, 1997), v, xi.

17. Josiah Royce, *Philosophy of Loyalty* (Nashville, TN: Vanderbilt University Press, 1995), 68.

18. John Rawls, *A Theory of Justice* (Cambridge, MA: Harvard University Press, 1971), 60.

19. Ibid., 3–4.

20. Jürgen Habermas, *Moral Consciousness and Communicative Action*, trans. Christian Lenhardt and Shierry Weber Nicholsen (Cambridge, MA: MIT Press, 2001), 200.

21. Ibid.

22. Confucius, *The Essence and Substance of the Analects* (*Lun Yu Zheng Yi* 论语正义), ed. Liu Bao Nan, in *Completed Works of Teachers* (*Zhu Zi Ji Cheng* 诸子集成), vol. 1 (Beijing: Unity Publishing House, 1996), 12.1.

23. Ibid., 12.17, 13.3.

24. Confucius, *Essence and Substance of the Analects*, 4.4.

25. Ibid., 4.3.

26. Mencius, *The Essence and Substance of Mencius* (*Mengzi Zheng Yi* 孟子正义), ed. Jiao Shun, in *Completed Works of Teachers*, vol. 1, 1A1–4.

27. Ibid., 6A10.

28. Ibid., 2A6, 6A6.

29. Ibid., 4A10.

30. Zhuxi and Lü Zhuqian, *Words of Reflection on Things at Hand*, ed. Li Zhuqian (Guangzhou: Flower Publishing House, 1998), 214.

31. Ibid., 197.

32. Brian Orend, *Human Rights* (Ontario, Canada: Broadview Press, 2002), 18.

33. Blaise Pascal, *Pensées* (Oxford, England: Oxford University Press, 1995), viii.154.

34. Korsgaard, *Source of Normativity*, 150.

35. Jürgen Habermas, *The Inclusion of the Other: Studies in Political Theory* (Cambridge, MA: MIT Press, 1998), 3–4.

36. Korsgaard, *Source of Normativity*, 157.

37. Habermas, *Inclusion of the Other*, 4.

38. Hannah Arendt, "Organized Guilt and Universal Responsibility," in *The Jew as Pariah*, ed. Ron H. Feldman (New York: Grove Press, 1978), 235.

39. Cf. Peter Singer, "How Can We Prevent Crimes against Humanity?" in *Human Rights, Human Wrongs* (New York: Oxford University Press, 2003), 92–137.

40. Orend, *Human Rights*, 76–77.

41. Richard Vernon, "What Is Crime against Humanity?" *Journal of Value Inquiry* 10, no. 3 (2002): 232.

42. Ernest Van Den Hagg, "The Ultimate Punishment: A Defense," *Harvard Law Review* 99 (1986): 1669.

43. Richard Rorty, "Justice as a Larger Loyalty," in *Justice and Democracy*, ed. Ron Bontekoe and Marietta Stepaniants (Honolulu: University of Hawaii Press, 1997), 9–10.

44. Bernard Williams, *Ethics and the Limits of Philosophy* (Cambridge, MA: Harvard University Press, 1985), 118.

45. Henry Rosemont, "Human Rights: A Bill of Worries," in *Confucianism and Human Rights*, ed. Wm. Theodore de Bary and Tu Weiming (New York: Columbia University Press, 1998), 55.

46. Mary I. Bockover, ed., *Rules, Rituals and Responsibility: Essays Dedicated to Herbert Fingarette* (La Salle, IL: Open Court, 1991), 191.

47. Orend, *Human Rights*, 242–50.

48. Thomas Nagel, "The Problem of Global Justice," *Philosophy and Public Affairs* 32, no. 2 (2005): 113.

49. Ibid., 114.

50. Ibid., 131.

51. Ibid., 121.

52. Lars Ericsson, "Two Principles of International Justice," in *Justice, Social or Global*, ed. Lars Ericsson (Stockholm: Gotab, 1981), 21, cited in Frederick Ochieng'-Odhiambo, "International Justice and Individual Self-Preservation," *Journal of Global Ethics* 1, no. 2 (December 2005): 100.

53. See Nichola Owen, ed., *Human Rights, Human Wrongs* (New York: Oxford University Press, 2003).

54. Nielsen, *Globalization and Global Justice*, 240.

55. Ibid., 243.

56. Ibid., 243–44.

57. Joshua Cohen and Charles Sabel, "Extra Rempublicam Nulla Justitia?" *Philosophy and Public Affairs* 34, no. 2 (2006): 149.

58. A. J. Julius, "Nagel's Atlas," *Philosophy and Public Affairs* 34, no. 2 (2006).

59. Cf. Ochieng'-Odhiambo, "International Justice."

60. Andrea Sangiovanni, "Global Justice, Reciprocity, and the State," *Philosophy and Public Affairs* 35, no. 1 (2007): 3–39.

61. Zisi, *The Great Learning*, in *The Four Books and Five Classics*, ed. Yang Xiaoming (Chengdu, China: Bu Chu Publishing House, 1996), 2: 4.

62. Ericsson, "Two Principles," 20–21, cited in Ochieng'-Odhiambo, "International Justice," 100.

63. Margaret Mitchell, *Gone with the Wind* (New York: Macmillan, 1964), 1034.

CHAPTER 4

~

Social Toleration: The Spirit
of Justice in Our Time

Ours is an age of diversity. Incommensurability, otherness, alterity, difference, diversity, and plurality are among the terms that give the present political and ethical ethos its distinctive color. Against this background, social tolerance and toleration become norms implicated by normative justice in our time. Speaking of social tolerance, David Heyd points out, "In the liberal ethos of the last three centuries, it has been hailed as one of the fundamental ethical and political values, and it still occupies a powerful position in contemporary legal and political rhetoric."[1] "Di shi kun. Junzi yi hou de zai wu" (地势坤. 君子以厚德载物 The way of the earth follows nature. A true person is of great mind and profound virtue and therefore can tolerate things), reads *Zhou Yi* (*The Book of Change*).[2]

Here, *social tolerance* is a kind of attitude and *social toleration* is a form of practice. The qualifier "social" indicates that what we discuss here are public attitudes and practices in public affairs and lives, not something such as a wife's tolerance of her husband's drinking habits, which I would like to call *private tolerance* and *private toleration* for the sake of distinction. Social tolerance and toleration are public obligations implicated by normative justice in our time; private tolerance and toleration are not obligations and have nothing to do with normative justice.

Under the principle of human rights, we ought to live and let live, to believe and let others to believe. Under the principles of human goods and humanity as the end, we must treat our own and others' humanity as an end, which in turn requires us to fully realize our humanity from where we are

93

and let others fully realize theirs from their own point of departure. Under the principle of human bonds, we must have a kind of relationship to fellow citizens and fellow human beings that is not alienated and not detrimental to the realization of our own or others' humanity.

Social tolerance and toleration are difficult and complicated. Bernard Williams summarizes the challenge succinctly: "The difficulty with toleration is that it seems to be at once necessary and impossible."[3] Herbert Marcuse characterizes the challenge of social tolerance in these words: "Today tolerance appears again as what it was in its origin . . . a subversive liberating notion and practice."[4] As Thomas Scanlon indicates, because of the inevitable indeterminacy of both the content of the idea of tolerance and the standards of toleration in a society in its formal and informal politics, the attitude of tolerance is difficult, though important.[5] Scanlon observes that tolerance

> can be given content only through some specification of the rights of citizens as participants in formal and informal politics. But such a system of rights will be conventional and indeterminate and is bound to be under frequent attack. To sustain and interpret such a system, we need a larger attitude of tolerance and accommodation, an attitude that is itself difficult to maintain.[6]

Some present approaches to the problems of social tolerance and toleration provide us with insights, but also leave much to be desired. For example, Jürgen Habermas suggests that social tolerance is something morally obligatory, but he fails to draw a distinction between the objects of social tolerance and those of rejection. Scanlon shows that tolerance is a median between wholehearted acceptance and unrestrained opposition and that an object of tolerance is something we strongly disapprove of, though he does not draw a clear distinction between tolerance and acceptance or endorsement. Michael Walzer points out that "tolerance (the attitude) takes many different forms and toleration (the practice) can be arranged in different ways," amid his erroneous suggestion that resigned acceptance, benign indifference, and enthusiastic endorsement are forms of social toleration.[7]

Therefore, some crucial questions remain to be answered here. What are social tolerance and toleration? What are their objects and requirements? Are their requirements ones of moral virtue or of social duty and obligation? What are the necessary conditions for stable, maintainable practices of social toleration?

Justification of Social Toleration

Why do we value social tolerance and toleration in our time? Why ought we to hold them at such high esteem? What do we aim at in practicing social tolerance and toleration? Social tolerance and toleration define a human way, but is this human way the right way today? These questions contour the justification question about social tolerance and toleration.

Walzer gives a popular answer to the justification question: Difference makes toleration necessary. That is, social tolerance and toleration are important because, in a democratic world, cultural diversity is an enduring reality, and thus it becomes a practical necessity to exercise social tolerance and toleration. Isaiah Berlin adds a voice to such a view:

> The world in which what we see as incompatible values are not in conflict is a world altogether beyond our ken; that principles which are harmonized in this other world are not the principles with which, in our daily lives, we are acquainted; if they are transformed, it is into conceptions not known to us on earth. But it is on earth that we live, and it is here that we must believe and act.[8]

The Walzer-Berlin answer is flawed, however. Social tolerance and toleration are demanded today not because of practical necessity. By practical necessity, social tolerance and toleration are not the only possible and effective responses to cultural diversity. In terms of practical necessity and effectiveness of management, a society can have a totalitarian response to diversity, eliminating it. Oppression and repression may be wrong, but they are not practically impossible nor ineffective. For example, intolerant religious fundamentalism and terrorism are wrong, but not because they are impossible or ineffective in eliminating diversity. If there is such a thing as political necessity for social tolerance and toleration, such a necessity is grounded in moral and ontological necessity, not in practical necessity. And such a political necessity should be understood as a political duty, not political causality—that is, as a free political choice to do the right thing in accordance with moral reason, not as some involuntary compliance with external coercion.

The fact that difference exists does not indicate that preservation of difference is a value or necessity. That diversity exists is not the normative reason to call for social tolerance and toleration. The value of allowing difference to continue is the normative reason for social tolerance and toleration. Preservation of diversity itself is not an intrinsic value. Then, what is the value that makes preservation of diversity an instrumental value and an important one in our time? That is the question!

Another answer to the justification question is a Confucian one. Confucius said, "Tolerance enables one to have the support of the mass."[9] From a Confucian perspective, social tolerance and toleration make it possible for a kind of mutually supportive relation to exist among the human members (the mass) of a community amid social diversity. That the human members of a society can mutually support each other is crucial for them to extend their lives together. Thus, a rule of humanity is social tolerance. From a Confucian perspective, social tolerance and toleration are instrumental values, serving to bring out a humanist community in which human beings can extend their lives together and realize their own humanity.

A further answer to the justification question is a contractualist one. To the question about why there is a need for social tolerance, Scanlon says, "The answer lies . . . in the relation with one's fellow citizens that tolerance makes possible."[10] He adds that "any alternative [to tolerance] would put me in an antagonistic and alienated relation to my fellow citizens, friends as well as foes."[11] According to Scanlon, we value social tolerance today because we want the kind of relations with our fellow citizens that only social tolerance and toleration can bring about. But what kind of social relation is that? Why do we want this relationship in the first place? To the first question, Scanlon indicates what we do *not* want: an alienated, antagonistic relationship with our fellow citizens. To the second, his view reveals that the problem of tolerance is about having a relationship with one's fellow citizens on the basis of rights, the rule of law, and the rule of reason.

Yet another answer to the justification question is the Habermasian one. According to Habermas, we practice social tolerance because of "the egalitarian and universalistic standard of democratic citizenship."[12] Social tolerance is demanded by "something that calls for equal treatment of the 'other' and mutual recognition of all as 'full' members of the political community."[13] Thus, the problem of social tolerance is of mutually recognizing and honoring each other's rights.

In light of the above, a reasonable answer to the justification question must, at a minimum, account for two things:

1. Why do we want the kind of relations with our fellow citizens that only social tolerance and toleration can bring in the first place? Is it our obligation to want such a relationship or is it merely a matter of virtue?
2. Why are social tolerance and toleration requirements of social obligation, more than something reasonable to do?

The kind of social relation to our fellow citizens that only social tolerance and toleration can afford us is a kind of communal bond that is essential to a human community. Globally, the kind of relations with fellow human beings that only international and cultural tolerance and toleration can provide is a common human bond that gives rise to human justice. It is our obligation to have such a relationship. This obligation is inscribed in the concept of normative justice. In A *Theory of Justice*, John Rawls argues for social toleration "solely on a conception of justice," insisting that "toleration is not derived from practical necessities or reasons of state."[14]

Social tolerance and toleration are norms of social obligation mandated by normative justice in our time. Conversely, social *intolerance* and *intoleration* involve rejecting the rights of those who disagree with us, treating them not as an end but as a means, and not honoring the universal human values and bonds. Social tolerance and toleration bring us human relations and bonds with others who disagree with us. We want this kind of relationship to our fellow citizens not because we may be practically much better off, but because we owe it to our fellow citizens to have this kind of relation, and because we want to be just.

Our attitude of social tolerance and our act of social toleration express this belief: even though there are other possible responses to those persons who disagree with us and to those beliefs and institutions that we morally, even strongly, disapprove of and want to disallow in our shared communal life, justice demands that we respect the rights of those persons who disagree with us; justice dictates, "No way of life can demand, such as prohibiting conduct by others, simply because one disapproves of it."[15]

Our attitude of social tolerance and acts of social toleration express this commitment: justice denies that any practical utility, expedience, or necessity can make it right for us to violate others' rights, not to treat humanity as the end, or not to honor what we owe to each other. Justice obliges us to give their due to institutions and beliefs that we disapprove of but that others have rights and good reasons to hold to.

The Object of Social Toleration

The answers to the justification question about social tolerance and toleration above lead us to the question of what should be tolerated. The justification question is internally related to the question of what the legitimate objects of social tolerance and toleration are. Justification of social tolerance and toleration lies partially in the objects of the tolerance and toleration.

Human beliefs, human institutions and practices, and members of a human community are three classes of the possible objects of social tolerance and toleration. I say "possible" here because no small number of philosophers believe that only persons, not beliefs and institutions, should be tolerated. As I shall demonstrate below, *not all* human beliefs, institutions, and persons *should* be tolerated. Here, we should first exclude what does not belong in the category of the objects of social tolerance and toleration.

Nonhuman animals and the institutions of any beings from other planets are not the objects of social tolerance and toleration. Stones, rivers, trees, bad weather, natural disasters, and so on are not the objects of social tolerance and toleration, either. A person's bad temperament or habits may be an object of private tolerance, but are not legitimate objects of social tolerance and toleration. Objects that are not, and cannot be, the objects of social tolerance and toleration are also not, and cannot be, the objects of concern of normative justice. Indeed, it is their irrelevance to normative justice that excludes them from the category.

Furthermore, not all human beliefs and institutions that we disapprove of nor all of those people who are in conflict with us are appropriate objects of social tolerance and toleration. Beliefs and institutions that have absolutely no socially redeeming values or that are totally reactionary, barbarian, perverting, and antihumanity cannot, and should not, be the objects of social tolerance and toleration. Institutions and beliefs that bring disproportionately greater evils than possible good to a normal society and its human members cannot, and should not, belong among the objects of social tolerance and toleration. For example, under the U.S. Constitution, not every speech and form of press belongs to the category of protected items in the name of freedom of thought and expression.

The concepts of social tolerance and toleration would be easy but pointless to defend if the institutions or beliefs that we should tolerate had no serious consequences to our lives and we could be totally indifferent to them. In certain contexts, institutions or beliefs that are too destructive to humanity should not be accorded social tolerance and toleration. For example, terrorism should not be a legitimate object of social tolerance and toleration today; to tolerate terrorism is to embrace crimes against humanity.

John Horton indicates two kinds of things that should not be the objects of social toleration: "On the one hand, some things should not be tolerated, because they should not be permitted; on the other hand, some things should not be objected to, hence are not appropriate objects of toleration."[16]

In some circumstances, Scanlon suggests, while those who hold certain views and beliefs should be tolerated as citizens or fellow human beings, their views and beliefs should not be tolerated.[17] Voltaire (François-Marie Arouet), who advocated universal tolerance, adopted such a strategy. This is also the strategy in Rawls's suggestion in *A Theory of Justice* that we should tolerate the intolerant in the name of justice.[18]

Throughout history, some philosophers also argued that some human members of a society should not be tolerated, though their arguments might not stand today. "With [St. Thomas] Aquinas and the Protestant Reformers the grounds of intolerance are themselves a matter of faith."[19] Jean-Jacques Rousseau believed that those who were dangerous to civil peace and order in a society should not be tolerated.

> Rousseau thought that people would find it impossible to live in peace with those whom they regarded as damned, since to love them would be to hate God who punishes them. He believed that those who regard others as damned must either torment or convert them, and therefore sects preaching this conviction cannot be trusted to preserve civil peace. Rousseau would not, then, tolerate those religions which say that outside the church there is no salvation.[20]

John Locke advocated religious toleration. His "Letter Concerning Toleration" is still a classic in philosophical writings even today.[21] But Locke also believed that we should not tolerate those people, beliefs, and practices that were dangerous to "public order."[22]

The trouble with social tolerance and toleration lies in the difficulty of determining what their legitimate objects are. Heyd points out:

> In the theory of rights, virtue, and duty, people who radically disagree about the analysis and justification of these concepts can still appeal to a commonly shared repertory of examples. But with tolerance, it seems that we can find hardly a single concrete case that would be universally agreed to be a typical object of discussion.[23]

Heyd indicates another difficulty: "Courage and *habeas corpus* are standard cases of virtue and rights, respectively. But would we agree on defining the attitude of restraint toward neo-Nazi groups as tolerance, or alternatively, would we describe as tolerance the way the heterosexual majority treats homosexuals?"[24]

Scanlon points out the conceptual problem of social tolerance:

> Although some specification of rights and limits of exemplification and advocacy is required in order to give content to the idea of tolerance and make it tenable, the idea of tolerance can never be fully identified with any particular system of such rights and limits, such as the system of rights of free speech and association, rights of privacy, and rights to free exercise (but nonestablishment) of religion. . . . Many different systems of rights are acceptable; none is ideal. Each is therefore constantly open to challenge and revision.[25]

Such a conceptual problem makes it difficult for us to define what the legitimate objects of social tolerance and toleration are.

One way to deal with the difficulty here is to turn the tables and ask the reverse question: What are the essential features of the object of social tolerance and toleration? What makes an object be an object of social tolerance and toleration? Thus, instead of trying to develop an exclusive list of the objects of social tolerance and toleration, we should discuss the basic criteria by which we select X as an object of social tolerance and toleration. I shall adopt this strategy here. Our questions now become: What essential properties must an object of social tolerance and toleration have? What distinguishes an object of social tolerance from the objects of other human attitudes such as benevolence and friendship?

Walzer says, "Toleration makes difference possible; difference makes toleration necessary."[26] Without difference, no social tolerance or toleration is needed. Therefore, difference is a necessary property of a legitimate object of social tolerance and toleration. It makes no sense for us to say that we should tolerate belief X if X is totally in congruence with our other beliefs.

However, while difference is a necessary condition for X to be an object of social tolerance and toleration, difference alone is not sufficient to make it so. Difference can be compatible or incompatible. With compatible difference, two different parties do not necessarily exclude each other. For example, British democracy and American democracy are different but compatible. On the contrary, with incompatible difference, two parties necessarily exclude each other and coexist only in conflict. Illustrative examples would be the pro-life and pro-choice beliefs in the abortion debate in America today.

A compatible difference is an object of problem solving, not one of social tolerance and toleration. At least, the idea of social toleration would be easy to defend but pointless if applied to a compatible difference. Thus, an object of social tolerance and toleration must be an incompatible difference. With an incompatible difference, one party cannot be absorbed by the other and must be endured if the two parties are to coexist. Only an incompatible difference can be a source of reasons and sentiments for disapproval, rejection, and prohibition. An incompatible difference will last as an object of social tolerance and toleration. For this reason, we often perceive and characterize the objects of tolerance and toleration as "thoroughly wrong or bad" (Williams), "morally disapproved" (Peter Nicholson), or "wrong" (Susan Mendus), things "that we strongly disapprove" (Scanlon) or "that we reject" (Habermas).

Williams goes so far as to say, "Toleration . . . is required only for the intolerable."[27] Scanlon notes that tolerance "applies to those who differ from us or disagree with us and who would like to make society something other than what we want to it to be."[28] Barbara Herman gives the following definition of an object of toleration: "The object of toleration has negative value to the tolerator: one tolerates what one dislikes or disapproves of."[29] In Buddhism, an object of social tolerance and toleration is something difficult, even apparently impossible, to tolerate. On this point, we can also draw some insights from practicing religious toleration. In religious toleration, what are tolerated are incompatible beliefs, persons, and religions.

Nonetheless, not all objects of incompatible difference are the legitimate objects of social tolerance and toleration, either. Incompatible differences that we can justly reject with sufficient reasons should not be considered as objects of tolerance and toleration. For example, we can justly reject crimes against humanity such as the genocides in Rwanda and Darfur, and they should not be tolerated. We can justly reject terrorism. We should not go to another extreme to tolerate things that we rightly should reject.

The standard of what is morally impermissible is an important but also delicate one. It sets a high bar for what ought to be rejected. It is easy for us to locate obvious cases of moral impermissibility such as the Rwanda and Darfur genocides that are totally repulsive to the moral conscience of humankind and that exemplify total bestiality, more than sadistic cruelty. Not surprisingly, things get more difficult when it comes to beliefs or practices such as racism, sexism, or other ideas that threaten our way of life but whose holders enjoy the same rights of freedom of conscience as we do. In some cases, we can adopt the exit strategy of drawing a distinction between the persons who hold the views and the views themselves. In other cases, our feet are stuck in the mud. Various forms of racism, sexism, or other rejectable beliefs may not reach the level of shocking the moral conscience of mankind; in addition, their definitions can be blurred.

A distinction between the object of social tolerance and toleration and the object of rejection is in order. What is tolerated is not rejected and what is rejected is not tolerated. Therefore, toleration and rejection cannot exist simultaneously, and an object cannot be an object of both toleration and rejection at the same time.

About religious tolerance, Habermas says:

> Rejection is a condition necessary for all kinds of tolerant behavior. We can only exercise tolerance towards other people's beliefs if we reject them for subjectively good reasons. We do not need to be tolerant if we are indifferent to other opinions and attitude in any way or even appreciate the value of such "otherness."[30]

Habermas correctly points out the distinction between an object of indifference and an object of tolerance. As Williams argues, "The attitude of tolerance is supposed to be more than mere weariness or indifference."[31] But an object of social toleration is not an object of rejection.

Habermas declares, "Tolerance can only come to bear if there is a legitimate justification for the rejection of competing validity claims."[32] Admittedly, tolerance is applied only to what we have good reason to reject. If we have no good reason to reject X, then X is not an object of tolerance; instead, it must be an object of either acceptance or indifference. Thus, Horton, quoting Joseph Raz, says, "A person can be tolerant only 'if the intolerant inclination in itself is worthwhile or desirable.'"[33]

Nonetheless, having good reason for rejection is one thing, and having a legitimate justification with sufficient reasons is quite another. One can have good reason to reject X and yet not actually reject it.

The criterion of "a legitimate justification with sufficient reasons" means that we are fully justified on good and sufficient grounds to reject something. In the situation in which we have a legitimate justification with sufficient reasons to reject X, then we do not tolerate X but actually reject it.

This puts us in a rhetorical drill. If we are fully justified to reject X, we are rationally, reasonably, and conclusively justified to reject it. If we should tolerate what we are reasonably and conclusively justified in rejecting, will we ever reject anything at all? If we are fully justified to reject both X and Y, but we end up tolerating X and rejecting Y, what is the justification for such a discrepancy and distinction then? And what will be the reasonable basis and rationality to reject anything if not that we should reject X if and only if we have a legitimate justification with sufficient reason to reject it?

The distinction between the intention to reject X and the act of rejection is also crucial here. Toleration and rejection of X cannot coexist. But the act of toleration of X and the *intention* to reject X can, even though in some cases such coexistence leads to bad faith. Admittedly, if rejection means opposing—or weaker still, disagreeing—then we can consistently claim both to reject and to tolerate something simultaneously. But this definition of rejection makes the concept of tolerance pointless. It is pointless to talk about tolerating X if X is something that we simply oppose or disagree with. The idea of social tolerance and toleration and our commitment to them are put to the test only when rejection of X means disallowing, prohibiting, and excluding X from a shared communal life. But speaking of rejection of X in this sense, we cannot consistently claim to reject and to tolerate something simultaneously. If rejection of X means disallowing, prohibiting, and excluding X, then when we reject X, we do not tolerate it. When we tolerate X, we do not reject it.

One may argue that we could reject X subjectively in consciousness and understanding, yet tolerate it objectively in action. This argument cannot stand. It suggests that we intentionally separate our consciousness and understanding from our actions. If we intentionally separate consciousness and action, how can we ever act rationally and reasonably when we act tolerantly? Or how can we say that our action of tolerance is rational and reasonable? To talk about tolerating X in action but rejecting it in consciousness is also to talk about what Jean-Paul Sartre called "bad faith." It makes toleration an act of running away from our belief and tolerance an attitude of ignoring our belief.

If we say that rejection means simply the recognition of the rejectability of what is tolerated, we are still at sea. We will be in a same situation as the situation of tolerating X while having a legitimate justification to reject it. We will encounter cognitive and moral problems when we talk about toleration of what is justifiably rejectable. If we can cognitively reject X, why should we tolerate it? If we can justly reject X as being morally impermissible, why should we tolerate it?

We do well here to note what Susan Mendus says: "Where toleration is based on moral disapproval, it implies that the thing tolerated is wrong and ought not to exist. The question which then arises is why . . . it should be thought good to tolerate."[34] If tolerance of what we morally disapprove of makes tolerance seem problematic, toleration of what we morally ought to reject makes toleration paradoxical. We contradict ourselves if we say that we should tolerate X while we are cognitively and morally justified in rejecting it. It would be irrational and unreasonable to tolerate X while we are fully and conclusively justified in rejecting it.

Do we solve anything by drawing a distinction between moral rejectability and moral impermissibility? The answer is no. This desperate move only draws a too-fine grip that cheapens the concept of moral permissibility. Even if moral irrejectability is not necessarily identical to moral permissibility, moral rejectability entails moral impermissibility.

Finally, a common exit strategy is to tolerate fellow citizens who have different beliefs but reject the beliefs that they hold to. As Voltaire beautifully said, "I disapprove of what you say, but I will defend to the death your right to say it."[35] When we tolerate fellow citizens but reject their beliefs, it appears that we both tolerate and reject something simultaneously. But the appearance is misleading. In reality, we tolerate fellow citizens, but reject their beliefs. We are not both tolerating and rejecting our fellow citizens nor both tolerating and rejecting their beliefs.

Thus, Habermas's insight needs a remedy. The remedy is to draw a distinction between the act of rejection and the intention to reject. I propose the following modification: an object of social tolerance and toleration is something that we have good *but not sufficient* reasons to reject; it is that whose defense we want to overcome but cannot reasonably and sufficiently overcome; it is that we want to reject, but do not reject. In the proposed modification, the idea that an object of tolerance and toleration is something we reject is replaced by the idea that it is something we desire to reject, but do not reject, in both consciousness and action.

In this modification, by "reasonably and sufficiently overcome," I mean overcoming by rational, reasonable, and conclusive arguments in accordance with rules that we cannot reasonably reject as just rules of regulating our social practices. Oppressive and repressive forms of overcoming, such as institutional sanctions by political, economic, or other forms of power, are ruled out here. The phrase "reasonably and sufficiently overcome" excludes things that are morally impermissible from the category of the objects of social tolerance and toleration. The phrase "we desire to reject, but do not reject" reaffirms that, first, we have strong, good reasons and sentiments to reject X and, simultaneously, listening to the voice of reason, we show restraint toward X because reasons for the defense of X are also good and weighty and therefore are worth our respect.

A further feature of an object of social tolerance and toleration is this: it is something that we have the right to prohibit. If we have no right to prohibit X, then X is not an object of our tolerance.[36] Instead, X is either an object of our acceptance or an object of our indifference. If we have no right to prohibit X, then X should not be prohibited by us; otherwise, the prohibition is pointless and unjust. For example, it makes no sense for us to ask whether we should tolerate or not tolerate the fact that the Chinese people celebrate the Spring Festival instead of Christmas. In this case, we have no right to interfere and impose our approval or disapproval.

This also amounts to saying that a person whom we should tolerate is a person who has the right to demand social tolerance and toleration from us. A belief or an institution that we strongly disapprove of but must tolerate is one that others have rights to hold to and whose defense of the belief or institution is reasonable and weighty.

In sum, an object of social tolerance and toleration can be defined as an object of significant, incompatible difference that we have a right and good reason to reject but do not have sufficient reasons to reject; it is an object that we cannot justly reject because there are reasons for its defense that are worthy and weighty, and because rejecting the object violates rules that we cannot reasonably deny as being fair and just rules of social and moral life. In short, an object of social tolerance and toleration has three distinctive properties:

1. Its rejection is within a tolerator's right
2. It is a significant and incompatible difference
3. It has reasonable and just defensibility

The property of "significant and incompatible difference" indicates that an object of tolerance and toleration is not just any difference, but a particular kind of difference. This characteristic is necessary to prevent us from trivializing the concepts of social tolerance and toleration and applying them to every difference that we deal with in real life. It accounts for the traditional labels for the object of tolerance and toleration as something "morally disapproved," "thoroughly wrong or bad," and "distasteful" without the problems and limitations of these labels. It explains our good reasons and desires to reject what we tolerate. It also indicates that the object of social tolerance and toleration has real significance and is difficult to bear.

Furthermore, the property demarcates the objects of social tolerance and toleration from the objects of other human attitudes or activities such as compassion, experimentation, and problem solving. An object of social tolerance and toleration is an irreducible, irritating, and discordant difference. It should be tolerated not because it is weak and needs compassion, but because it is strong and is entitled to be treated with due respect and to be free from prohibition and exclusion. It should be tolerated not because it can be absorbed, but because it is irreducible. It should be tolerated not because we can play with it, but because of the danger and wrong which exclusion of it will incur.

The idea that "we have the right and good reason to reject but do not have sufficient reasons to reject and cannot justly reject" is also crucial. It accounts for the normative aspect of social tolerance and toleration. Horton suggests, "Toleration involves two sets of considerations: reasons for showing restraint toward that which is regarded as objectionable; and reasons (or sentiments) that makes something objectionable—the considerations that make it appropriate to countenance prohibition or interference in the first place."[37] According to him, both sets of reason can be disputed and rejected and, therefore, toleration is a virtue.

Horton's view is suggestive, but I want to make a modified claim: In situations in which social toleration is evoked, both sets of reasons are weighty, and the reasons (sentiments) for showing restraint are not reasonably rejectable and cannot be justly disregarded. Therefore, social toleration is a public duty and obligation. When tolerance and toleration of X are required, both the reasons for rejection of X and those for restraint are acceptable and worth consideration; the reasons for restraint are not reasonably rejectable and cannot be justly disregarded. If the reasons for restraint can be reasonably refuted, then social toleration is neither a virtue nor an obligation, but some practical necessity and expedience.

The concept of reasonable defensibility underscores the following truth. In public life, toleration of X should not be what we ought to practice if the reasons for showing restraint toward X can be reasonably refuted, that is, if disallowance of X is morally and cognitively reasonable and just. In such a circumstance, it is not toleration but rejection that should be evoked. On the other hand, toleration of X is not appropriate if the reasons for rejecting X have no value and are themselves unreasonable. In such a circumstance, it is not toleration but acceptance and endorsement that are required. Correspondingly, X should not be tolerated if its defense is not reasonable or sufficient to counter the reason for its rejection. It is not the case that X should be tolerated as long as someone puts forward an argument for it and claims a right to it. For example, terrorism should be rejected even though there are individuals or groups who defend it for various reasons.

The extremes here would be either tolerating all incompatible differences or rejecting every incompatible difference. Going to either pole, we team with totalitarianism and oppression. In appearance, acceptance of all incompatible differences is maximum toleration, but in reality, it is something else and unsustainable. By accepting all incompatible differences, we turn social toleration into some form of resignation, indifference, or disengagement. In addition, accepting all incompatible differences demands that we accept the impermissible. This is to "demand an attitude that is almost unattainable,"[38] which will lead us to intoleration. When we tolerate the impermissible, such as religious terrorism, we endorse intoleration. At the other extreme, if we reject every incompatible difference, we practice outright intoleration.

The Requirements of Social Toleration

This leads us to the requirements of social tolerance and toleration. What is required of the attitude of tolerance and the act of toleration? Horton points out, "The core of the concept of toleration is the refusal, where one has power to do so, to prohibit or seriously interfere with conduct that one finds objectionable."[39] According to him, social toleration consists of the act of refusing to prohibit or to seriously interfere with the tolerated.

Horton's view is basically correct. Social toleration presupposes a refusal to prohibit or disallow the tolerated. But more than this is required of social toleration. Differences exist between toleration and indifference or neglect. Indifference or neglect also implies a refusal to prohibit or disallow the incompatible difference. Walzer and some philosophers believe that neglect, indifference, and negligence are forms of social toleration. Others disagree. Williams, Habermas, and Horton all think that social toleration is more than simple indifference.

Indifference, neglect, and negligence are not forms of toleration. As an analogy, neglect of one's duty is not toleration of one's duty. Negligence in one's responsibility to a child is not toleration of the child. But what else, in addition to a simple refusal to prohibit the incompatible difference, is required of social toleration?

Habermas's answer is that social tolerance includes treating others as equals. Scanlon agrees that social tolerance involves "accepting as equals those who differ from us."[40] For them, social tolerance and toleration involve treating others as equals, recognizing our opponents' rights and entitlements. "Tolerance requires us to accept people and permit their practices even when we strongly disapprove of them."[41]

For example, Scanlon argues,

> Tolerance requires that people who fall on the "wrong" side of the differences . . . should not be . . . denied legal and political rights: the rights to vote, to hold office, to benefit from the central public goods that are otherwise open to all, such as education, public safety, the protections of the legal system, health care, and access to public accommodations.[42]

We can add that "equal entitlement" means that "all members of society are equally entitled to be taken into an account in defining what our society is and equally entitled to participate in determining what it will become in the future."[43]

The idea that social tolerance and toleration involve treating others as equals is insightful. Social tolerance and toleration differ from patronizing benevolence and compassion. Social toleration is not an act of compassion of the stronger to the weaker. To tolerate someone's beliefs is not to bestow kindness on or grant benefit to that person, but to recognize the person's rights and to include him or her as a legitimate member in a shared communal life. In tolerance and toleration, one treats the other in a way that is proportional to what the other is entitled to, whereas in patronizing benevolence and compassion, one treats the other as the weaker who needs to be taken care of. Tolerance and toleration must not be excessive or insufficient, but benevolence can be. In other words, toleration and tolerance emphasize proportionality; benevolence does not. Justice—not compassion, benevolence, or generosity—mandates tolerance and toleration.

Another distinction is this: Toleration is not bearing with something in humiliation or exploiting others from a stronger position. Instead, it is bearing with others with mutual respect and in full dignity. Toleration is not the situation in which one party, because of a lowly or weak status or being overpowered, puts up with the oppression and abuse of another, stronger party. When one weaker party, because of its status, must live in humiliation dictated by the stronger party, this is not toleration by the weaker party; nor is it toleration, but rather exploitation, by the stronger party.

Walzer does not think that treating others as equals is a component of toleration. For him, "tolerating and being tolerated is a little like Aristotle's ruling and being ruled: it is the work of democratic citizens."[44] Walzer's view is true of many historical cases of social toleration, but it is flawed in several aspects. It is not applicable to a vast numbers of cases in our times. If the relationship between tolerating and tolerated were akin to Aristotle's ruling and being ruled, social tolerance and benevolence could be identical, at least from the ruling party's point of view. Walzer's conception leads us to a slippery position.

What is involved in the act of accepting the other as an equal? With regard to fellow citizens, accepting them as equals means accepting them as legitimate, autonomous participants of a shared communal life. It means respecting and honoring their equal rights—as citizens—in our shared community. Toleration does not require us to take incompatible beliefs as having equal truth and value or to accept those incompatible institutions as being equally good. It does not require us to consider those who disagree with us as being equally correct in their beliefs. Toleration simply requires us to treat others as having an equal right to their own beliefs and institutions as we do to ours.

Further qualifications are in order. With regard to toleration of fellow citizens, egalitarianism may be noble, but is not sustainable. Politically and legally, we should recognize the basic liberties and rights of fellow citizens—no question about that. However, we must respond with discretion to their beliefs or practices that may change society in a direction that we do not desire. We should recognize fellow citizens' equal political and legal rights, but we cannot grant all beliefs and institutions that they hold to have equal entitlement to be tolerated. Scanlon makes such a qualification on this point: "It is not that their point of view is entitled to be represented but that they (as fellow citizens, not as holders of that view) are entitled to be heard."[45]

If we consider those incompatible beliefs to be as true as our own and those incompatible institutions to be equally good, we hold to an unreasonable, implausible position. How can we reasonably consider them equal when we have good reason to believe that they are wrong? Here, to say that we recognize the value and the reason for showing restraint toward these beliefs is one thing, but to say that we consider them to have equal truth and value is quite another. For example, it is one thing to say that, because of the rights of those who hold to them, we should not disallow these beliefs to be advocated and to compete with our own beliefs, playing themselves out in the intellectual and moral discourses of our community. It is quite another to say that we should consider these beliefs to be true and valuable.

When we suggest that incompatible beliefs have equal truth and value, we in effect endorse them. However, social toleration is not endorsement or approval, whether wholehearted or half-hearted. Social tolerance is "an attitude that is intermediate between wholehearted acceptance and unrestrained opposition."[46] Social toleration is an intermediate act between endorsement and complete rejection or exclusion. It makes us both endure and disapprove of incompatible beliefs or institutions, neither oppressing them nor endorsing them. Endorsement of X signifies that we no longer consider X to be objectionable. But if X is no longer objectionable, it loses its qualification as an subject of social tolerance and toleration.

In light of the above, social tolerance and toleration involve more than treating others as equals. They imply the idea of inclusion. In indifference, neglect, and negligence, we consider others as equals; we acknowledge their rights but do not care about them, are indifferent to them, have nothing to do with them. However, neglect, indifference, and negligence are not forms of tolerance and toleration. A crucial element of tolerance and toleration is inclusion—better yet, active inclusion. The term *active inclusion* indicates that in toleration, one is not indifferent or negligent to what is tolerated, but actively engages it.

On this point, perhaps, the Chinese counterpart of the English word *toleration*, kuanrong (宽容), may give us some perspective. It consists of two words: *kuan* (宽 broad, taking it easy) and *rong* (容 containing, including). The concept of *kuanrong* connotes broadening, including, and bearing with. On the one hand, one is *kuan*—broad-minded or open-minded—to accommodate what is disagreeable. On the other hand, one must *rong* (contain, include) what is disagreeable. The concept of *kuanrong* excludes the ideas of both indifference and rejection.

We now arrive at a new concept of toleration: Toleration is bearing with, refusing to disallow, and actively including an incompatible difference in a shared communal life. With regard to fellow citizens, toleration means bearing with and actively including them in our shared communal life. Toleration requires us to allow our opponents to exercise the same rights that we have, to enjoy the same freedoms that we enjoy, and to advocate their views and beliefs publicly in words or even by examples. In this new definition, the requirement of social tolerance and toleration to treat others as equals is implied, and simultaneously a new requirement that social tolerance and toleration involve actively including others in a shared communal life is added and emphasized.

In this view, social tolerance and toleration presuppose reciprocity, that is, mutual tolerance and toleration between two incompatible parties. Social tolerance is not benevolence that one party bestows upon the other, and social toleration is not compassion or sympathy that one party has toward another. Instead, social tolerance and toleration, respectively, imply the act and the attitude of mutual recognition and inclusion between two incompatible but equal parties.

Much has been said about the requirement of treating others as equals in social toleration. A few words on the additional requirement of inclusion are in order. For the most part, philosophers today have failed to recognize this requirement. For example, Herman argues:

> Someone who exemplifies the virtue of toleration thus need not approve of, be interested in, or willing to have much to do with the object of her toleration. It is a *laissez-faire* virtue. If I must tolerate the public speech of minority groups because suppression of speech is politically dangerous over the long run, I do not have to listen. If we may not prevent groups with special histories and traditions from continuing objectionable practices, we do not have to live with them among us (though we might not be able to pass restrictive zoning, we can move).[47]

Here, Herman identifies the attitude of tolerance with indifference and the act of toleration with laissez-faire acts. In essence, her view belongs to the Walzer camp. But tolerance and indifference should not be identified with one another, nor should toleration and laissez-faire.

Some objects of indifference cannot be the objects of social tolerance. For example, we can be indifferent to what is good for us, but it makes little sense to say that we should tolerate what is good for us. The reverse is also true: Some objects of tolerance cannot be the objects of indifference. For example, significantly incompatible beliefs and social institutions that will redefine our way of life in a profoundly different direction may become the objects of social tolerance, but they cannot be the objects of indifference. "We all have profound interest in how prevailing customs and practices evolve."[48] In short, indifference and tolerance each have their own objects and range of concern.

The act of social toleration cannot be defined as a laissez-faire outlook, either. Declining to act may be appropriate for objects that have nothing to do with us or that we have no right to interfere with one way or the other, but the act of social toleration can be performed only on objects that we are involved with and have a right to interfere with. The reverse is also true. Social toleration should be adopted only for objects that we cannot avoid or run away from, whereas we can be laissez-faire with objects that we can avoid. We do not need to tolerate X if we can simply run away and have nothing to do with it. When we run away from X, we let it have its way. In Herman's example above, if we move away, we run away from some groups of people who are incompatible to us and from objectionable practices; we do not tolerate them, we simply have nothing to do with them. We have nothing to tolerate once we move away from what we are challenged to tolerate. It makes no sense for us to say that we tolerate X when we run away from it and, as a result, have nothing to do with it.

Meanwhile, toleration of incompatible social institutions requires us to allow these institutions to exist in our shared communal life, to let them compete with our institutions. It does not require us to endorse or accept these institutions, but it does require us not to be indifferent to them and not to run away from them. The presence of incompatible social institutions may affect the evolution of prevailing institutions and practices in a direction and to a degree that we do not desire. Thus, while we tolerate them, we continue to engage them as opponents. In this way, "tolerance can allow the possibility of peaceful and harmonious coexistence without compromising the integrity of reasonably held and valuable convictions."[49]

Toleration of incompatible beliefs also requires us intellectually and morally to allow them to be advocated publicly in word and deed and requires that we actively engage them in discourse. Habermas says, "The expectation of tolerance assumes that we can endure a form of ongoing nonconcurrence at the level of social interaction, while we accept the persistence of mutually exclusive validity claims at the cognitive level of existentially relevant beliefs."[50] However, social toleration does not require us to endorse incompatible beliefs and treat conflicting claims about good, right, value and meaning as equally correct. Social toleration does not require us to endorse any cognitive difference, incompatibility, contradiction, incommensurability, and conflicting validity claims about truth either. What is cognitively required is "to socially accept mutual cognitive dissonance that will remain unresolved for the time being."[51] What is required is to live with the difference.

In light of the above, we can summarize the positive requirements of social tolerance and toleration of X as follows:

1. To treat X as equal and to allow it in a shared communal life
2. To actively bear with, endure, and engage with X in a shared communal life; to actively include X in a shared communal life, not just to forget, neglect, or marginalize X or leave it alone
3. To critically engage with X, but not to endorse it

We also can summarize the negative requirements of social tolerance and toleration of X:

1. Not to treat X without dignity and with humiliation
2. Not to bear with X under humiliating conditions
3. Not to exploit X as a means to one's own end

Accordingly, there can be several forms of extremity pertaining to social tolerance and toleration. One of them is either to endorse X or to simply neglect and disengage from X. Going to either extreme, that is, endorsement or indifference, we will turn social tolerance and toleration into social intolerance and intoleration or something else. If we endorse an incompatible difference, we either must suppress the difference to make it the same to us and agreeable to us and our institutions and beliefs—at least to suppress the incompatible to make it compatible to us—or we suppress ourselves, our institutions, and our beliefs to become compatible with what is tolerated. Either way, we turn social tolerance into social intolerance, and toleration into intoleration, whether of others or of ourselves, our institutions, and our beliefs. To leave an incompatible difference alone, we either must marginalize the incompatible difference or totally separate it from us. In either case, we exclude it from our shared communal life. This is just another form of social intolerance and intoleration.

The Necessary Conditions to Stabilize and Maintain Social Toleration

We now face the issue of the stability of social tolerance and toleration. To tackle the issue, let me introduce two new concepts here: primary value and secondary value. *Primary value* is value that is not derivative; *secondary value* is derivative. The distinction between the two is not the same as the distinction between intrinsic value and instrumental value. While all secondary values are instrumental, some primary values may also be instrumental.

Stability is not a primary value, but a secondary one. Stability is desirable if and only if that which is stabilized is itself desirable. This amounts to saying that the value of stability is derived from the value of what is stabilized. In other words, when the thing that is stabilized is desirable, stability is desirable; when it is undesirable, insistence on stability is reactionary.

Given that social tolerance and toleration are desirable in our time, stability of practicing them is valuable. Accordingly, the scope and limit of social tolerance and toleration and the conditions under which they can be achieved, stabilized, and sustained become important here. The danger is that social tolerance and toleration can become unstable, that is, turn themselves into their opposites or something else altogether. Here, the concern is not about the instability of social tolerance and toleration caused by parties' desires to avoid social tolerance and toleration, the kind of instability of social tolerance and toleration that George P. Fletcher points out.[52] Rather, the matter at hand is how desirable social tolerance and toleration can be stabilized and sustained.

Two immediate concerns arise here. One is that social tolerance and toleration may turn themselves into their opposites. The other is that they may turn themselves into something else, for example, benevolence. Social tolerance and toleration can transform by the law of *wu ji bi fan* (物极必反 extremity produces self-destruction).

If social tolerance and toleration are unrestrained, they will begin to change into social intolerance and intoleration or something else. When we apply social tolerance and toleration to objects that should not be tolerated, or practice tolerance and toleration beyond their requirements, we will alter them. In other words, social tolerance and toleration should be neither excessive nor insufficient. A crucial difference exists between tolerance and toleration on the one hand, and anarchy or rulelessness on the other.

When we practice social tolerance and toleration, our practice itself must be not excessive or insufficient. Suppose we tolerate pornography. Our toleration must be proportional. If it is excessive, we must oppress those legitimate concerns about the undesirability of pornography and those legitimate reasons to resist pornography. If it is insufficient, we oppress and repress certain legitimate interests in and of pornography. In either situation, we "tolerate" pornography with oppression or repression, and our toleration heads toward intoleration. Thus, laws that regulate production and transmission of pornography must balance the concerns of both freedom of speech and the evolution of society in which people have legitimate investments and rights to interfere.

Dao De Jing states: "When things reach their limits, they turn into their opposites. Going to the limit of a thing violates the *dao*. What violates the *dao* will perish."[53] Another Chinese classic, *He Guan Zi: Huan Liu* (鶡冠子：

环流), advocates the same idea. It reads, "Wu ji ze fan, min ye huan liu" (物极则反，明曰环流 Extremity produces self-destruction, this is the universal law of movement).[54] *Dao De Jing* therefore warns us:

> From calamity, happiness arises. From happiness, calamity is latent. Who knows when the limit is reached? Is there not normality? Then normality turns into abnormality [when it reaches its limit and] good turns to evil. . . .
>
> The Way of the universe is to reduce whatever is excessive and to supplement whatever is insufficient. Mankind practices the wrong and unnatural way. The way of mankind is to reduce the insufficient to offer to the excessive [this is why the way of mankind is wrong].[55]

Perhaps we may argue that X turning into its opposite is not a bad thing; accordingly, instability of social tolerance and toleration might not be a bad thing. Has G. W. F. Hegel not indicated that beings have made progress by following the path of position, negation, and negation of negation? Has he not suggested that X's self-negation designates progress, not a regression? However, this argument cannot stand. We must appreciate the differences between the concept of *wu ji bi fan* and the Hegelian concept of dialectics of being here.

The Hegelian self-negation is a characteristic of the path of X's progress. X's self-negation, in the Hegelian sense, refers to its acquiring characteristics that make it appear to be opposed to its former self. In a Hegelian dialectical movement of X, it is X that evolves and makes progress. According to the rule of *wu ji bi fan*, when X arrives at its limit, it turns itself into its opposite, which means that X loses itself. What the principle of *wu ji bi fan* brings home is not X's self-negation in a progressive sense, but the loss of X in a negative sense. It is one thing to say that X makes progress in a way that its next advanced state of existence has characteristics and properties opposed to X's present characteristics and properties. It is quite another to say that X loses itself by becoming its opposite or something else. For example, it is one thing to say that a person who used to be arrogant has become moderate now, yet quite another thing to say that a person now has lost himself or herself by becoming a totally different person or thing.

While some beings follow a pattern of self-negation in order to make progress, not all of X's self-negation necessarily entails progress, nor is X's self-negation a sufficient condition for progress. We can easily imagine a case in which X's self-negation is a regression, instead—for example, a person's health turning from good to poor. We can also easily imagine a case in which X makes qualitative progress without self-negation. For example, after some revisions, my manuscript is qualitatively improved. In the same way, we may make qualitative personal progress in personality, knowledge, wisdom, or a sense of duty and honor without a self-negation.

The law of *wu ji bi fan* underscores the idea of normative justice as the foundation of social tolerance and toleration. Social tolerance and toleration will be unsustainable if our practices of them are not grounded in normative justice. When we do not ground social tolerance and toleration in normative justice, social tolerance and toleration will be excessive or insufficient. And when that happens, the act of social toleration and the attitude of social tolerance oppress and repress what is due in some aspects. For example, if we ground social tolerance in the idea of benevolence, we cannot avoid excessive tolerance, which eventually will lead us to intolerance.

As Williams points out, social toleration can be grounded in "a Hobbesian equilibrium, under which the acceptance of one group by the other is the best either of them can get. This is not, of course, a principled solution. . . . The Hobbesian solution is also notoriously unstable."[56] We can also practice social toleration with "an active skepticism against fanaticism and the pretensions of its advocates; conviction about the manifest evils of toleration's absence."[57] However, if the ground for social toleration is merely active skepticism, we still do not see the true obligation of social toleration, which in turn makes social toleration unstable.

A qualification is in order here. With regard to people, social toleration is centered on redeeming the rights of freedom of thought and autonomy of our fellow citizens. The limit of rights is also the limit of social toleration. For example, in America, our fellow citizens have the right to religious freedom. However, they have no right to demand independent statehood. Thus, Muslims in America can believe in Islam, but an Islamic community within America has no right to demand an independent Islamic state on U.S. territory. Neither a Chinese community nor any other ethnic or religious community has such a right. True, as Scanlon points out, the reality is that "many different systems of rights are acceptable; none is ideal. Each is therefore constantly open to challenge and revision."[58] But that does not alter the fact that the limit of rights is the limit of social toleration.

In short, there are some necessary conditions for stable, sustainable practices of social tolerance and toleration. Among them is the balance of different relevant factors mandated by the law of *wu ji bi fan* (物极必反 extremity produces self-destruction). Unconditional, unconstrained, and extreme social tolerance and toleration are self-destructive.

Toleration, Truth, and Reason

While balance is the ontological condition for stable, sustainable practice of social tolerance and toleration, loyalty to truth and reason is the necessary condition to make the tolerance and toleration just and desirable. While public trust is a needed atmosphere for social tolerance and toleration in a diverse world, loyalty to truth and reason is a key to building public trust. The belief that social tolerance and toleration are antitheses to loyalty to truth and reason is wrong. Instead, loyalty to truth and reason is a needed bridge to just, stable, and maintainable social tolerance and toleration.

Loyalty to Truth

Tolerated beliefs are incompatible beliefs that are reasonably defensible; they are beliefs that we have good reason, but not sufficient reason, to reject. In other words, tolerated beliefs are beliefs that other people have a right and good reason to believe, even though we do not believe in them.

One implication here is that social toleration does not involve a battle between loyalty to truth and disloyalty to truth; instead, the battle is between loyalties to different concepts of truth. These good reasons on which our fellow citizens subscribe to those incompatible beliefs can constitute a kind of "ought" for these citizens to believe those beliefs. If these beliefs are that others ought to believe, to believe in them is not to be disloyal to truth, but loyal to truth. As William James says, truth is "what would be better for us to believe," "what we ought to believe."[59] If subscribing to these beliefs is not disloyal to truth, then neither is toleration of them.

Habermas rightly suggests that social tolerance is grounded in loyalty to truth; it is geared to redeem the truth claim of social practice. In the context of discussing religious tolerance, Habermas asks, "Could religious conflicts have been brought to an end if the principle of tolerance and freedom of belief and conscience had not been able to appeal, with good reasons, to a moral validity independent of religion and metaphysics?"[60] According to Habermas, the principle of social tolerance can be upheld if and only if we can appeal to ideologically neutral truth in practicing religious tolerance and toleration. Operating within a critical tradition that can be traced back to Karl Marx, Friedrich Engels, and Hegel, Habermas identifies religion and metaphysics with ideology here.

For Habermas, the commitment to truth enables the conflicting parties to be willing to go beyond their ideologies, engaging each other in dialogues and communications, which in turn leads to true social tolerance and toleration. By this token, truth provides true social tolerance and toleration a neutral and solid footing to ground themselves. In Habermas's view, there is a distinction between loyalty to truth and loyalty to one's own ideology. Loyalty to truth is being loyal to the objective truth, not to the concept of truth in a given ideology. True social tolerance and toleration are not disloyal to truth, but imply going beyond loyalty to one's own ideology.

This brings us back to the popular exit strategy—drawing a distinction between the view-holder and the view itself; tolerating the former while rejecting the latter. According to Heyd, true social toleration involves suspension of judgment of truth and focusing only on the holders of beliefs. Heyd dubs his concept of toleration a "perceptual" model:

> I call toleration a perceptual virtue, because it involves a shift of attention rather than an overall judgment. Tolerant people overcome the drive to interfere in the life of another not because they come to believe that the reasons for restraint are weightier than the reasons for disapproval, but because the attention is shifted from the object of disapproval to the humanity or the moral standing of the subject before them.[61]

By this account, social tolerance is a virtue of perceptual attitude that focuses on the perception of the rights and moral standing of the holders of beliefs, not on the judgments of the truth of the beliefs. The popular exit strategy, as exemplified in Heyd's strategy, involves bad faith: running away from truth and suspending the difficult task of judgment and decision making. As bad faith, social toleration of incompatible beliefs would never be true social toleration in the sense of bearing with and including them in a shared common life; it would be nothing but a pretense of social toleration.

True social toleration does involve a shift of focus, from loyalty to a particular ideology to loyalty to truth and justice. True social tolerance and toleration require a shift to loyalty to what Habermas calls "communicative rationality or reason."

Loyalty to truth has four distinctive contributions to true, stable social tolerance and toleration. First, it constitutes a source of inspiration and motivation for incompatibly conflicting parties to tolerate one another and be willing to coexist together. Thus, Habermas confidently insists that truth is one of the four validity-claims of universal communicative rationality, which reveals itself in rational communicative discourses. Second, loyalty to truth preserves a common ground on which incompatibly conflicting parties that tolerate one another can set their feet to work out their differences and to create and expand the common ground. Third, it maintains the possibility and the condition for the conflicting parties to be loyal to normative justice as setting human affairs right in accordance with the principles of human rights, human goods, and human bonds. Finally, loyalty to truth liberates parties from indulgence in politics and contributes to create public trust, the difficult but necessary atmosphere for stable social tolerance and toleration in a diverse world.

Conversely, we will not appeal to the moral force of a true belief in the first place if we do not honor the principles of social tolerance and freedom of conscience! And only through social tolerance and toleration, in which we let different voices have chance to speak for themselves, do we follow the voice of truth when we accept or reject a belief. In oppression and repression, we do not appeal to the voice of truth, but to the will of institutional power.

From a practical and historical point of view, social tolerance and toleration are necessary for us to welcome newly discovered truth. William James characterized the typical journey of a new theory's career as something like this: "First, it is attacked as absurd; then it is admitted to be true, but obvious and insignificant; finally it is seen to be so important that their adversaries claim that they themselves have discovered it."[62] What James said indicates that it takes social tolerance and toleration to allow newly discovered truth, especially newly discovered truth that is incompatible with orthodox beliefs.

Michel Foucault also pointed out:

> Truth is not the reward of free spirit. . . . Each society has its regime of truth, its "general politics" of truth: that is, the types of discourse which it accepts and makes function as true; the mechanism and instances which enable one to distinguish true and false statements, the means by which each is sanctioned; the techniques and procedures accorded value in the acquisition of truth; the status of those who are charged with saying what counts as true.[63]

We should bear in mind that in real life, in many extreme cases, "speaking one's truth can be treacherous . . . as Socrates, Antigone (Sophocles), Copernicus, Rameau's (Detrot), Thomas Paine, Black Hawk, Sojourner Truth, The Cherokee, Emma Goldman, Malcolm X, and other more obscure persons have discovered."[64] When he finished writing his great novel *The Red and the Black*, Stendhal claimed that the novel was for readers fifty years later! Stendhal knew then that he had the truth and a better argument. It would require social tolerance for his novel to be accepted!

In short, true and stable social toleration presupposes loyalty to truth. Furthermore, social tolerance and toleration are necessary for loyalty to truth. This is a reason why social tolerance and toleration can embody the timely spirit of normative justice in our time.

Loyalty to Reason

Social tolerance and toleration also imply loyalty to reason. Following the voice of reason is a necessary condition for any possible stable, true social tolerance and toleration. Richard Brown points out that we listen to the voice of reason when we practice "tolerance in other people's way of thought."[65]

Unfortunately, reason today "evokes images of domination, oppression, patriarchy, sterility, violence, totality, totalitarianism, and even terror."[66] This is due in great measure to the fact that the Enlightenment reason is considered to be totalitarian, for example, by Max Horkheimer and Theodor Adorno. One way to overcome the totalitarian reason of the Enlightenment is to replace it with a more inclusive, tolerant human reason. Having just, stable, and sustainable social toleration presupposes loyalty to the true voice of human reason, rejecting the sabotage of desires, interests, powers, and practical expediencies.

Habermas indicates that the problem of the Enlightenment reason is its subject-centeredness; the Enlightenment reason therefore lacks self-reflection and is exclusive and intolerant. About the exclusiveness of the Enlightenment reason, Habermas tells us:

> The spatial metaphor of inclusive and exclusive reason reveals that the supposedly radical critique of reason remains tied to the presuppositions of the philosophy of the subject from which it wants to free itself. Only a reason to which we ascribe a "power of the key" could either include or exclude. Hence, inside and outside are linked with domination and subjugation; and the overcoming of reason-as-power holder is linked with breaking open the prison gates and vouchsafing release into an indeterminate freedom. Thus, the other of reason remains the mirror image of reason in power.[67]

The Enlightenment reason is exclusive; it is akin to a key holder that excludes all others and allows only its own kind; to such a exclusive and intolerant reason, others become merely mirrors to its power.

For Habermas, intoleration and exclusion lead the Enlightenment reason to be self-idolizing, lacking self-reflection. But the problems of the Enlightenment reason invite us to reconstruct human reason. Habermas's proposed fix is to replace it with communicative reason. Communicative reason, which has the normative claims of comprehensibility, subjective truthfulness, propositional truth, and normative rightness, has three virtues. It is:

- inclusive and tolerant
- democratic and uncoercive
- just and fair

Being inclusive and tolerant, communicative reason enables us to give other voices their due. Being just and fair, it affords us with loyalty to truth and being truthful to ourselves and others without relying on institutional or political powers and oppression.

This amounts to saying that, according to Habermas, we do not become irrational by being tolerant and inclusive; instead, we become truly rational and reasonable when we are tolerant and inclusive. Only when human reason is tolerant and inclusive can it be true and the best. The Habermasian insight accords well with Taoist wisdom: the true reason is inclusive and all-embracing, not exclusive and partial. Laozi said that the *dao* was inclusive—"Dao tung wei yi" (道通为一 The *dao* synthesizes all reasons and truths together as one). The key word here is *tung* (通 connecting, relating). The *dao* connects and relates all together and thus includes all as one (unity).

While listening to the voice of true human reason implies listening to the voice of tolerance, toleration, and inclusion, to have stable and true social tolerance and toleration, we must listen to the true voice of human reason. We can appreciate this especially by recognizing the existence of what Larry Krasnoff calls "a stubborn and consensus-hindering fact":

> Suppose, however, that there exists a stubborn and consensus-hindering fact that is ascribed not to the limits of individual rationality, but to the working of reason itself. Suppose, that is, that individuals exercising their rational capacities in a full and undiminished manner produce a state of affairs that make it impossible, or nearly impossible, to achieve a normative consensus around a particular set of beliefs.[68]

Another argument is the old Socratic one. It goes something like this: If we do not follow human reason, we will follow our desires, passions, and the will to power and domination. As a result, true, stable social toleration is impossible; at most, we may have some degree of inclusion for the sake of benevolence and compassion, or some degree of compromise for practical necessity and negotiation of interests and desires. Following desires, passions, and the will to power, we can never distinguish the legitimate objects of social tolerance and toleration from the illegitimate ones and can never detect the limit and scope of social tolerance and toleration.

Finally, the law of *wu ji bi fan* brings home the voice of human reason. If social tolerance and toleration are not grounded in reason, they will not follow such rational rules as proportionality, rational balance, and giving what is due. Laozi thus said:

Zhi chang yue ming. Bu zhi chang, wang zuo xiong. Zhi chang rong, rong nai gong, gong nai wang, wang nai tian, tian nai dao, dao nai jiu. (知常曰明. 不知常, 妄作凶. 知常容, 容乃公, 公乃王, 王乃天, 天乃道, 道乃久 Knowing the laws is enlightenment. Without knowledge of the law and acting arbitrarily, one endangers oneself; having knowledge of the law, one becomes tolerant and inclusive; being tolerant and inclusive, one is fair; when one is fair, one is kingly; being kingly, one follows the rule of the heaven; following the rule of the heaven, one follows the *dao*; following the *dao*, one can endure in existence.)[69]

Cultural Toleration and Global Justice

The preceding discussions now lead us to the problems of cultural toleration and global justice in global human affairs. Globalization brings together different nations, peoples, cultures, and traditions. The metaphor of the global village is no longer a fairy tale, but connotes a substantial reality. Globalization raises questions about balancing the aspiration of modernity and respect for local contexts and nations' sovereignty, defense of the integrity of modernity and cultural toleration of local diversity. It calls for global justice, especially global normative justice. In turn, global normative justice implicates toleration to be a norm in global human affairs.

The main spheres in which cultural toleration is demanded in global human affairs do not differ essentially from its domestic application. Religious toleration, political toleration, and value toleration are among the paradigmatic cases of cultural toleration in the global arena, as they are on the domestic front. In 1981, the United Nations published the Declaration on the Elimination of All Forms of Intolerance and of Discrimination Based on Religion or Belief.[70] It proclaims:

> It is essential to promote understanding, tolerance and respect in matters relating to freedom of religion and belief and to ensure that the use of religion or belief for ends inconsistent with the Charter of the United Nations, other relevant instruments of the United Nations and the purposes and principles of the present Declaration is inadmissible.[71]

The UN declaration was published in a historical context in which religious intolerance became a major source of international conflict.

In 1993, Harvard University professor Samuel P. Huntington published a thought-provoking article in the journal *Foreign Affairs* entitled "The Clash of Civilizations?"[72] In it, Huntington predicted that in the twenty-first century, the main source of international conflict would be differences of civilizations, especially a clash between Christianity-centered cultural-religious allies and Confucian- and Islamic-centered cultural-religious allies. Setting aide the controversy over Huntington's particular conclusions, his essay is instructive and leads us, from a different direction, to see the importance of cultural tolerance and toleration in global human affairs today.

We can now confirm that cultural, especially religious, intoleration around the globe is a major source of international conflict today, regional as well as global. For example, as Louis P. Pojman notes, "Religion is surpassing nationalism as the foremost threat to world peace and stability."[73] Indeed, religious and cultural intolerance and intoleration currently pose the greatest challenges to global justice and humanity.

On November 16, 1995, the United Nations Educational, Scientific, and Cultural Organization (UNESCO) published its Declaration of Principles of Tolerance and designated November 16 of each year as International Tolerance Day.[74] The declaration indicates that religious tolerance and toleration are of great importance to global justice and humanity. Its preamble states:

> *Bearing in mind* that the United Nations Charter states: "We, the peoples of the United Nations determined to save succeeding generations from the scourge of war . . . to reaffirm faith in fundamental human rights, in the dignity and worth of the human person . . . and for these ends to practice tolerance and live together in peace with one another as good neighbors,"
> *Recalling* that the Preamble to the Constitution of UNESCO, adopted on 16 November 1945, states that "peace, if it is not to fail, must be founded on the intellectual and moral solidarity of mankind."[75]

In this declaration, UNESCO points out both the fact that cultural, religious, and political toleration is the inherent spirit of the UN Charter and the importance of cultural tolerance and toleration in global human affairs. Isaiah Berlin keenly observes:

> Every nation has its own tradition, its own character, [and] its own face. Every nation has its own moral gravity, which differs from that of every other; there and only there its happiness lies—in the development of its own national needs, its own unique character.[76]

It is also the case that every civilization has its own face, life, center of gravity, and center of happiness. Cultural and national diversity is a profound reality, not some passing phenomenon. Accordingly, cultural tolerance and toleration—and only cultural tolerance and toleration—embody the timely spirit of global normative justice. Berlin says: "Different nations, different roots, different laws, different peoples, different communities, different ideals. Each has its own way of living—what right had one to dictate to the others?"[77]

Global normative justice implicates the norms of religious toleration, political toleration, value toleration, and other forms of toleration in global human affairs today. To start with, global normative justice calls for respect for the national sovereignty of a people. The national sovereignty of a nation or people constrains the rights of other nations and peoples to interfere or prohibit what are deemed to be domestic affairs. The national sovereignty of a nation or people also demands that other nations and peoples respect and honor their rights and their due in international affairs.

In terms of global normative justice, the principles and requirements of cultural tolerance and toleration in global human affairs include:

- bearing with other nations and peoples and refusing to interfere in their domestic affairs except for situations where there are serious human rights violations or crimes against humanity
- including, not isolating, nations and peoples even if we disapprove of them
- promoting mutual cultural understanding and communication
- refusing offensive wars and conflicts based on religion, race, or political ideologies; that is, rejecting offensive wars and conflicts based on religious imperialism, racism, nationalism, and political-ideological fundamentalism

In short, in terms of global justice, when nations and peoples become the members of an international community and part of the integral lives of the international human community, they and their cultures become the objects of cultural tolerance and toleration. They should be shown forbearance and included as legitimate members of the international human community and its life. They should be allowed to hold to their institutions and advocate their beliefs and values in words and actions, in a peaceful manner.

Meanwhile, so far as the requirements of cultural toleration in global human affairs are concerned, we are always at a point at which the problem of indeterminacy is aggravated. The exact contents of the requirements of international and cultural tolerance and toleration are even less determinate than the requirements of social toleration on the domestic front. Domestically, especially in developed countries where there is the rule of law, the scope and limit of social tolerance and toleration are well defined in the constitutions and relevant laws; therefore, the requirements of social toleration are relatively determinate. But in global human affairs, the scope and limit of international and cultural toleration are not well defined in many areas; in some aspects, they are not defined at all.

But one thing about international and cultural toleration around the globe is always clear: in global normative justice, a people's rights and sovereignty are always recognized and honored; global normative justice mandates that a nation or people must be tolerant of other peoples and cultures. Global justice demands peaceful coexistence of nations, which in turn demands international and cultural toleration. It may be that ways of life of other nations and peoples are not compatible with one another, but still, global justice demands toleration of incompatible differences, not oppressing them in the shared life of international human community.

A people should defend its values or beliefs. But by the same token, peoples must also tolerate each others' values and traditions. Only if they do so can they coexist peacefully. In addition, only if they do so, will they act justly. Modernity and globalization are historical tasks of humankind today. Truth, righteousness, and reason will stand straight in modernity and globalization when social, political, and cultural tolerance and toleration exist in global affairs and when hegemony, colonization, totalitarianism, oppression, repression, and aggression in international affairs are rejected as unjust.

It is possible that from a certain nation's or people's perspective, other nations' and peoples' values, practices, and institutions are incompatible with modernity. Still, global justice implicates the norms of cultural tolerance and toleration. Here, we should recall Zhuangzi's teaching:

> Yi zhi yu zhi zhi fei zhi, bu ruo yi fei zhi yu zhi zhi fei zhi ye; yi ma yu ma zhi fei ma, bu ruo yi fei ma yu ma zhi fei ma ye (以指喻指之非指，不若以非指喻指之非指；以马喻马之非马，不若以非马喻马之非马 One should not take one's finger as the standard and therefore say that others' fingers are not fingers; instead, one should take the universal finger as the standard and see that a particular finger is not identical to the [universal] finger; one should not take a particular horse as the standard and therefore say that other [particular] horses are not horses; instead, one should take the universal horse as the standard and therefore see that a particular horse is not identical to the [universal] horse).[78]

To develop a new, just global order, just international laws and global institutions need to be developed. New international laws will be just when they embody the aspiration of modernity and also the timely spirit of social tolerance and toleration amid the historical reality of cultural, religious, and local diversity. Equally crucial, new international laws will be just when they embody the spirit of reason, which in turn calls for tolerance and toleration, rejecting imperialism, hegemony, and colonization.

Social Toleration and the Spirit of Our Time

In conclusion, as a state of consciousness and an attitude of a society, social tolerance is demanded by normative justice in our time. As a form of practice, social toleration is called for by normative justice. Robert P. Wolff suggests:

> The virtue of a monarchy is loyalty. . . . The virtue of a military dictatorship is honor; that of a bureaucratic dictatorship is efficiency. The virtue of traditional liberal democracy is equality, while the virtue of a socialist democracy is fraternity. The ideal nationalist democracy exhibits the virtue of patriotism . . . the virtue of the modern pluralist democracy . . . is tolerance.[79]

What Wolff says has a kernel of truth. I would like to add, as it is demonstrated by discussions in this chapter, that the norms of social tolerance and toleration are not norms of virtue, but norms of public obligation. Social tolerance and toleration may not be attractive, but they are obligatory. We do not do fellow citizens a favor or bestow upon others kindness and benevolence when we are tolerant of them; we fulfill our obligations to our fellow citizens and give them what they are entitled to. Similarly on a global scale, we do not do other nations or peoples a favor when we are tolerant of them and tolerate them; we fulfill our global obligations implicated by global normative justice. Global justice also mandates that international laws and global institutions be culturally tolerant.

Meanwhile, the spirit of social tolerance and toleration does not call for unreflective pluralism, but asks for reflective pluralism. One manifestation of unreflective pluralism is the postmodern tendency that celebrates otherness, diversity, and division; that associates all emphases on social unity and harmony as oppression and repression; and that advocates "anything goes." Reflective pluralism emphasizes the value of pluralism on the one hand and stresses public good, communal unity, and social harmony on the other. Wolff observes:

> Pluralism is humane, benevolent, accommodating, and far more responsive to the evils of social injustice than either the egoist liberalism or the traditionalistic conservativism from which it grew. But Pluralism is fatally blind to the evils which afflict the entire body politics and as a theory of society it obstructs consideration of precisely the sorts of thoroughgoing social revision which

may be needed to remedy those evils. Like all great social theories, pluralism answered a genuine social need during a significant period of history.[80]

Wolff correctly associates social intolerance and intoleration with social injustice. However, he incorrectly associates the norms of social tolerance and toleration with humanitarian morality, not with the duty of justice. Humanitarian morality may be a part of the spirit of our time. But social tolerance and toleration are norms implicated by normative justice in our time.

Social tolerance and toleration are the norms of obligations in a democratic society or a nation-state in the traditional sense. They are also the norms of obligation of a Kantian-style cosmopolitan republic. Such a republic is not a traditional nation-state; instead, it is an empire of humanity in a new sense.

In summary, social tolerance and toleration are the norms of justice of our time, as diversity is the enduring reality of our time. The Bible tells us: "One believes he may eat everything, while the weak man eats only vegetables. Let not him who eats despise him who abstains, and let not him who abstains pass judgment on him who eats."[81]

Notes

1. David Heyd, "Introduction," in *Toleration: An Elusive Virtue*, ed. David Heyd (Princeton, NJ: Princeton University Press, 1996), 3.

2. *Zhou Yi* (周易), ed. and trans. Fang Fei (U Lu Mu Qi, China: XinJiang Youth Publishing House, 1999), 25.

3. Bernard Williams, "Toleration: An Impossible Virtue?" in Heyd, *Toleration*, 18.

4. Herbert Marcuse, "Repressive Tolerance," in Robert P. Wolff, Barrington Moore, and Herbert Marcuse, *A Critique of Pure Tolerance* (Boston: Beacon Press, 1965), 81.

5. Thomas Scanlon, *The Difficulty of Tolerance* (Cambridge: Cambridge University Press, 2003), 195–201.

6. Ibid., 201.

7. Michael Walzer, *On Toleration* (New Haven, CT: Yale University Press, 1997), xi.

8. Isaiah Berlin, *The Crooked Timber of Humanity* (Princeton, NJ: Princeton University Press, 1997), 13.

9. Confucius, *The Essence and Substance of the Analects* (*Lun Yu Zheng Yi* 论语正义), ed. Liu Bao Nan, in *Completed Works of Teachers* (*Zhu Zi Ji Cheng* 诸子集成), vol. 1 (Beijing: Unity Publishing House, 1996), 20.1.

10. Scanlon, *Difficulty of Tolerance*, 192.

11. Ibid., 201.

12. Jürgen Habermas, "Religious Tolerance—the Pacemaker for Cultural Rights," *Philosophy* 79, no. 1 (Spring 2004): 10.

13. Ibid.

14. John Rawls, *A Theory of Justice* (Cambridge, MA: Harvard University Press, 1971), 214.

15. Scanlon, *Difficulty of Tolerance*, 197.

16. John Horton, "Toleration as a Virtue," in Heyd, *Toleration*, 33.

17. Ibid.

18. For details of Rawls's view, see Rawls, *Theory of Justice*, 216–21.

19. Ibid., 216.

20. Ibid., 215.

21. John Locke, "A Letter Concerning Toleration," in *Locke, Berkeley, Hume* (London: William Benton, 1952), 1–22.

22. Cf. Rawls, *Theory of Justice*, 216.

23. Heyd, *Toleration*, 3.

24. Ibid.

25. Scanlon, *Difficulty of Tolerance*, 198.

26. Walzer, *On Toleration*, xii.

27. Williams, "Toleration," 18.

28. Scanlon, *Difficulty of Tolerance*, 190.

29. Barbara Herman, "Pluralism and the Community of Moral Judgment," in Heyd, *Toleration*, 61.

30. Habermas, "Religious Tolerance," 10.

31. Williams, "Toleration," 20.

32. Habermas, "Religious Tolerance," 10.

33. Horton, "Toleration as a Virtue," 32.

34. Susan Mendus, *Toleration and the Limits of Liberalism* (London: Macmillan, 1989), 18–19.

35. Cited in Scanlon, *Difficulty of Tolerance*, 197.

36. Horton, "Toleration as a Virtue," 33.

37. Ibid., 32.

38. Scanlon, *Difficulty of Tolerance*, 197.

39. Horton, "Toleration as a Virtue," 28.

40. Scanlon, *Difficulty of Tolerance*, 190.

41. Ibid., 187.

42. Ibid., 189.

43. Ibid., 190.

44. Walzer, *On Toleration*, xi.

45. Scanlon, *Difficulty of Tolerance*, 196.

46. Ibid., 187.

47. Herman, "Pluralism," 61.

48. Ibid., 191.

49. Horton, "Toleration as a Virtue," 34.

50. Habermas, "Religious Tolerance," 10.

51. Ibid.

52. See George P. Fletcher, "The Instability of Tolerance," in Heyd, *Toleration*, 154–92.

53. Laozi, *Dao De Jing*, ed. Wei Yuan, in *Completed Works of Teachers*, vol. 3, chap. 55.

54. *Si Ku Chaun Shu* (*Collections of All Traditional Chinese Classics of All Disciplines*), (Tianjin, China: Tianjin Classics, 1998), vol. 2, p. 554. He Guan Zi (鶡冠子) is a person of the Spring and Autumn and Warring States periods. His real name is unknown. His works were collected under the title of *He Guan Zi*. See also Ruo Ji, *The Tradition of I Jing and the Cultural Paradigm of Thinking in China* (Wu Han, China: Wu Han Publishing House, 1994), 146.

55. Laozi, *Dao De Jing*, chap. 58, chap. 77.

56. Williams, "Toleration," 21.

57. Ibid., 27.

58. Scanlon, *the Difficulty of Tolerance*, 198.

59. William James, *Pragmatism* (1907; reprint, Indianapolis, IN: Hackett, 1981), 37.

60. Habermas, "Religious Tolerance," 17.

61. Heyd, "Introduction," 12.

62. James, *Pragmatism*, 81.

63. Michel Foucault, *Foucault Reader*, ed. Paul Rabinow (New York: Pantheon, 1984), 72–73.

64. Andrew R. Smith and Leonard Shyless, "On Ethnocentric Truth and Pragmatic Justice," in *Recovering Pragmatism's Voice*, ed. Lenore Langsdorf and Andrew R. Smith (Albany: State University of New York Press, 1995), 71.

65. Richard H. Brown, *Society as Text* (Chicago: Chicago University Press, 1987), 65.

66. Richard Bernstein, *New Constellation: The Ethical-Political Horizon of Modernity/Postmodernity* (Cambridge, MA: MIT Press, 1992), 32.

67. Jürgen Habermas, *The Philosophical Discourse of Modernity*, trans. Frederick G. Lawrence, (Cambridge, MA: MIT Press, 1993), 309.

68. Larry Krasnoff, "Consensus, Stability, and Normativity in Rawls' Political Liberalism," *Journal of Philosophy* 95, no. 6 (June 1998): 275.

69. Laozi, *Dao De Jing*, chap. 15.

70. "Declaration on the Elimination of All Forms of Intolerance and of Discrimination Based on Religion or Belief," G.A. Res. 36/55, 36 U.N. GAOR Supp. (No. 51) at 171, U.N. Doc. A/36/684 (1981). Available at http://www1.umn.edu/humanrts/instre/4deidrb.htm.

71. Ibid.

72. Samuel P. Huntington, "The Clash of Civilizations?" *Foreign Affairs* 72, no. 2 (Summer 1993).

73. Louis P. Pojman, "The Cosmopolitan Response to Terrorism," in *The Moral Life*, ed. Louis P. Pojman (New York: Oxford University Press, 2004), 965.

74. "Declaration of Principles on Tolerance," http://www.unesco.org/webworld/peace_library/UNESCO/HRIGHTS/124-129.HTM.

75. Ibid.

76. Berlin, *Crooked Timber of Humanity*, 37.

77. Ibid., 33.

78. Zhuangzi, *Zhaungzi Ji Jie*, in *Completed Works of Teachers*, vol. 3, chap. 2.

79. Robert P. Wolff, Barrington More Jr., and Herbert Marcus, *A Critique of Pure Tolerance* (Boston: Beacon Press, 1969), 3–4.

80. Ibid., 52.

81. Rom. 14:2–3.

CHAPTER 5

~

Democracy: The Vehicle of Justice in Our Time

While normative justice implicates social tolerance and toleration as the norms of our time, it also seeks democracy as its instrument for realization in our time. As a form of government and a form of life, democracy may be one of the best vehicles to realize normative justice. In a normal society, its human members should be both the receivers and the coauthors of justice. Internationally, nations, peoples, and individuals should be the receivers and coauthors of global justice.

The allure and pitfalls of democracy are as conspicuous as ever. We cannot take for granted the association of normative justice and democracy. A good democracy can be an instrumental value to justice; a bad one, a disvalue. Conversely, only a just democracy is a good one; only a just democracy is worth having and can be stable and endurable. An unjust democracy is a bad one that is not worth having and cannot be sustained. Many democracies in the world today are hijacked by the rich, the powerful, and the privileged.

What a democracy is remains an open question. Christopher Hollis vividly describes democracy as meaning "one thing at Moscow, one at Rome, a third in Sudan and a fourth at home."[1] What is democracy? How is a just, wise democracy possible? These questions remain outstanding today.

The waters are further muddied by the fact that there is also a long tradition of debunking democracy as a form of unjust government and an antithesis of justice and reason. Indeed, an asymmetry exists between the faithful commitment to democracy nowadays and a long tradition of suspicion and skepticism of democracy throughout history. There is some conspicuous disharmony between the persistent hope for democracy and the blistering criticism of it. Is democracy evil or good? That is the question which human civilization bequeaths us! Global democracy and democratization—good or bad? That is the question which we face today.

While the summit of the truth of democracy is within our horizon, various paths by which we ascend to that summit are slippery, and any carelessness will lead to our downfall. We must demonstrate that true democracy is the vehicle for normative justice in our time and, simultaneously, that true, just democracy is the only form of government and form of life we ought to vote for. We must demonstrate both that justice demands democracy and that democracy must be grounded in justice in order to be true, acceptable, and endurable. We must demonstrate that a good democracy provides a good vehicle to humanity, enabling humankind to flourish and to fully self-realize, while bad democracies will bring humanity and humankind to ruin. All the same, an unexamined democracy is not worth having.

Democracy and Its Discontents: The Chinese Story

I will travel a particular path by taking as the guide here the Chinese struggle for democracy from the nineteenth century to the twenty-first. The struggle is an illustrative paradigm for us to study the allure and pitfalls of democracy and global democratization. It gives us a good window offering a titillating view of the promises, issues, discontents, and challenges of democracy as a vehicle for justice and international democratization as part of the ongoing globalization. It serves as an outstanding case for us to look at the prickly matters of a people's sovereignty, the rights of nations and peoples, the historical temperaments and cultural characters of democracy, and the precarious relations between *ethnos* and *demos*.

The Chinese struggle reveals that different historical climates create different historical temperaments, which produce different kinds of what Nietzsche calls humanity's "artistic cruelty," and that in turn contributes to the diversity of democracy in the globe today. The Chinese example reaffirms that, just as the various planets are different but all move around the sun, all true democracies must move around the idea of justice; just as all stars are within the universe, all true democracies must be within the horizon of justice; just as the laws of the universe and of nature preserve their dignity in the cosmos, so do the laws of the human family preserve theirs in the human kingdom.

The Enlightening Volcano

The idea of democracy was first introduced to China in the 1890s. At that time, among the Chinese people, there were profound feelings of national humiliation, being powerless before foreign aggressors, and there was a prominent threat to China's national independence and internal unity, as well as frustration over China's economical, political, and military backwardness. Accordingly, the Chinese people were totally preoccupied with the issues of *jiu wang tu cun* (救亡图存 saving the nation from extinction and assuring its survival) and of China's reempowerment.

In such a historical context, "Mr. Democracy" and "Mr. Science," as the Chinese protagonists dubbed them, presented themselves as the princes to empower China, not some relatives to social justice. In such a historical context, all Chinese protagonists argued for one thing in common: a democracy that could empower China most effectively. Thus, for example, a group of protagonist intellectuals led by Kang Youwei (1858–1927) advocated a constitutional monarchy because, as Andrew Nathan notes, Kang and his comrades believed that this form of government was the "secret of the strength of Japan and the Western countries."[2] It was the Mr. Democracy of power, not the Goddess Democracy of justice, that was in favor with the Chinese people then.

In the Chinese New Culture Movement in the 1910s and 1920s, democracy was advocated not as a form of just government but as a form of government that could empower China. The approaches to democracy in the movement shaped China's struggle for democracy thereafter. Focused on the aspiration to empower China, different concepts of democracy were proposed: a rationalist bourgeois republic versus an egalitarian people's democracy from 1927 to 1937, a bourgeois republic versus a multiparty democratic republic from 1937 to 1945,[3] a bourgeois republic versus a people's democratic dictatorship from 1946 to 1949. None of these proposals advocated democracy as the vehicle for justice, however. They all conceived democracy as the way to make China a world power again.

Nothing is wrong with seeing the power of democracy. The twentieth century itself was a century in which democracy empowered human civilization. Nonetheless, in welcoming the democracy of power rather than that of justice, a people welcomes the wrong guest. To aspire for democracy in order to have power, and not justice, a people will end up having a false or illusive democracy. This is the problem with the Chinese approaches to democracy. The absence of the idea of justice in their struggle for democracy has led to serious consequences.

First, a conceptual inadequacy exists in the Chinese understanding of democracy. China has claimed to have had democracy since 1949. Since that time, there have been various official versions of new democracy in Mainland China. From 1949 to 1966, it was called the "people's democratic dictatorship," which Mao Zedong defined as "democracy for the people and dictatorship for the enemy."[4] In the period of the Great Proletarian Cultural Revolution (1966–1976), it was called "the proletarian dictatorship." Since the late 1970s, the concept of people's democratic dictatorship has been restored. In all these "democracies," what the core value and principle of democracy was is not clear.

Second, there was a failure to develop a set of concepts such as basic human rights, liberties, legitimacy, fairness, lawfulness, humanity as the end, and the like to serve as analytical tools for critical assessments of basic social powers and institutions in China. An absence of such a set of analytical tools in turn makes it impossible for a deep understanding of the oppressive nature of China's socialist democracy. Despite its long cultural tradition, the present Chinese instrumental mentality or instrumentalist concept of rationality has de facto marginalized the idea of humanity as the end in socialist democracy. Democracy becomes a factory to produce a certain kind of product. We can call these individuals in China's socialist democracy socialists, communists, or builders of a red world, as we like. But make no mistake: it is that they are for the great cause, not that the great cause is for them; they are the means, not the end.

Third, there was a failure to develop a reasonable mechanism for mass participation. To be fair, there was no lack of calls for mass participation in public life and government. The problem was the failure to find a way for true mass participation. Mao was thrilled in the beginning with the Cultural Revolution, because he thought that China had finally found its means of mass participation. But in the end, even he found that it was an illusion.

The problem is systemic. The failure to find a way of true mass participation in formal and informal politics of the nation has a deep cause: mass participation is not conceived as the necessary means to exercise individuals' rights and for individuals to act as the end and to extend their lives together. Instead, it is conceived merely as some kind of instrumental necessity, some compassionate gift of a humane government; it is emphasized as the necessary extension of the benevolence of the government toward the people.

All these glaring errors gathered the upcoming storms that would shake China profoundly. Instead of having the morning sun of democracy, China had one volcano after another of democratic revolution.

The Raging Storm

When the People's Republic of China was established in 1949, the Chinese people believed that democracy was a reality in Mainland China. Everything appeared to belong to the people, too: the People's Newspaper, the People's Congress, the People's Government, the People's Liberation Army, and so on. Above all, Mao historically proclaimed, "The Chinese people now have stood up," in Tiananmen Square on October 1, 1949. But the belief was soon crushed by the silent reality, especially the remorseful *da min zhu* (大民主 great democracy) of the Cultural Revolution.

The political catastrophe of the "great democracy" of the Cultural Revolution caused a new wave of outcry for democracy and passionate debates over the nature, scope, and limit of democracy in the later 1970s. The new demands for democracy called for a correction of the political, ideological oppression and feudalist totalitarianism in the Cultural Revolution. It also called for a government of humanity, wisdom, and reason.

It was no wonder that the outcry for democracy called for a correction of the *da min zhu* of the Cultural Revolution. The notion of *da min zhu* was derived originally from the "four *da*'s" (*da* 大 big):

1. *da ming* (大鸣 speaking out loudly and freely)
2. *da fang* (大放 airing views fully and loudly)
3. *da bian lun* (大辩论 great, heated debate)
4. *da zi bao* (大字报 big-character poster)

Da min zhu thus originally connoted freedom to do these four "bigs." It was at first a call for mass democracy in formal and informal politics; in the words of Mao, "Let those little men talk," "Down with the monster, liberation of the little men." However, in the Cultural Revolution, *da min zhu* (great democracy) turned itself into an unchecked ultrademocracy and anarchism.

The first crucial change of the Constitution of the People's Republic of China after the Cultural Revolution was the legal ban on *si da zi you* (四大自由 four great freedoms)—the four bigs: *da ming, da fang, da bian lun,* and *da zi bao*. Meanwhile, even at this point, no question about social justice was raised.

Instead, in the context of China's aspiration for "four modernizations"—modernization of industry, agriculture, science and technology, and national defense—the question abut democracy was still the question of which form of democracy was the most effective form of government. Accordingly, three conflicting proposals for democracy were put forth in the late 1970s and early 1980s:

1. Communist Party–led democratic centralism—a neo-authoritarian democracy

2. an elite- and intellectual-led rationalist democracy
3. a liberal, egalitarian democracy based on the principles of the Paris Commune

At the core of democratic centralism were three beliefs. First, democracy should have a Chinese style. Such a form of democracy should embody traditional Chinese values such as social harmony, discipline, political unity and stability, trust, propriety, and wisdom, all bearing Chinese cultural marks. Second, democratic centralism—or people's democratic dictatorship, in the official language—requires the leadership of Chinese Communist Party of China. Third, there should be the rule of the knowledgeable and the rule of law. Unfortunately, for those who advocate democratic centralism, the concern was not which form of government or form of life would bring social justice and protect citizens' rights, but which form of government was more effective in leading China to the four modernizations.

Chinese radical liberals and liberal rationalists both rejected the idea of democratic centralism and came up with two different proposals: egalitarian liberalism and liberal rationalism. The focus of the egalitarian democracy was not on political stability, law, and order, but on the political liberation of the Chinese masses. Even with the experience of the Cultural Revolution in the background, Chinese egalitarian liberals called for a "socialist mass democracy . . . gradually to realize the principles of the Paris Commune."[5] Some activists in the democratic movement of 1979–1980 went so far as calling for destroying the old state machinery and the rule of the party, replacing them with a mass participatory democratic system modeled on the Paris Commune.

Though they also called for protection of citizens' political rights and elimination of oppression and alienation of political powers, Chinese egalitarian liberals in 1970s and 1980s had no idea that the first duty and obligation of a government was that of social justice. They called for a "proletarian democratic revolution" without an understanding of what such a revolution was for. Their intellectual inspiration was the example of Paris Commune, not traditional Chinese values such as humanity, propriety, and wisdom. They aspired for democracy as a free form of life, but had no concept of the rule of law and the importance of basic laws such as the constitution of a nation.

Chinese rationalists did not fare any better. They invoked the early idea of a rationalist democracy, but "they intended to identify it very strongly with the rational, efficient management of government by people of trained expertise. Their most general concern was with the project of modernization."[6] Rationalist intellectuals "were very radical in their critique of the communist rule. But their call ultimately was for a kind of reform in which the best trained, most elite experts would advise the government, not for a mass mobilization of the Chinese people."[7] As Craig Calhoun observes, "Fang [Lizhi] spoke frequently of democracy. His emphasis, however, was not egalitarian. Rather than mass participatory institutions, he advocated a government by experts. At the extreme, it seemed as though he would like to see government by physicists."[8]

Rationalist intellectuals also called for individual rights and freedom. Fang insisted, "Democracy means every human being has his own rights and that human beings, each exercising his own rights, form our society."[9] Rationalist intellectuals also rejected the so-called four cardinal principles. While they believed that the best-qualified persons should rule, they rejected the idea that the best-qualified persons came from the party cadre corps. They believed that reason and science should rule, but rejected the concept that Marxist-Leninist-Maoist thought was science. Meanwhile, rationalist intellectuals such as Fang and his comrades had no idea of the rule of law and its role in democracy.

In short, during China's struggle for democracy in the 1970s and 1980s, the question about democracy was still not which form of democracy was just, but which form of democracy could lead China to modernization and make China a world power again. China's struggle for democracy in this period involved the effort to set China's affairs right, but the problem was still that the endeavor was not to set things right in accordance with justice. This resulted in the violent conflicts in the end of 1980s, highlighted by the Tiananmen Square massacre in 1989.

After the Rolling Thunder

China's inability to develop democracy in terms of justice continued in the 1990s. The struggle for democracy was still driven by two different calls alternatively: the neo-authoritarian call for the rule of law, order, and rationalization of the government; and the egalitarian call for liberation, human rights, and freedom. But neither of these was about having a just form of government and life, only about having a democracy that could lead China to modernization.

In his Work Report to the Fifteenth National Congress of the Communist Party, Jiang Zemin said:

> To develop socialist politics with the Chinese style is to govern the country by laws and to develop a socialist democratic polity under the leadership of the

Chinese Communist Party and based on the principle of the sovereignty of the people. This means . . . making perfect the system of People's Congress and the system of multiparty cooperation under the leadership of the Communist Party of China, and political consultation.[10]

Jiang's statement highlights two themes of Chinese rationalism in the 1990s: the rule of the law and the real empowerment of the People's Congress, the national congress. Equally important is what Jiang did not spell out explicitly: the call for socialist formal and informal politics with a Chinese style; the insistence on a stable political environment for China's modernization.

Western observers complain that Jiang failed to call for radical democratization of China's political system. Richard Baum, for example, says, "Although Jiang used the word 'democracy' no less than 32 times in his report, structural reform of the political system was not revived."[11] The criticism is that China does not practice a Western form of democracy. But such a criticism misses the crucial point. There is nothing unjustified in China wanting to develop a form of democracy fitting its own historical, cultural reality. There is no universal form of democracy in the world. The real question is whether the kind of democracy that China practices now can be just. Had the question about justice been asked, issues about social toleration would have been addressed and the role of social toleration in sociopolitical stability would have been emphasized.

Chinese neoliberals in the 1990s did not argue for democracy in terms of justice, either. They recognized that China's political system itself was the problem, that the four cardinal principles were oppressive and the core of the problems. However, they had no solution. Some neoliberals tempered their call for radical democracy with the concern about political stability; others, for the first time, advocated two ideas explicitly: human rights and individual freedom. In 1994, several scientists and social scientists even wrote an open letter to the National People's Congress, claiming that "ignorance, neglect and disregard of human rights constitute the main cause for the misfortune of the populace and for the corruption in the government."[12] However, none of Chinese neoliberals ever talked about democracy in terms of justice.

As a result, Chinese neoliberals also had their Achilles' heel. They were intolerant of different views, especially those that they deemed to be conservative. They did not see the important connection between democracy and social toleration. They had no idea of the intrinsic connections among human rights, democracy, and toleration.

The Long-Awaited Call for Social Justice

In February 2005, in a speech to an internal conference of the provincial Communist Party leaders, Chinese president Hu Jintao called for establishing *she hui gong ping zheng yi* (社会公平正义 social fairness and justice) in China. In his National Day speech on October 1, 2006, Chinese premier Wen Jiabao also asserted that China should "shi xian she hui gong ping zheng yi, wan shan she hui zhu yi zhi du" (实现社会公平正义, 完善社会主义制度 realize social fairness and justice and perfect its socialist system).[13] Some Chinese intellectuals and theorists immediate hailed the speech as a call to restore the concept of role duty or public duty of the government.

The call for social justice is a call for a harmonious democracy and a harmonious society (*he xie she hui* 和谐社会). Here, the concept of social fairness and justice (*she hui gong ping zheng yi* 社会公平正义) calls for "fairness in rights and benefits, fairness in opportunities, fairness in laws and rules, and fairness in distributions"—in short, distributive justice. What is important here is the emerging awareness that a basic duty of government is to bring about and realize social justice. Promoted by Hu's support, China's ongoing discourse on democracy and justice now focuses more on the rule of law and fairness of laws, but not on basic rights, liberties, social responsibility, and human values. The push for social toleration is still conspicuously absent, but the concept of social justice is on the discussion table.

There is no question that the Chinese people aspire for democracy to empower China for good historical reasons, yet one cannot help asking: Why has the question about justice in democracy evaded the Chinese people for more than a century? There is a deep philosophical reason: the absence of an explicit concept of normative justice. This is exhibited even in the present Chinese discourse on social justice. Today, the concept of justice brings to the Chinese mind still only two kinds of justice: distributive and corrective. The concept of normative justice is yet to be developed. The traditional Chinese rejection of *bao zheng* (暴政 government by violence and repression), *nude zheng* (虐政 abusive, oppressive, and repressive government), and *yin zheng* (淫政 government by excessive desires and violence) has not produced a concept of normative justice in the present discourse on social justice and democracy in China.

The Chinese experience of democratization offers a mirror of global democratization today. That is, it mirrors a vast majority of cases of democratization around the globe. There should be no question that a nation has a right to choose a model of democracy that fits the cultural, historical, and regional contexts of the situation in which the nation or people is situated. However, the fundamental questions remain: What is a just democracy? What are its basic features?

The Ancient Skepticism and Promise

Today, democracy has become a most promising form of government and life in the world. In 1995, the seventh East–West Philosophers' Conference, "Justice and Democracy," took place in Honolulu. As Ron Bontekoe and Marietta Stepaniants report, the conference

> attracted well over a hundred philosophers and political theoretists from every continent and religion in the world, and they agreed perhaps on only one thing—that today democracy (understood in a number of quite different ways, however) is the only government that enjoys moral legitimacy.[14]

In June 2000, the inaugural meeting of the Community of Democracies was held in Warsaw. "Representatives of the governments of 106 countries signed the 'Warsaw Declaration,' recognizing the universality of democratic values, and agreeing that 'the will of the people shall be the basis of the authority of government.'"[15] If the seventeenth and eighteenth centuries constitute the Age of Reason and the nineteenth century the Age of States Rights, then the twentieth and twenty-first centuries should constitute the Age of Democratization.

Some disharmony still exists. Ancient philosophers, including Plato, Confucius, Aristotle, and many others, all considered democracy to be a bad form of government and of life. Some of their criticisms on democracy are still illuminating to us today.

Plato and Pericles

The Platonic just government is a rationalistic one, that is, a government ruled by reason, philosophical wisdom, knowledge, truth, and the best. This implies that a just government is a wise one. Indeed, the primary virtue of the Platonic guardianship or rulership is wisdom. Accordingly, democracy is bad because it equates to the rule of desires, not the rational, and it cannot bring social harmony.

Plato's concept of democracy is an egalitarian one. *The Republic* singles out several features of democracy in the Platonic sense:

1. The rule of the working class, or "the poor," in Socrates' words
2. The rule of desires and passions
3. Equality for all on everything
4. Licensed and unchecked individual liberty
5. Diversity of forms of life and disunity of a people
6. Anarchic and motley conditions[16]

The first and third features of the Platonic democracy share common points with the kind of egalitarian democracy that China had struggled for. The others are rejected by both the egalitarian and rationalist democracies proposed in China. Feature 6 was a feature of China's so-called great democracy in the Cultural Revolution as discussed above. The experience of China's struggle for democracy indicates that democracy will be healthier if the first five features are constrained by human reason and the sixth is rejected.

Plato's concept of democracy differs significantly from Pericles's characterization of the Athenian democracy. In his address to his fellow Athenians in the period of Peloponnesian War, Pericles said:

> Our constitution is called democracy because power is in the hands not of a minority but of the whole people. When it is a question of settling private disputes, everyone is equal before the law; when it is a question of putting one person before another in positions of public responsibility, what counts is not membership of a particular class, but the actual ability which the man possesses. . . . We are free and tolerant in our private life; but in public affairs we keep to the law. . . . We give our obedience to those whom we put in positions of authority, and we obey the laws themselves, especially those which are for protection of the oppressed, and those unwritten laws which it is an acknowledged shame to break.[17]

In this statement, Pericles defines the essence and features of the Athenian democracy in terms of two properties:

1. Power in the hands of the people as a whole
2. Freedom in private life and law-abiding behavior in public life

Thus, crucial differences exist between the Periclesian democracy and the Platonic one.

In the Periclesian democracy, political power is in the hands of the whole of the people, not merely those of a handful or of the poor masses or working class as in the Platonic democracy. In the Platonic democracy, by contrast, the poor rule and exclude members of other classes, forming a kind of dictatorship of the working classes. In the Periclesian democracy, citizens are free in private life but abide by the law in public life. In the Platonic democracy, such a distinction does not exist, and thus the Platonic democracy is anarchic. In the Periclesian democracy, citizens obey those unwritten moral laws "which it is an acknowledged shame to break," but in the Platonic democracy, individuals disregard moral rules and everyone acts on their own passions and desires, enjoying shameless liberty. The Platonic democracy is thus a market where individual persons trade cooperation to fulfill their interests, desires, and passions.

But Plato's criticism of democracy and Pericles's praise of it share one common point: that a just government is a government of reason, not of desires; a just form of life is the form of life led by reason, not by desires. Therefore, what Plato de facto rejected was a specific kind of democracy: the dictatorship of the proletarian class with extreme egalitarianism, anarchism, extreme pluralism, and the rule of passion and desire. His criticism of democracy suggests something important: When it becomes the kind of polity Plato described, a democracy is unjust. First, such a democracy is unreasonable and irrational. On this point, the Chinese democracy of the Cultural Revolution period provided a good example of the madness of a dictatorship of the proletarian classes, exactly the kind of democracy that Plato criticized. Second, such a democracy is not a polity in which humanity can thrive. In such a democracy, humanity is neither a value nor a virtue. Instead, it is turned into a commodity. Third, as the Chinese experience indicates, the kind of democracy that Plato rejected cannot endure.

To appreciate the Platonic criticism, we are better off in noting Cass R. Sunstein's division of democracy today into three kinds:

1. Democracy as a political system for protecting individual persons' basic rights. In this form, "democracy is seen principally as a way of securing those rights."[18]
2. Democracy as a mechanism for aggregating private preferences. This type of democracy ensures that "the number and intensity of preferences are reflected in governmental outcomes. . . . Democracy is thus a kind of market, one that is specially suited to the pervasive problem of aggregating preferences."[19]
3. Democracy as a deliberative republic that combines "a measure of popular sovereignty and commitment to justifications for the distribution of benefits and burdens."[20]

The first type of democracy has some merits, but is significantly flawed. It is based on the concept of individual rights. This democracy has elements of justice by recognizing and honoring individual persons' rights, and the principle of human rights is one of the three principles of normative justice on which human affairs are set right. However, the democracy of individual rights does not emphasize the harmony of the republic as a whole. Without a minimal level of social harmony, a democracy cannot be healthy or stable, let alone effective. Plato would be right in rejecting this form of democracy.

The second form of democracy is seriously flawed, and again Plato would be right in rejecting it. He indeed called democracy a bad form of government when he identified it exclusively with this form. Aristotle, who did not see democracy to be as lawless as Plato did, nevertheless also rejected democracy as a bad form of government. In Aristotle's eye, it was a kind of market. Democracy should not be akin to a market where individuals bargain for the best of their own interests.

It is the third type of democracy that is most desirable, and Plato and Aristotle could have accepted this form of democracy. We should aspire for this form of democracy.

Returning to Plato, we see that he rejected democracy because he identified it with a specific form of democracy—the dictatorship of the proletarian class, plus democracy as a market. As the human experience in the twentieth century indicates, a proletarian dictatorship is totalitarian, undemocratic, and essentially unjust. The proletarian class cannot be the most progressive and cannot represent the most advanced productive force of our epoch. It cannot be the most unselfish, revolutionary force. Plato is not wrong to reject the kind of democracy that combines the dictatorship of the proletarian class and a market. From the point of the view of normative justice, such a form of democracy sets human affairs wrong and warps humanity. It increases the chance of violating human rights, selling out common human goods, and commercializing human relationships.

In *The Republic*, Plato also put forth three illuminating ideas:

1. Guardianship is a science, and those who would be guardians should be properly trained to be so.
2. Political power must not be arbitrary; that is, it should neither be an expression of a tyrannical individual's arbitrary will, nor an expression of the arbitrary will of the majority of the mass.
3. The idea of Good, not desire or passion, should be the governing principle of life.

Plato is right on all three points. Governing is an art, if not a science; it requires not only practical skills and knowledge but also political wisdom, philosophical insights, and a capacity for strategic thinking. Political power should not be arbitrary. Democracy is not naturally free of political arbitrariness. The will of the majority can be arbitrary. The rule of the majority can from time to time violate the minority's rights or individuals' rights. The "great democracy" of the Chinese Cultural Revolution is a good example. The Platonic rejection of that type of democracy should remind us of the Confucian rejection of *bao zheng, nude zheng,* and *yin zheng.*

In short, the Platonic criticism of democracy still provides us with insights. We should not discard these insights because of the shortcomings of Plato's arguments.

The Confucian Resistance

We can also learn something from traditional Confucian humanism. Confucianism is relevant here for three reasons. First, some present democracies in East and Southeast Asia can be called Confucian democracies. Second, an interesting fact of China's struggle for democracy after 1949 is that, in all times, the political philosophy that inspires the Chinese people to correct their mistakes in their struggle for democracy is traditional Confucian humanism. This is true even of the newly developed discourse on building a harmonious society with social justice. Third, the Confucian rejection of *bao zheng, nude zheng,* and *yin zheng* is still illuminating for us today in building a more viable democracy.

A Confucian ideal polity is one of humanity, righteousness, propriety, wisdom, and trust. It differs from the Platonic republic. First, the Confucian ideal polity is not a republic but a community in which concrete human relations such as familial and communal relationships are the foundation. While Plato considered the ideal structure of a just republic to be the extension of the structure of a just soul of an individual, traditional Confucians considered the ideal structure to be the extension of the just structure of a good human family. Second, in the Confucian ideal polity, the ideas of humanity, righteousness, propriety, wisdom, and trust are the five governing norms of sociopolitical life, while in Plato's ideal republic, wisdom, courage, and moderation are the governing principles. Here, the most crucial difference is that in the Confucian case, the norms of humanity and trust are emphasized, while such an emphasis is totally absent in Plato's republic. Third, in the Confucian ideal polity, culture and tradition are appropriated as the matrices of wisdom and understanding, while in Plato's ideal republic, culture and tradition constitute the prisoners' cave that imprisons us in prejudice, illusion, and falsity. The Confucian insight enables us to see the significant gaps in Western democracies today.

In present Western democracies, despite the recognition of and respect for individual political rights and entitlements, there is no emphasis on humanity as a central quality or as the end goal. First, no emphasis on the human purpose and the destiny of humanity are found in present democracies. The idea of human excellence in terms of certain human qualities is dead. The concept of human character has retired. While democracy is supposed to be a form of life in which individuals extend their lives together and common humanity also thrives, in present Western democracies, people pay for the increase of their freedom and rights with alienation from their humanity. Societies and communities pay for the rule of majority with the high prices of individual character and virtues. Human excellence is replaced by collective commonplace. The spirit of George Washington, Thomas Jefferson, and Abraham Lincoln is given away to the selfish, vulgar pretension of double-faced demagogues. Common human good is traded for individuals' material gains and practical expedience.

Second, no emphasis on the values and qualities of human relations is found in present Western democracies. The qualities of human relations decline steadily. A good democracy is built on the trust on individual persons who can exercise reason. But a democracy cannot be a shining city in a human desert where individuals are like disassociated pieces of sand and where human relations, human bonds, and neighborly human love are absent and forgotten. A good democracy has as much dependence on real human relations as it does on trust in individual reason. A good democracy, like a good marriage, requires bonds and relations, not merely a certified contract.

Third, in present Western democracies, trust as a norm and standard of government is something alien. But an untrustworthy government is also a bad government and a democracy governed by it is a improper one. In democracy, there should be a bond between the government and the people. Otherwise, the concept of democracy as a government of the people, by the people, and for the people would become empty words. When the government is untrustworthy, the bond between the government and the people is violated. A true democracy can be stabilized only on various forms of social cooperation. But there can be no true social cooperation without various forms of social trust.

In light of the above, Confucian humanism still provides needed insights into democracy. A good democracy is a polity of humanity in which human character counts, human bonds are emphasized, and human trust is an obligatory norm. A democratic government ought to be a government of human character, care, and trustworthiness. Democracy has a compelling interest in promoting human bonds, communal solidarity, common identity, and communal loyalty. A good democracy ought to be a good family, not a mad market or trading house.

The Modern Promises and Skepticism

If, for ancient thinkers, democracy has a bad taste, for modern thinkers its taste is uncertain. Since the eighteenth century, democracy has given us both hope and anxiety, creating a sense of uncertainty and skepticism in the West. Since the 1990s, the collapse of socialist governments in the former Soviet bloc has begun a new wave of democratization in the globe. But the new wave is accompanied by a vast asymmetry between the glamour of popular sovereignty on one side and chaos, conflict, and even genocide on the other. Against the background of global democratization, a tradition of distrusting democracy continues.

The Enlightenment Thinkers' Suspicion of Democracy

Leading Enlightenment thinkers of the eighteenth and nineteenth centuries distrusted democracy. John Locke, who advocated religious toleration and representative government, believed that "the great bulk of mankind wallows in 'passion and superstition.'"[21] Voltaire, a crusader against tyranny and bigotry, considered the masses to be like cattle and "doubted that the multitude should even be educated"; he "observed that attempting to instruct the masses was like building a huge fire under an empty pot."[22] Voltaire's famous disciple the Marquis de Condorcet (Marie-Jean-Antoine-Nicolas de Caritat) wondered, "What operation capable of producing any double good can be understood by the people?"[23] David Hume "thanked God (if such existed) that he did not live in a democracy."[24]

Immanuel Kant was a republican, not a democrat. "Kant regarded democracy as one illegitimate form of government because it is based not upon reason and right as found in the eternal order of things, but upon the caprice of majorities."[25] Georg W. F. Hegel was no democrat, either.

> Democracy was, for him, a form that had become obsolete in modern state; it belonged to a bygone era of small communities. In the last year of his life the greatest thinker of his age opposed the British Reform Bill, enacted in 1832 to extend the right to vote somewhat (but by no means to all) and to make representative fairer.[26]

Why did the leading Enlightenment thinkers mentioned above reject democracy? What did they see to be wrong with democracy? These modern philosophers' criticisms of democracy share a striking common point with Plato's criticism: that there is an inherent opposition between reason and democracy; that democracy was governed by the desires of the majority, not by the human reason embodied in human members of a society. William

Godwin in 1793 indignantly referred to democracy as "that intolerable insult upon all reason and justice" and insisted that truth "cannot be made more true by the number in its votaries."[27]

In the eyes of modern thinkers, democracy is a kind of polity and a form of life that represents a kind of intolerable insult to human reason and justice. According to Locke, democracy is not ruled by reason. Roland N. Stromberg quotes John Milton as arguing that "it was better that an enlightened minority compel the majority to be free 'than that a greater number, for the pleasure of their baseness, compel a less most injuriously to be their fellow slaves.'"[28] The Kantian republic is a kingdom of reason and of humanity as the end. In short, it was the belief in government by reason and justice that led those great Enlightenment thinkers to reject modern democracy, as Plato had done centuries earlier.

In the views of the Enlightenment thinkers mentioned above, democracy is wrong because it does not operate by reason; democracy could not be right or set things right because it itself could not be set right to operate by reason. The period of time in which the leading Enlightenment thinkers lived is called the Age of Reason. They believed that human reason was embodied in individuals' reason. What they did not believe was that the mass of a society, who were poorly educated or were not even educable, were capable of following reason.

Enlightenment thinkers believed in human rights. However, for them, democracy is not the proper form of government or form of life for protecting human rights. They believed in social justice, but did not think that democracy was a just form of government or of life. They believed in truth and reason, and government by reason, but saw an inherent opposition between democracy and the government of reason. Essential to these thinkers is still the concept that a good government is also a wise government, and that democracy does not create a wise government.

The Enlightenment thinkers' skepticism about democracy again returns us to one simple but often forgotten fact: Democracy itself is not an intrinsic value; it is only an instrumental value—that is, it will be valuable if and only if it is an instrument to realize social justice in government and public life. Democracy itself, as a form of government and a form of life, must first be set right before it can be a vehicle to establish justice in a society. With this in mind, democracy as it was conceived in the seventeenth through twentieth centuries was significantly flawed. Democracy so conceived was not adequate to set things right in terms of human rights, human goods, and human bonds. Democracy has a great potential to be a just form of government, but it is yet to be a form of government of true justice and wisdom.

Political Liberalism

With regard to democracy, the present political liberalism leaves much to be desired. According to political liberalism, democracy is the sociopolitical system to protect the basic rights and liberties of individual citizens inscribed in the idea of justice as fairness. In political liberalism, the project of democracy is greatly improved and the ideas of justice and reason are explicitly emphasized as being at the core of democracy. Indeed, in political liberalism, justice is the foundation for social cooperation and society-building and is thus the foundation of democracy.

At a first blush, one crucial criticism of democracy by the Enlightenment thinkers is answered by political liberalism. However, the politically liberal concept of justice, as exemplified in Rawls's political concept of justice, is seriously inadequate. According to Rawls, the idea of justice as fairness includes two basic principles:

1. Each citizen has a set of basic rights and liberties compatible with the same rights and liberties of others in a democratic regime.
2. Social and economic inequalities can be justified if they are either reasonably expected to bring advantages and benefits to every citizen in a democratic regime or attached to positions and offices open to all.[29]

The two principles "serve as guidelines for how basic institutions are to realize the values of liberties and equalities."[30] Here, justice is identified exclusively with distributive justice, but this concept of justice is inadequate to set democracy right.

In a political liberalist democracy, public reason is the ruling power. According to Rawls, "In a democratic society, public reason is the reason of equal citizens who, as a collective body, exercise final political and coercive power over one another in enacting laws and in amending their constitution."[31] He also points out:

> [In democracy] knowing that they affirm a diversity of reasonable religious and philosophical doctrines, [citizens] should be ready to explain the basis of their actions to one another in terms each could reasonably expect that others endorse as consistent with their freedom and equality. Trying to meet this condition is one of the tasks that this ideal of democratic politics asks of us. Understanding how to conduct oneself as a democratic citizen includes understanding an ideal of public reason.[32]

So far, so good. However, we start to enter into capricious high seas when we move one step further. In political liberalism, public reason differs from both nonpublic reason—for example, the reason of a particular institution such as a church or a university or the reason of particular individuals in a society—and what Kant calls "practical reason" or moral reason. What is missed in the concept of public reason is philosophical wisdom, knowledge, and understanding of humanity.

Furthermore, democracy in political liberalism in essence is still merely an individual-centered democracy. Democracy in political liberalism still emphasizes only individuals—individuals' rights, the inviolatabilty of an individual person as a person, individual persons' basic liberties, and so on—not the community. Concepts such as a people, a nation, and a community are consciously marginalized. Communal values and bonds, let alone universal bonds and universal human goods, disappear from the democratic consciousness in political liberalism. As a result, democracy becomes a giant building on a surface of loose sand, not on solid ground. Though Rawls's political liberalism draws heavily from the American experiences, there is something valuable of the American experiences of democracy—the concept of one nation, one people, under God—that is unjustifiably abandoned. Democracy without a unified democratic community has a serious inadequacy!

Furthermore, other missing pieces of democracy in political liberalism include a government of public trust and a form of social life that emphasizes trust; a government and form of life in which human character, qualities of human relations, and human excellence—both what Aristotle would call intellectual excellence and moral excellence—count; and a government and form of life that is wise.

Habermas's Proposal

Jürgen Habermas's concept of procedural democracy contributes some original insights to the subject, but is also akin to the Hindu god Shiva, who does both good and evil. Habermas provides a sharp analysis and criticism of both liberal and republican democracies, offering procedural democracy as the alternative.

Habermas's procedural model of democracy has three distinctive features. First, a procedural model of democracy is grounded in what he dubs "constitutional patriotism." In such a democracy, the *demos* of citizens is not based on the *ethnos* of a nation; that is, the *demos* is not ethnic and is independent of a nationalist consciousness. Second, the procedural model of democracy emphasizes normative justification of the democratic process. In a procedural model of democracy, the basic liberal principles and values that ground the democracy have been written into a constitution. Therefore, democracy does not focus on an ethical discourse that creates a communal self-understanding and consciousness. Instead, it focuses on procedural implementation of a democratic process. Third, a procedural model of democracy emphasizes democratic inclusion and defends a concept of universal human rights that is sensitive to cultural differences. In a procedural democracy, there is a public sphere in which different views converse, and there are also legal and political institutions that facilitate the cultivation of plural cultural and religious identities in a community.

As far as the two issues that hang on the neck of democracy—reason and justice—are concerned, Habermas offers some solutions. With regard to the rule of reason, the procedural model of democracy emphasizes and is grounded in communicative rationality; thus, procedural democracy involves the rule of reason. With regard to the issue of justice, procedural democracy emphasizes rights and inclusion, which implies social toleration. But something crucial is also missing here: the concept of reason as an ethical reason, and the humanity of the members of a democratic community as the end, not the means, in a democracy.

Habermas resists both liberal democracy and republican democracy. According to him, in the liberal model of democracy, "the democratic process takes place exclusively in the form of compromises between competing interests."[33] Liberal democracy, according to Habermas, is pretty much a combination of what Sunstein calls democracy as a political system protecting individuals' basic rights and democracy as a contractual market, that is, a contractual mechanism for aggregating private preferences, a mechanism that ensures that the number and intensity of preferences are reflected in governmental outcomes and a process that is specially suited to the pervasive problem of aggregating preferences, as described above. The liberal concept of democracy fails to see that democracy has normativity and is a form of life in which there is normative deliberation.

In a republican democracy, the democratic process is a process of will-formation that "is supposed to take the form of an ethical discourse of self-understanding; here deliberation can rely for its content on a culturally established background consensus of the citizens."[34] Thus, republican democracy is essentially a process of ethnic culture-building or ethnic nation-building; it is a process of building a collective *ethnos*, a collective self-identity. According to Habermas, the republican concept of democracy fails to see the contractual feature of democracy and cannot be inclusive. For example, it cannot be tolerant of the Other—the Other must either become the same as us or get out.

According to Habermas, the procedural model of democracy is the remedy. A procedural democracy is contractual, for it is structured by the constitution of a community, say, a nation. It is thus deliberative and has an ethical life. But this ethical life is not geared to self-understanding or to an understanding of an ethnic self, but to a communal intersubjectivity that is brought out by a shared constitutional patriotism. Therefore, a procedural democracy weaves together the contractual feature, the feature of self-understanding—the replacement of an ethnic self-understanding with constitutional patriotism—and justice.

The theory of the procedural model of democracy is called the discourse theory of democracy. "Discourse theory invests the democratic process with normative connotations stronger than those of the liberal model but weaker than those of the republican model."[35]

Habermas suggests that a procedural democracy is a form of government that embodies justice and is a form of life in which justice can be realized. According to him, in procedural democracy, "the procedures and communicative presuppositions of democratic opinion- and will-formation function as the most important sluices for the discursive rationalization of decisions of a government and an administration bound by law and statute."[36] Here, the communicative presuppositions refer to the presuppositions of the validity claims of comprehensibility, truthfulness, propositional truth, and normative rightness in the communicative dimension of democratic life. In other words, the communicative presuppositions are the norms—the four communicative norms—in which a rational communicative action must ground itself. These communicative presuppositions are also the source for the justice of democracy as a form of life.

Therefore, in Habermas's view, a procedural democracy has several features that make it just: its emphasis on the rule of law (especially, the primacy of the constitution of a society), political rationality, and normativity grounded in communicative rationality, truth, and individual rights. So far, so good. But Habermas has not solved the crucial problem of liberal democracy: being too individual-centered and an absence of the concepts of one nation and one people. Instead, he actually makes the problem worse by the idea of postnational democracy. A postnational democracy is a democracy grounded merely in citizens' loyalty to a publicly established constitution, not in their sense of being a people or a nation.

Habermas's intention is noble. The concept of postnational democracy is meant to address the problem of social inclusion, which is crucial to democracy today amid the diversity in a democratic society. However, without the concept of being a people or a nation, a true and stable democracy is impossible. The first sign of the trouble with a democracy without such a concept is the social alienation of the members of a society: people are so estranged and alienated from one another that a sense of a bond among them is gone. A sense of constitutional patriotism can ease a temporary pain of a postnational democracy, but it cannot heal the illness. Marginalizing the crucial role of ethical self-reflection in a democracy, Habermas ignores the need of a democracy to have substance, character, temperament, and human excellence. In procedural democracy, procedure is everything; humanity is pushed to the background and sidelined.

In short, Habermas's proposal will only turn the disassociated individual persons of a liberal democracy into anonymous players of a political game in a procedural democracy, not into democratic citizens of a republic. While procedural democracy raises the hope of social justice through social inclusion and toleration, it damages such a hope, and the substance of the hope, by a concept of social inclusion at the cost of losing the selves. In this form of democracy, a self is a lost abstract. What we need here is a new concept of democracy that is individual and community intersubjective, not individual-centered subjective. We also need to develop a concept of democracy with human character, excellence, and standards, recovering a sense of humanity as the end for a democracy. But before we come to this task, we should deal with another paradox first.

The Paradox of the Egalitarianism–Rationalism Dichotomy

Many philosophers today identify true democracy with an egalitarian polity. This is a mistake. There is no question that a just democracy values the idea of equality, but it also has equal respect for rights and entitlements of all members of a human community or society. Everyone counts, and no one is discounted or marginalized—at least no one is supposed to be discounted and marginalized. However, democracy should not be conflated with egalitarianism. Democracy should not be overlaid with the idea of equality. As Stromberg indicates, "An egalitarian society could be politically most undemocratic, in the sense of being ruled by a despot or an oligarchy."[37]

The Chinese experience offers an example: Mainland China between 1949 and 1978 was egalitarian, but not democratic. Conversely, a relatively democratic society may be less egalitarian than a totalitarian one. Mainland China is more egalitarian, but less democratic; Taiwan is less egalitarian, but more democratic. North Korea is egalitarian, but totalitarian; South Korea is relatively more democratic, but not egalitarian. The United States is relatively democratic, but not egalitarian; Cuba is more egalitarian, but totalitarian.

Also, as Stromberg notes, "The nineteenth century, it has been said, was about equality. Equality of rights spelled liberalism; equality of votes, democracy; equality of good, socialism."[38] In short, historically, democracy takes equality most seriously, but is not identical to equality. Also, one of the two Rawls principles of justice mentioned above is: "Social and economic inequalities are to be arranged so that they are both (a) reasonably expected to be everyone's advantage, and (b) attached to position and offices open to all."[39] In other words, in accordance with Rawls, justice does not exclude inequality.

This brings us to the egalitarianism–rationalism dichotomy, one of the most misleading assumptions in the discourse on democracy today. In this assumption, egalitarianism and rationalism are situated as two necessarily antagonistic alternatives, and a democracy is, and ought to be, one or the other. The assumption is erroneous. Egalitarianism and rationalism need not exclude one another. On the contrary, history reveals that rationalism and egalitarianism are, and ought to be, akin to the yin-yang forces in a good democracy, contrasting, complementing, and enhancing one another. A good democracy is not an ultraegalitarian or ultrarationalistic one. Stromberg notes:

> As the eighteenth-century British statesman Robert Walpole explained, "the monarchical and the aristocratic and the democratic forms of government are mixed and interwoven so as to give us all advantages of each without subjecting us to the dangers of either." An unadulterated democracy was perhaps the most dangerous form of all.[40]

Indeed, as the Chinese experience indicates, ultraegalitarian democracy is self-destructive. So is an ultrarationalistic one.

A just democracy should be reasonable and rational. It emphasizes individual rights and freedom but is governed by public reason and laws. In addition, a true and just democracy values individual rights and freedom but is governed by the ideal of political rationality and rationalization of politics. A just democratic government is accountable to the citizens it represents and governs. It makes decisions but must be ready to explain and justify its decisions to the people.

A just democratic form of life must also be reasonable and rational. In a just democratic sociopolitical life, citizens make choices and are ready to explain and justify their choices to their fellow citizens. Equally crucial, a just form of democratic life is, and ought to be, governed by a set of rational norms such as rights, freedoms, responsibility, fairness, care, propriety, wisdom, and public good.

A just democracy should have the support of human feelings. No democracies are true and can endure if the idea of the rule of reason is marginalized or the idea of rationality is marginalized.

Those democracies that have unprecedented vitality today are combinations of egalitarianism and rationalism, not completely one or the other. Correspondingly, the ultraegalitarian and ultrarationalistic democracies in the world today are the most unstable ones. When a democracy one-sidedly moves toward extreme egalitarianism, it betrays the idea of the rule of reason and, eventually, the rule of the ideas of justice, good, and truth. It will be short-lived. The Paris Commune and the ultrademocracy of the Chinese Cultural Revolution are good examples. When a form of democracy unilaterally pursues rationalism, it becomes totalitarian.

The assumption of a dichotomy between egalitarianism and rationalism is built on the either/or mode of thinking. According to this thinking, in the final analysis, the only alternative available for democracy is either egalitarianism or rationalism. But this is not a law of nature nor a precept of natural law. In addition, the either/or mode of thinking is applicable only when two alternatives necessarily exclude each other. This is not the case of the relationship between egalitarianism and rationalism in public life—at least, this is a case that remains to be made. In short, the assumption of the dichotomy between egalitarianism and rationalism is unjustified and, more than misleading, is indeed paradoxical.

Democracy, Social Toleration, and Integration

Thomas Scanlon says that a tolerant society is one that is "democratic in its informal politics."[41] More than that, a truly democratic society is tolerant in both its formal and informal politics. Habermas's procedural democracy has one virtue of a just democracy: inclusiveness. A truly democratic society is inclusive as much as deliberative in both its formal and informal politics.

Most democracies today exist in a diverse world. Diversity makes democracy a necessity. Democracy in turn maintains diversity, turning it into strength. A democratic form of government and a democratic form of life are the necessary choices in a diverse world. They are the necessary vehicles to realize justice. Simultaneously, only a democratic form of government and of life can be truly inclusive and therefore can allow real, endurable diversity. Only democracy makes true social toleration possible, and social toleration, which sustains diversity, is a necessary condition for a true and enduring democracy.

A true democracy should be a democracy of citizens. These citizens may not have the same ethnic origins, ancestries, ideologies, or cultural backgrounds, but they come together from different avenues to form a common community. For different, even incompatible, citizens to come together, such citizens must tolerate each other and be both the authors and receivers of tolerant laws and other social institutions. On this point, two extremes must be avoided. One extreme is attempting to eliminate all differences in order to have an identical entity. The other is marginalizing those differences. A true democracy is marked by the practice of including all, instead of privileging some, even the majority.

Meanwhile, even in a most liberal, tolerant democracy, there should not only be common norms, standards, and values of a community but also a sense of common or communal identity. Even the most liberal, tolerant democracy must be an integrated one. It cannot be anarchy. Therefore, even in such a democracy, the concepts of human goods and common bonds are indispensable. For this reason, democracy and constitutionalism, or the belief of the rule of law, are internally connected. True, constitutionalism has "even more ancient roots."[42] However, a true and stable democracy today relies on principles of constitutionalism, for example, the idea of positive laws as the necessary means for social integration and cooperation.

In addition, democracy is also internally associated with the ethical self-understanding of a people. Is it part and parcel of the duty of democracy to make a people? My answer is yes. The belief that a true democracy can exist without a people—that is, different groups of people joined together as a people with a shared identity and *ethnos*—in the proper sense has no truth. Democracy should allow diversity, no doubt about that. However, it should also emphasize identity—that is, the sameness, oneness, and unity. A true democracy is not a market, a coffee shop, or a department store. It is a family. And a democratic family should not be one in name only, but should also in substance. In short, a true democracy makes a true family, and a true family has one people. Therefore, "one people and one nation" is not merely a political slogan for a democracy, but its duty, burden, ideal, and mission.

The concept of substantial unity, which connotes substantial sameness and oneness, is deliberately used here to contrast the kind of merely procedural solidarity Habermas's constitutional patriotism entertains. The concept of substantial unity is also evoked here to emphasize the centrality of a unified national *ethnos* in democracy. Democracy encourages diversity, but diverse elements can form an integrated whole, just as a man and a woman can get married and form an integrated family and, eventually, with their children, an enlarged but integrated family. Such a family can have democracy, but democracy should not disintegrate the family. For this reason, the procedural model of democracy proposed by Habermas is self-handicapped.

Inclusion and integration are not antitheses of one another. On the contrary, true inclusion requires integration. Just as different individuals from different walks of life can join together to form a common community, different peoples of different religious, ethnic, and cultural origins can join together to form one people and one nation. Equally crucial, nothing is un-justified for a people and a nation to ask those who want to join as members of this group. To be true members of a community, these newcomers should actively integrate themselves into the communal life, which in turn requires adoption of some justified changes. For example, if one wants to be a true citizen of the United States and lives a happy life in America, one should learn to speak English, whether one's original mother tongue is Russian, French, Chinese, German, Czech, or Korean. One should abide by the laws in America, including the Constitution. In short, true inclusion demands true integration.

Democracy and Global Justice

Discussion of the issue of global democracy is in order. Global democratization is a part of globalization today. However, a just process of globalization is not simply a process of compressing a diverse world into an undifferentiated one and reducing different peoples to a clones of the strongest group. Just globalization is not colonization. Instead, just globalization brings unity among diversity, integrating diverse peoples and civilizations as one, in which both diversity and unity exist. For this reason, democracy and democratization are crucial to just globalization and to international politics.

Global democracy is a call for global normative justice as setting human affairs right in terms of human rights, human goods, and human bonds around the world. It is instrumental to global justice both that democracies spread throughout the globe and that basic international institutions are democratized. When democracies spread, the opportunities for peoples to set their affairs right in terms of normative justice are increased. With democratization of basic international institutions, the opportunities for the global community of humankind to improve human affairs in international fields collectively are increased. With democratic participation from more and more nations and peoples in global affairs, the chances of setting global human affairs right and correcting the human wrongs and evils are greatly increased.

Global expansion of democracies and the democratization of international institutions such as the United Nations provide good vehicles to realize global justice, especially global normative justice. Democratic governments, forms of life, and institutions provide the human and institutional resources to promote global normative justice. They involve institutional embodiment of the ideas of human rights and dignity, self-consciousness, self-determination, and self-realization. They create the conditions and atmosphere for collectively creating and realizing common human goods and cultivating common human bonds globally.

World democracy and democratization are also the concerns of global justice, especially global normative justice. Joshua Cohen and Charles Sabel note:

> An idea of inclusion, both procedural and substantantive, is central to the domain of global justice. Conceptions of global justice offer accounts of human rights, standards of fair governance and norms of fair distribution. . . . Competing conceptions can be understood, then, as advancing alternative accounts of what inclusion demands: of the kind of respect and concern that is owed by the variety of agencies, organizations and institutions (including states) that operate on the terrain of global politics.[43]

Cohen and Sabel do not explicitly spell out that global justice demands global democracy. However, the concept of democratic inclusion, both substantive and procedural, in international politics and affairs is a call for global justice today.

In terms of substance, global justice calls for democratic inclusion of nations and peoples in global affairs in order to make concrete the ideas of human rights, humanity as the end, and human bonds. It calls for democratic participation of nations and peoples to prevent and eliminate human rights violations, crimes against humanity, and various social evils. In terms of procedure, global justice calls for democratic participation of nations and peoples and democratization of international institutions; it calls for fair procedures, norms, and standards of international politics and regulation of international affairs.

Global democracy involves the democratic participation of nation-states and peoples in establishing international laws and orders as well as in determining issues of global significance in international affairs, instead of letting a few stronger powers and rich nation-states determine the fate of the whole of humankind. Global democracy differs from domestic democracy in some crucial aspects. We can appreciate this simply through recalling that not long ago, during the so-called Cold War period, the fate of the world was more or less determined by two superpowers, the United States and the Soviet Union. Which is the more just world, the one today or the one in the Cold War? The answer should be self-evident.

Today, more and more nations and peoples participate in global affairs of a wide range: social, economical, political, cultural, environmental, security, religious, and so on. This honors not only the idea of global distributive justice but also the ideas of global normative justice and of global corrective justice. With regard to global distributive justice, global democratization is the movement toward more fairness in the distribution of powers, responsibility, burdens, opportunities, resources, and benefits. With regard to global normative justice, internationalization of democracy is the movement toward respect for rights, emphasis on humanity as the end, and renovation of common human bonds. With regard to global corrective justice, it is the movement toward correction of existing wrongs.

Furthermore, global justice implicates norms of global democracy and global democratization. They include:

1. Mutual respect and recognition among nations and peoples
2. Reasonable and fair arrangements for nations and peoples to have their voices and votes in international organizations and in the establishment of international institutions such as international laws and treaties
3. Active inclusion of nations and peoples in international affairs, from peacekeeping missions and international interventions to stop human rights violations or crimes against humanity in a region to international assistance in resolving historical and current international conflicts
4. Active inclusion and participation of nations and peoples in international socioeconomic, political, educational, health, and environmental cooperation
5. Active inclusion and participation of nations and peoples in promoting human rights–centered consciousness and democratic mentality
6. Active inclusion and participation of nations and peoples in discourses on global justice
7. Active inclusion and participation of nations and peoples in articulating a blueprint for humankind in the globe

Cohen and Sabel observe:

The idea of inclusion, in both its procedural and substantive aspects, calls attention to a process: the reflective exploration, by a variety of actors in the setting of global politics, of the character of the moral norms, both procedural and substantive, that are suited to the forms of association that already connect them.[44]

Global democracy advances global inclusion of nations and peoples. True global inclusion implies global integration. This amounts to saying that global democracy establishes a global family that has a family ethics and ethos. The global family needs not be akin to a superstate, but it must be a family in a profoundly meaningful sense.

This invites us to revisit the relationship among democracy, peoples, and humanity. Traditionally, democracy is of people, not of humanity. Carl Smith's view sheds some light onto the history of democracy. He claimed: "The central concept of democracy is the people, not humanity. If democracy is indeed a political form, it can only be a democracy of the people, not of humanity."[45] Democracy is first about how a people governs itself. However, as I understand it, democracy is also meant to integrate different peoples into a people. A democratic community is a diverse but integrated community. Accordingly, global democracy is meant to bring different peoples together as a people, a people of humanity. By this interpretation, democracy is also of humanity. Global democracy is to build a family of humanity. We can call it a Kantian kingdom of the ends, a cosmopolitan republic. It is a family of humanity.

Therefore, we are currently in a historical period in which democracy is both of the people and of humanity. It is of the people in a twofold sense: it is a form of life and a form of government that a people chooses for itself and in which a people is the democratic sovereign subject; simultaneously, it is the important form of international interactions between nation-states and peoples today. Meanwhile, democracy is also of humanity today. Justice as loyalty to human rights, human goods, and human bonds is what democracy should realize in a domestic community and what global democracy should realize in the world today. The evolution of an international community facilitated by international laws and organizations makes all human beings into a united people. Global democracy is for and of all human beings. It is about how humanity as a species should govern itself.

While a basic component of global democracy involves the continuous democratization of nation-states in the globe, international institutions—international organizations, laws, organized practices, and so on—should be more democratized. They should be reinvented not to serve only a few rich, developed nations and people, but to serve all nations and peoples. Equally crucial, they should be reinvented to create a people in the world community, to realize the Kantian kingdom of the ends and create the Kantian cosmopolitan republic of humanity. And democracy, as the forging of a people and a nation, and democracy, as the creation of global humanity, are compatible with one another, though each has its own focus and emphasis.

Democratization of Earth's nations and peoples continues to be the basis of global democracy. It promotes further democratization of international laws, institutions, and affairs. In turn, continuous democratization of international laws, institutions, and affairs will stimulate the democratization of nations and peoples throughout the world. Global democratization is still a long and uneven process; its burden is heavy. But global democracy can be instrumental to global justice: distributive, corrective, and normative.

The concept of global democracy differs from Habermas's postnational democracy. But his concept involves insight that is illuminating to global democracy and democratization. According to the concept of postnational democracy, the foundation for a people today is no longer shared common ancestry, language, history, and experience or ethnic commonality, but is instead the shared liberal and democratic values defined by a collectively established constitution of a state or society. The idea of postnational democracy may not be applicable to many domestic democracies, such as those in Asian nations, but it indicates the possibility and plausibility of international democracy and democratization.

Just as different groups of peoples in a community can become one people on the basis of shared democratic values and aspiration, different peoples can come together to form a single people under a unified concept of humanity in the world. In other words, the concept of postnational democracy raises the hope of global democracy and democratization, which raises the value of the stock of the idea of global humanity. Good global democracy does not dig trenches to divide nations and peoples. To have good democracies in the world and a good global democracy is an ontological and moral imperative, as it is a political and practical task.

Toward a Just and Wise Democracy

It is time to make the crucial point now. Justice calls for democracy as it calls for social toleration and inclusion. But justice does not call all democracies; it calls for only good and wise democracies. This returns us to the question: What is a good and wise democracy? This is as historical and practical a question as it is a theoretical one. Different peoples have their own answers, tempered by their own particular cultural, historical, and regional contexts. But all good democracies should share some common features that make them good and just in the same sense.

In light of the preceding discussions, I believe that, as a working map, a good democracy should have the following general features. It should be:

1. Grounded in the idea of justice—distributive, corrective, and normative
2. Grounded in the idea of the rule of reason

3. A reasonable combination of popular sovereignty and deliberate institutions, with the existence of reasonable, public spheres
4. Capable of creating a people, a community, and a shared form of life, treating humanity as the end and promoting human bonds, both communal and universal, with the idea that humanity stands straight as an ideal and a standard
5. A vigilant republic in which the advancement of individuality goes hand in hand with the advancement of citizenship, that is, where an ideal extension of individual lives is married with an ideal extension of common, public good
6. A vigilant form of life in which an emphasis on liberty is joined by an emphasis on public responsibility and obligation, freedom with the rule of fair law, and diversity with solidarity
7. A vigilant form of life in which rights, liberty, equality, truth, good, rationality, righteousness, and duty are core vocabularies
8. A place where public trust is a norm and standard in social, political, and communal life
9. An inclusive polity and form of life in which social toleration and integration each works better with the company of the other
10. A reflective polity and form of life in which propriety, trust, and wisdom are among the core norms of government and public conduct and policies

The core of the model here is the idea of a democracy that balances what are traditionally postulated as two poles of democracy—for example, rationalism and egalitarianism, individuals and society, individuality and citizenship, equality and difference, freedom and responsibility, individual rights and public good, creativity and rationality, liberty and the rule of law, context and normativity. A good democracy recognizes the law of *wu ji bi fan* (物极必反 extremity produces self-destruction).

A good democracy enables humanity as a quality and humankind as a species to thrive. A just democracy emphasizes humanity as the end, as well as fundamental human relationships such as familial and communal bonds, as essential. Thus, a good democracy is a humanist democracy. In addition, a just democracy is tolerant and inclusive, recognizes the rule of reason, and emphasizes public reason as much as it recognizes public will. It is thus a wise democracy.

A good democracy also emphasizes the importance of the development of human character in communal life. It values trust and wisdom as the necessary aims for a healthy communal life. While it conceives communal cooperation to be crucial to the members of a democratic society to extend their lives together, it also recognizes that true, productive, and sustainable communal cooperation requires public trust and wisdom as the necessary atmosphere.

The above roadmap rejects two concepts of democracy: democracy as a market and democracy as a factory. Democracy is a form of life in which sovereign individuals extend their lives together. However, it is not, and ought not to be, a market where the only important activities are individuals exchanging their interests and the only relationships among the members of a democratic process are those of business partners. Democratic processes involve contractual activities, but these activities in a true democratic process not only should be an exchange of interests among individual persons but also should include activities in which political ideas, moral and political norms of sociopolitical practices, and communal standards of human rights, goods, and bonds are collectively established and developed.

Meanwhile, a good democracy is not a factory that molds different people into the same kind of individuals, repetitive and replaceable, after an established model. A just democracy emphasizes the rule of the law. However, *wu ji bi fan*. When the emphasis on laws and procedures in a democracy turns to promoting bureaucracy and mere proceduralism, a democracy will turn itself into a bureaucratic factory and, therefore, begin its self-destruction.

In conclusion, while democracy becomes more and more part of a universal vocabulary, our road to a true, wise democracy is still long and uneven. Democratization in the globe is still a form of tango that we must learn to dance well. It is still a great novel to be written, a great poem to be composed, and a great painting to be painted. It is a beautiful melody in which ideals are expressed and in which truth and beauty are experienced, but has yet to be composed.

Notes

1. In Roland N. Stromberg, *Democracy: A Short Analytical History* (Armonk, NY: M. E. Sharpe, 1996), 4.

2. Andrew J. Nathan, *Chinese Democracy* (New York: Afred A. Knopf, 1985), 46.

3. Mao Zedong, *The Selected Works of Mao Zedong* (Beijing: People's Publishing House, 1964), 353.

4. Ibid., 1364.

5. Nathan, *Chinese Democracy*, 10.

6. Craig Calhoun, "The Ideology of Intellectuals and the Chinese Student Protest Movement of 1989," *Praxis International* 10, nos. 1/2 (April/July 1990), 140.

7. Ibid., 137.

8. Ibid., 141.

9. Ibid.

10. *People's Daily*, overseas edition, 13 September 1997.

11. Richard Baum, "The Fifteenth National Congress: Jiang Takes Command?" *China Quarterly*, no. 153 (March 1998), 28.

12. *World Daily*, 11 March 1994.

13. Quoted at http://www.sina.com.cn.

14. Ron Bontekoe and Marietta Stepaniants, eds., *Justice and Democracy: Cross-Cultural Perspectives*, (Honolulu: University of Hawaii Press, 1997), 1.

15. Peter Singer, "How Can We Prevent Crimes against Humanity?" in *Human Rights, Human Wrongs* (New York: Oxford University Press, 2003), 122.

16. Plato, *The Republic*, 557a3–c6.

17. Pericles, "The Funeral Oration," in Thucydides, *History of the Peloponnesian War* (New York: Penguin Books, 1972), 145.

18. Cass R. Sunstein, "Deliberation, Democracy, and Disagreement," in Bontekoe and Stepaniants, *Justice and Democracy*, 93.

19. Ibid.

20. Ibid.

21. Stromberg, *Democracy*, 19.

22. Ibid.

23. Ibid.

24. Ibid.

25. Ibid., 20–21.

26. Ibid., 30.

27. Ibid., 20.

28. Ibid., 21.

29. John Rawls, *A Theory of Justice* (Cambridge, MA: Harvard University Press, 1971), 60; John Rawls, *Political Liberalism* (New York: Columbia University, 1993), 5–6.

30. Rawls, *Political Liberalism*, 5.

31. Ibid., 214.

32. Ibid., 218.

33. Jürgen Habermas, *Inclusion of the Other* (Cambridge, MA: MIT Press, 1998), 246.

34. Ibid.

35. Ibid., 248.

36. Ibid., 250.

37. Stromberg, *Democracy*, 7.

38. Ibid.

39. Rawls, *Theory of Justice*, 60.

40. Stromberg, *Democracy*, 17.

41. Thomas Scanlon, *The Difficulty of Tolerance* (Cambridge: Cambridge University Press, 2003), 190.

42. Stromberg, *Democracy*, 5.

43. Joshua Cohen and Charles Sabel, "Extra Rempublicam Nulla Justitia?" in *Philosophy and Public Affairs* 34, no. 2 (2006): 149.

44. Ibid., 174.

45. Carl Smith, *Verfassungslehre* (Berlin: de Gruyter, 1928), 234.

CHAPTER 6

~

Justice: The Crowning
Glory of Virtues

In the history of humankind, no ideas have inspired more hope and faith, commanded more commitment and devotion, motivated more reflection and discourse, or created more sentiment and enthusiasm than the concept of justice does. "You shall not pervert justice. . . . Justice, and only justice, you shall follow," reads Deuteronomy 16:19–20. "Xing yi yu da dao" (行义以达道 practice righteousness to arrive at the *dao*), said Confucius. Justice is the common bond of humankind, the principle of hope, the ideal of civility, the standard of excellence, and the norm of being.

This book began with an examination of the concept of justice as setting things right and erecting righteousness. It then put forth its signature concept: the concept of normative justice as setting human affairs right in terms of human rights, humanity as the end, human goods, and human bonds. It demonstrated that normative justice is a distinctive family of justice, having a concern, focus, content, standard, and scope that differ from those of distributive justice and corrective justice. Normative justice implicates norms of obligation that differ from fairness in distribution and correction, but are no less compulsory and obligatory; they also differ from the requirements of humanitarian morality. Conversely, our loyalty to our humanity identity is a crucial source of our motivation to be just.

The concept of normative justice serves the *novus ordo seclorum*. It engenders a family of duty and obligation of humankind to humankind. It addresses those urgent concerns of justice in our time, including those of global justice in globalization, global cooperation, modernity, regional and global security, regional and global peace, human liberties, social responsibility, cultural toleration, democracy, democratization, and cosmopolitan order. Normative justice refuels the idea of human justice. It challenges us to rethink of the nature, duty, and function of basic social institutions in terms of humanity. It impels us to broaden our horizon of global justice and to develop needed global institutions for global humanity.

Reason, More Reason, and Always Reason

This book has defended the idea of justice as the rule of reason. Its inquiry into justice was from the outset informed by a conviction that the internal connection of justice and human reason exists amid our age of postmodernism. Not only has the conviction been reinforced by the inquiry hitherto but it also has become evident that the idea of justice and the idea of the rule of reason entail each other. Justice makes human institutions and activities most reasonable. Reason is the source of justice's truth, good, beauty, and sublimity. The principle of justice is the most reasonable principle for social cooperation among the human members of a society. Justice exalts reason and wisdom over terror, passion, desire, and practical expedience.

Admittedly, the present discourses on justice are infused with vocabularies such as incredulity to grand narrative, freedom, irony, diversity, others, and equality. In such a postmodern climate, the concept of reason "often evokes the images of domination, oppression, patriarchy, sterility, violence, totality and totalitarianism and even terror," whereas traditionally "the call to 'Reason' elicited association with autonomy, freedom, justice, equality, happiness and peace."[1] The association of human reason with injustice is absurd. It surely strikes us as self-evident that unreasonable social practices and institutions are wrong; no righteous ways of humankind are unreasonable. It follows that human justice cannot be unreasonable. Conversely, a human community in the absence of human reason is not a human community at all, but a community of beasts. "El sueño de la razón produce monstruos" (The sleep of reason produces monsters), said Francisco Goya in 1799.[2] Victor Hugo wrote "the volcano enlightens, the morning sun still enlightens better."[3] While human will inflames, human reason enlightens. Human reason is not justice's bête noire, but its head and soul. Justice is not the reign of terror, but the rule of wisdom, truth, and good.

Truth is justice's blood, and human reason, its head. As rationality, human reason brings to human justice several properties:

- authentic reality
- justified form and structure
- justified norms and standards
- justified principles, grammar, and maxims
- real value and meaning
- true unity and coherence
- consistency and integrity

Reality, form, structure, norm, standard, grammar, maxim, value, meaning, unity, coherence, consistency, and integrity are indispensable for true justice, and none of them can exist in justice without human reason; otherwise they would not be reasonable, let alone justified. As a faculty, human reason is the author, administrator, judge, and guardian of justice. As natural light, human reason illuminates justice. It is by human reason that we reject religious fundamentalism as insane, international terrorism as mad, and new imperialism as absurd. It is in terms of human reason that we call for global peace, global democracy, and the global family of humanity. It is on human reason that we evoke global justice implicating norms of global duty and obligation of humankind and a global standard of acceptability of basic human institutions and human conduct in the human family.

Normative justice implies the rule of human reason. While human rights are the righteous reasons to treat human beings in a certain way, human reason as a faculty is the administrator, judge, and guardian of human rights. Human reason as rationality justifies human rights as the righteous reasons; human reason as the natural light enlightens human rights as the righteous reasons. While human goods and humanity as the end are righteous reasons for human beings to act or abstain from action, human reason as a faculty is the administrator, judge, and guardian of human goods and humanity as the end, and human reason as rationality justifies human goods and humanity as the righteous reasons to act or abstain from action. Human reason as the natural light enlightens human goods and humanity as the righteous reasons. While human bonds are righteous reasons for human beings to act or abstain from action, human reason as a faculty is the administrator, judge, and guardian of human bonds, and human reason as rationality justifies human bonds to be the righteous reasons to act or abstain from action. Human reason as the natural light enlightens human bonds as the righteous reasons.

Normative justice *par reason* brings home the truth that Isaiah Berlin keenly observes: "Man is, above all, a creature endowed not only with reason but with will. Will is the creative function of man."[4] In justice, reason establishes an outstanding working relationship with will: reason brings normativity; will produces novelty. While reason can benefit from will's Leonian creativity, will becomes fruitful through reason's Aquarian vision and rationality. Reason carries with it the enduring. Will consists of spontaneity. If human history is a perpetual saga of normativity and novelty or creativity, it is also an enduring romance of reason and will. Justice is the righteous union of reason and will in which will's artistic urge of creation is united with reason's "artistic cruelty"; will's Leonian desire for novelty is married to reason's Aquarian aspiration for rationality. Creativity is not an enemy of structure. Nor is normativity the foe of creativity. The planets Saturn and Uranus do not block the sun. Instead, each shines more brilliantly in the other's company in the cosmos. The Socratic dream of justice in which philosophical wisdom is integrated with political power is still enlightening and inspiring today. Reason is still justice's immortal soul and head.

Justice brings about the perfect marriage of humankind's Leonian creativity and Aquarian normativity. Normative justice choreographs human will's passionate ballet with human reason's graceful principles of human rights, goods, and bonds, rejecting the perverting voices of power, force, greed, desires, and interests. It orchestrates human will's sensational opera with human reason's enduring themes of rights, humanity as the end, goods, and bonds, rejecting the perverting sounds of power, force, greed, desires, terror, and interests. While justice is reason's answer to the sabotage of powers, greed, desires, and interests, normative justice is human reason's rejection of perversion and subversion of humanity by powers, greed, desires, interests, and bestiality.

The rule of human reason in justice is not the same as the rule of the absolute. Human reason sets human affairs right in terms of historical and developing universal norms and standards. True, human reason makes universal claims. However, the claims of human reason are not absolute; they can be revised in the future. It is proper to recall one of Michael Walzer's arguments here. Walzer points out:

> No architect, for example, aims to design the last building (not even the last church or school) and make architecture henceforth unnecessary—even though he aims to get his particular building right. . . . Architecture is a reiterative activity. . . . Criticism is also a reiterative activity.[5]

But no architect can get his particular building right if he or she does not have a "universal building" in mind, that is, what makes a building a building and not a bridge or a stone wall.

Universality connotes timelessness. But timelessness does not mean transcending above and outside all time frames. Instead, it means participating in all times. A universal claim can be timeless in the sense not of transcending above and outside time but of participating in all times, of being "classic." From this perspective, the tyrant of the absolute can be retired, while the leader of the universal and the normative still dances. Similarly, universality does not mean being above and outside all space, but rather participating in all space—for example, not separating from any cultural space, but participating in all cultural space. The universal and normative need not be oppressive and repressive, but can be inclusive and tolerating. Reason's claim on the normativity and universality of justice is a claim not on the distance between justice and space, but on the enduring presence of justice in all space.

It is because of human reason that there can be global justice. Global justice is not the alleged "justice" defined by tanks, missiles, and airplanes. Granted that justice must cross swords with injustice and inhumanity in the globe. Still, what a dreadful absurdity for anyone to think that human affairs can be set right by bullets and bombs! What a gloomy irony that would be, finding the alleged "global justice" to be no longer reasonable anymore! In reality, global justice sets global human affairs right by the unforced power of reason. Human reason leads us to recognize the profound truth and value of global humanity and brings us to meet the standard of global humanity, away from domination, oppression, repression, colonization, and so on. Global justice has the ability of reason to bring about mutual understanding, respect, peace, and cooperation among nations and peoples.

Admittedly, at times, the realization of global justice requires the support of institutional sanctioning forces, which become more and more available. For example, with regard to distributive justice, more and more international legal institutions such as the WTO Dispute Settlement Panels and the Permanent Court of Arbitration and international laws are established today. For global normative justice and global corrective justice, we have international organizations such as the United Nations, the International Court of Justice, and the International Criminal Court, as well as some internationally recognized norms of justice pertaining to human rights and human goods such as the UN Declaration of Human Rights (1948).

Nevertheless, global justice exists first because of human reason, not anything else. International and global institutions are products of and useful auxiliaries to human reason; no question about that. However, it is human reason that establishes the norms and standards of global justice, implicating the global duty of justice. It is human reason that defines certain inhumanities, evils, and crimes against humanity as global injustices. Basic international and global institutions are vehicles of human reason to articulate global justice historically.

A note on the relationship between reason and social institutions is in order. Richard Brown indicates: "Social structures canalize rational thought; reasoning creates and recreates social structures. Economic reasoning creates a market system, legal reasoning creates a world of law, and moral discourse creates a moral order."[6] Basic social institutions canalize justice and contribute to its historical development; justice makes social institutions reasonable.

In sum, it is justice, and only justice, that we should follow. Correspondingly, it is human reason, and only human reason, that we should listen to. Normative justice is human reason, more human reason, and always human reason.

Humanity, More Humanity, and Always Humanity

This book has defended both the idea of justice as the rule of humanity and the concept of normative justice—one of the three general families of justice—as setting human affairs right in terms of humanity. The inquiry into justice from the outset has also been informed by the conviction that a true, viable concept of social justice always presupposes as its counterpart a plausible, true concept of humanity; true justice exalts humanity over bestiality and terror. Not only has this conviction been reinforced by the outcome of the inquiry hitherto, but it also has become evident that, in addition to distributive justice and corrective justice, there is the third family of justice: justice in terms of humanity. Justice is humankind's duty, obligation, and path; humanity is justice's home. More crucially, there is a distinctive family of justice that implicates a set of norms of obligations exclusively in terms of human rights, humanity as the end, human goods, and human bonds. This family of justice erects humanity as the end, quality, standard, and ideal for humankind. It dictates a particular class of standards for evaluating basic human institutions and human activities exclusively in terms of the obligation of humankind to humankind. Justice is humanity's triumph over bestiality.

Not surprisingly, at the core of the matter is humankind's humanity identity. Loyalty to this identity makes human beings into humankind in the full sense, which means that the name of humankind names a correspondent reality and substance called humanity. In justice, names always name the profoundest reality and substances. The Chinese word for "justice," *zhengyi*, brings that home. In justice, humankind embodies humanity and righteousness to the extent that humanity stands straight in the human society. Only in this way does the name *humankind* designate the profoundest reality and substance. Thus, humanity is justice's only home, while justice is humankind's only correct path and the crown jewel of duty. Humanity is justice's burden and destiny, while justice is humankind's duty and obligation. Justice is the enduring presence of humanity, and humanity thrives under the guidance of the lasting ideal of justice. While justice dictates the correct way for human beings to interact with one another, humanity indicates the standards for that way.

The idea of humanity contributes to the idea of justice several crucial elements, including the end, purpose, and *telo*; the center of values and substantial content; the subject and object; agency; the source of normativity and obligation; form and structure; substance and character; temperament; and standards. Humanity humanizes justice, while justice civilizes humanity. Immanuel Kant thus says profoundly: "Out of the crooked timber of humanity, nothing straight can be made."[7] When humanity as a quality and principle is crooked, when humanity as the end is crooked, no justice, and nothing righteous and good, can exist. When humanity is not straight, the end, center, subject, object, agency, form, structure, substance, character, temperament, and standard of justice are not straight. Conversely, when justice is crooked, humankind is of crooked end, center, subjectivity, agency, form, structure, substance, character, temperament, and standard of existence.

Copernican astronomy may tell us that it is not the sun that moves around the Earth, but the other way around. Notwithstanding this, humankind is the center of the great cosmic drama of salvation and sin, justice and injustice, good and evil, beauty and ugliness, truth and falsity. Salvation and redemption of humankind is still the central theme of the historical dramas of justice and injustice, good and evil, beauty and ugliness. The resurrection of humanity is still the central theme of the global opera of human civilization. It should strike us as self-evident that the universe is not a problem for humankind; instead, humankind itself is the problem for humankind. The battles are waged between human justice and human injustice, human good and human evil, truth and falsity of humanity, beauty and ugliness of humankind as a species, the human way and the way of bestiality, human aspiration and the bestial propensity. Justice is not about the permanent universe, but about the making and struggling of humanity and humankind.

Therefore, the duty of justice is the duty of humanity, and the duty of humanity is the duty of justice. Injustice is that which perverts humanity. This is why injustice is the greatest evil. And crimes against humanity are paradigms of the greatest evils and belong to the family of the greatest injustice. Justice sets humanity standing straight, and humankind makes justice great. Inhumanity is injustice. Great inhumanity is great injustice.

Normative justice implicates the obligation of humankind to humankind. There are three kinds of obligations:

1. The obligation to respect human dignity, rights, and liberties
2. The obligation to recognize humanity as the end, to serve human goods, and to honor universal human values
3. The obligation of solidarity in the family of humanity—that is, the family of all men and women, the members of a particular community, family, village, city, province, state, nation, or people

The obligation of justice is beyond the requirement of compassions and benevolence. It is unconditional, compulsory, and sanctionable.

It is tempting to succumb to the idea that the norms and standards of justice have been established by a divine power. However, the norms and standards of justice within the human horizon and sphere are human norms and standards that are developed by human beings, for human beings. This is not to say that religious hypostatization of the divine rules is mischievous. Rather it is simply to say that they are human artifacts. The same is true of the philosophical hypostatizations of the rules of justice as the rules of the universe—they are not Newton's apple falling from the heavens, but Beethoven's music composed. Equally crucial, the principles of human rights, human goods (humanity as the end), and human bonds constitute a particularly important, and independent basis for norms of human conduct and standards of evaluating basic social institutions. Thus, while justice civilizes humanity and humankind, humanity humanizes justice among humankind.

The principles of human rights, human goods (humanity as the end), and human bonds implicate a distinctive family of obligations of humankind and human institutions. In turn, this family of obligations serves as a paradigmatic illustration that justice brings human principles, structures, and values to the world; justice brings humanity's Aquarian vision to realization through humanity's Leonian creativity; justice humanly reproduces the human world in terms of humanly interpreted truths, purposes, goods, and beauty from the human perspective; and justice inspires humankind to cultivate itself after the image of truth, good, and beauty.

The rise of global humanity is the rise of global justice, as the eclipse of local humanity is the eclipse of local normative justice. Today, as Tu Weiming observes, "The universality of human rights broadly conceived in the 1948 Declaration is a source of inspiration for the human community."[8] Other international treatises such as the United Nations' Declaration on the Elimination of All Forms of Intolerance and of Discrimination Based on Religion or Belief (1981) and UNESCO's Declaration of Principles of Tolerance (1995) contribute significantly to the rise of global humanity. All these bring new dynamics to global justice and also indicate the great challenges to it. They indicate both the rise of and the challenges to global humanity.

Fundamentally, global justice and global humanity require one another, just as global injustice and global inhumanity imply each other. Global normative justice erects human rights, human goods, humanity as the end, and human bonds in the human family. The gross inhumanity in the world such as gross violation of human rights per se, human enslavement, massacres, genocides, ethnic cleansings, and other crimes against humanity is gross injustice on Earth. Correspondingly, the call for global justice to defend humanity and stop crimes against humanity is not a call of humanitarian morality or a demand of practical necessity, but the mandate of global humanity. Global peace and cooperation are summoned because they are the instruments for global justice in terms of global humanity. Global toleration, inclusion, and democracy are called today because they can be instrumental to global justice in terms of humanity.

The drive for global justice, especially global normative justice, revives the promise of the Kantian cosmopolitan republican order in which humanity is the end and, in comparison to humanity as the end, the sovereignty of a nation or a people is secondary. Without humanity as the end, the people as the end, there can be no true sovereignty of a nation or a people. Real sovereignty does not lie in the fact that a nation has a clear border, but in the fact that a people truly stands up, that the humanity of a people truly stands straight.

In short, justice is for and of humanity, and humanity demands justice. Justice is humankind's path, and humanity, its home. While justice civilizes humankind, humanity humanizes justice. Justice exalts nations, peoples, and individuals, and they in turn contribute to expand justice. While justice obliges nations, peoples, and individuals, humanity is the obligation of justice. Normative justice is about humanity, more humanity, and always humanity. Global normative justice is about global humanity, more global humanity, and always global humanity.

Harmony, More Harmony, and Always Harmony

This book aims at restoring the idea of justice as social harmony. The inquiry into justice has from the outset been further informed by the Confucian-Taoist-Platonic conviction that justice brings social harmony. Not only has this conviction been reinforced by the outcome of the inquiry hitherto, but it also has become evident that, while social justice brings social harmony in a normal society, global justice brings global harmony of humanity on Earth.

Both the concept of social harmony and the concept of the harmony of humanity worldwide are of greater importance today. Peace, cooperation, and humanity are inseparable in a just globalization.

It may sound out of season to talk about justice bringing about social harmony in a postmodern climate, amid the irreducible cultural diversity today. However, our only hope springs from our only challenge, just as our only love may spring from our only hate. These should strike us as self-evident:

1. Justice implicates basic principles, norms, and standards of regulating basic human institutions and existence.
2. These principles, norms, and standards are reasonable, consistent with truth, good, and beauty.
3. These principles, norms, and standards set human affairs right in the world and bring order, cooperation, reasonable peace, and stable communal relationships to a normal human society.

It should also strike us as self-evident that it makes no sense for us to say that setting human affairs right brings not harmony, but discord; not order, but chaos; not peace, but conflict into a normal human world. Moreover, if in justice, the profoundest truth of humanity stands straight and righteousness stands straight, then humanity stands straight. And when humanity stands straight, harmony among humankind exists. Since things that are self-evident and relevant normally provide the most solid and reasonable argument and justification, the idea that justice brings about social harmony is solidly, reasonably defended here.

Philosophers today, including John Rawls, would like to evoke the concept of well-ordered society instead of a harmonious one. There can in fact be differences between these two concepts, but both lead to some of the same ideas:

1. In a just society, there is a good, stable social order.
2. In a just society, all reasonable human members value mutual cooperation and desire to extend their lives together in a well-defined public framework or scheme.
3. In a just society, there is most reasonable social cooperation on a great scale and most general level.

Berlin argues, "The notion of a harmonious solution of the problems of mankind, even in principle, and therefore the very principle of Utopia, is incompatible with the interpretation of the human world as a battle of perpetually new and ceaselessly conflicting wills, individual or collective."[9] Berlin's view is both instructive and flawed. It is instructive because a harmonious, final solution of all problems of mankind is not feasible; every solution of humankind in a given historical context is inevitably historical. However, humankind can reasonably, rationally resolve its problems to the extent that the human world becomes more harmonious (than it was before) and minimally harmonious in a given historical circumstance.

A harmonious solution need not be a final solution, but can be a historical solution. A historical just world need not be like Grecian art in which there is glamour and a perfection of symmetry. However, a just world has harmony and unity. Justice sets things right. When things are set right and fit into their space and times, the harmony and unity of the world arise. Just as the rule of reason and the rule of humanity are not the rule of the absolute, the aspiration for justice as social harmony is not an aspiration for the absolute.

In the human world, there is a constant battle of perpetually new and ceaselessly conflicting wills, individual or collective. There are always competitions and rivalries among various Leonian creations and among various Aquarian visions. There are also always conflicts of interests, desires, passions, and cravings. Still, a historical solution of human conflicts is possible and a relatively harmonious human world can be created by continuous historical solution of human problems and conflicts. Historical, social harmony can be constantly achieved historically, and justice as setting human affairs right is meant constantly to bring social harmony to humankind historically.

Georg W. F. Hegel and Karl Marx might have wrongly believed that "there is a march of history—a single ascent of mankind from Barbarism to rational organization."[10] However, the progress of humankind in history indeed involves marches from barbarism to humanity along different avenues. There is no incompatibility between the concept of justice as social harmony and the concept of the human world full of perpetually new and conflicting human wills, individual or collective. Social harmony brings to a normal society amid diversity several necessary conditions of stability and endurance:

1. It makes it possible for that which differs from one another to mutually grow with one another, not destroy one another, turning diversity into social theater, not a "black hole."
2. It makes it possible for that which differs from one another to enhance, not hinder, one another, turning diversity into a strength, not an Achilles' heel.

3. It makes it possible for that which differs from one another to mutually cooperate and coordinate with one another, not be at odds with
one another, turning diversity into a symbol of beauty, not a sign of
ugliness.

The concept of social harmony does not connote some kind of timeless
serenity, but rather indicates a kind of reasonable unity, peace, and stability.
Meanwhile, the concept of social harmony is broader than the concept of
social cooperation. Social harmony implies social cooperation, but is more
than that. It presupposes the existence of true communal bonds among the
members of a human community and the existence of a communal *ethnos*.
By true communal bonds, I mean the kind of bonds consisting of familial,
neighborly, social-structural, cultural, and nation-people connections.

While social harmony is the goal, social toleration and democracy are the
timely vehicles of justice in our time. In a world of diversity, social toleration
and democracy are crucial and necessary to bring about social harmony. In
turn, whether they are able to bring about social harmony is an important
criteria and standard to judge whether they are good or bad. The kind of social toleration that creates and accelerates division, antagonism, and discord
should be rejected as bad. A form of democracy that creates and accelerates
division, antagonism, and discord should be rejected as a bad form of democracy. Social toleration, true and stable social toleration, just and enduring social toleration—that is the challenge of our time! Democracy, true and stable
democracy, just and enduring democracy—that is the challenge of our time!

Communal bonds are part of our human identity, that is, part of the identity of us as the kind of persons that we know. Accordingly, loyalty to these
bonds is an obligation to us, and justice means giving these bonds their due
claims. Part of the due claims of these bonds is the claim that we must preserve such bonds in stable, historically harmonious conditions. The concept
of social harmony brings home our sense of our social identity and social
obligation. It indicates that justice is proper loyalty to such a social identity
and faithful fulfillment of such social obligation.

The idea that justice brings about harmony of humanity excludes social
oppression, repression, subjugation, and enslavement. Emphasizing social
harmony does not require advocating elimination of differences and diversity.
Instead, it calls for social unity through social toleration and democracy. Normative justice demands respect for difference, even if some differences may be
incompatible. Justice demands us to have a humanistic attitude toward difference, being both tolerant of another's way of thought and responsible for the
consequence of one's own cognitive and moral choices. Meanwhile, normative

justice reminds us of the rule of *wu ji bi fan* (物极必反). It reminds us of the limit of diversity and difference as much as the limit of sameness and identity. Therefore, social toleration and democracy are desirable for justice, though they have their limits. Social toleration and democracy bring social inclusion, integration, and unity without oppression, repression, and subjugation. At the same time, the forms and limits of social toleration and democracy must be appropriate to bring social harmony to a normal society.

In short, resolving social conflicts, overcoming social evils, and affirming basic humanity are among the tasks of normative justice. Accordingly, securing global peace, promoting just globalization and democratization, and developing global harmony of humankind are among the tasks of global justice. Regulation of global affairs among nations and peoples, elimination of global conditions of human destruction, reinvention of universal human bonds, and creation of an atmosphere of global human harmony—these are among the tasks and challenges of global justice.

This amounts to saying that global justice means turning a world in which human beings know each no more into a world in which human beings know each as neighbors, turning a world in which exploitation is the form, "justice" is the stronger's interests and desires, and power and domination are the watchwords into a world in which the rise of global humanity, global cooperation, and the development of nations and peoples are not merely ideals, but realities.

Justice brings out social harmony. Social harmony realizes justice. Global justice brings about global security, peace, and cooperation. Global democratic cooperation facilitates conditions to realize global justice. Justice harmonizes humankind in the world. Social harmony among human beings indicates the glory of the crown of justice.

Conclusion

The conclusion of this book boils down to three central concepts:

1. *Normative justice.* Justice is setting human affairs right in terms of human rights, human goods (humanity as the end), and human bonds. Justice makes the truth of humanity shine and erects humanity as a substance and value. Accordingly, global normative justice sets global human affairs right in terms of human rights, human goods (humanity as the end), and human bonds.
2. *Normative justice singles out a distinctive family of obligations of humankind to humankind.* Normative justice establishes a distinctive family of

standards of evaluating human practices and institutions. Global normative justice is a distinctive family of global justice, and global human rights–centered politics in global affairs in our time is defended.

3. *Human justice has exclusive priority among all possible classes of justice in our social, moral, and political consideration.* Human justice is the only justice in the universe that is really within the human horizon, that really matters to us, and that is really meaningful to us. Justice for all is justice only for all human beings, not for all species of beings.

In connection with the above, this book demonstrates that social toleration and democracy can be instrumentally valuable in our age; they can be the timely vehicles of normative justice. Social toleration is the song with all the colors of the mountains and rivers; democracy, the rose with thorns.

"Justice is the crowning glory of virtues," said Cicero millennia ago. But the road to this crowning glory is still long and uneven for humankind. The road is long, and the burden heavy—this is the challenge for humankind's search for the true, full justice in the world today.

Notes

1. Richard J. Bernstein, *New Constellation: The Ethical-Political Horizons of Modernity/Postmodernity* (Cambridge, MA: MIT Press, 1992), 32.

2. David Couzens Hoy and Thomas McCarthy, *Critical Theory* (Cambridge, MA: Blackwell, 1994), 1.

3. Victor Hugo, *Les Misérables* (New York: Modern Library, 1992), 564.

4. Isaiah Berlin, *The Crooked Timber of Humanity* (Princeton, NJ: Princeton University Press, 1997), 41.

5. Michael Walzer, *Thick and Thin* (Notre Dame, IN: University of Notre Dame Press, 1994), 52.

6. Richard H. Brown, *Society as Text* (Chicago: University of Chicago Press, 1987), 77.

7. "Aus so krummem Holze, als woraus der Mensch gemacht ist, kann nichts ganz gerades gezimmert warden." Immanuel Kant, *Gesammelte Schriften* (Berlin: de Gruyter, 1923), 8:23; cited in Berlin, *Crooked Timber of Humanity*, v, xi.

8. Tu Weiming, "Epilogue: Human Rights as a Confucian Moral Discourse," in *Confucianism and Human Rights*, ed. Wm. Theodore de Bary and Tu Weiming (New York: Columbia University Press, 1998), 297.

9. Berlin, *Crooked Timber of Humanity*, 44.

10. Ibid.

Index

absolute, 88, 168–69, 175, 180
Arendt, Hannah, 71
Aristotle, 49, 108, 140, 143, 149
asymmetry, 1, 57, 78, 131, 146, 180

Bacon, Francis, 2
bao zheng (暴政), 34–36, 63, 139, 144
Barry, Brian, 12
beauty, 2, 7, 15, 162, 166, 171–72, 174, 176
benevolence, 45, 55, 69–71, 100, 107–8, 110, 113, 115, 120, 125, 134, 172
Berlin, Isaiah, 18, 95, 122, 126, 167
bestiality, 5–6, 14–15, 51, 55, 73, 101, 168, 170–71
bond, 2, 5, 12, 14–17, 22, 49–59, 62–65, 67–71, 73–74, 77–80, 83–85, 94, 96–97, 145, 147, 149, 152, 155–59, 161–62, 165, 167–68, 170, 172–73, 176–77; of humanity, 87; communal, 58, 64, 67, 77, 96, 161, 176; human, 5, 12, 14–17, 22, 49–58, 62–75, 78–80, 83–87, 94, 96, 118, 145, 147, 156–57, 161, 165, 167, 170, 172–73, 177; moral, 57; national, 84

Burke, Edmund, 2

causality, 15, 95
Chun Qiu Zheng Yi (<<春秋正义>>), 22
Ci Yuan (<<词源>>), 22
Cicero, 3, 178
Cohen, Joshua, 59, 82, 157–58, 164
colonization, 16, 84, 124–25, 156, 169
communitarianism, 57
Condorcet, Marquis de (Marie-Jean-Antoine-Nicolas de Caritat), 146
Confucius, 6, 22–23, 25–26, 28, 31–32, 34–35, 38, 45, 62–63, 95, 140, 165
contractualism, 58
contradiction, 1, 3, 43,111
cruelty, 1, 71, 101; the artistic, 7, 132, 168

dao (道), 12, 23–24, 26–34, 36, 38, 45, 76, 87–88, 113–14, 120–21, 128, 165
Dao De Jing (<<道德经>>), 18, 124, 29, 46, 113–14, 128
democracy, 1–2, 17, 83, 100, 125, 131–62; democratic centralism, 135–36; global, 132, 156–60, 167;

179

liberal, 125, 150–52; republican, 150; procedural, 149–52, 154

demos, 132, 149

Deschamps, Eustache, 2

dignity, 8, 30, 44, 51–52, 61, 63–68, 73–74, 77–78, 84, 108, 112, 122, 132, 156, 172

diversity, 12, 36, 41, 44, 93, 95–96, 121–22, 124–26, 132, 140, 148, 151, 154–56, 161, 166, 174–77

domination, 1, 15, 74, 84, 109–20,

duty, 2–16, 23, 35, 41, 44–45, 51, 53, 55–85, 94–95, 99, 105–6, 115, 126, 136, 139, 155, 161, 165, 171; of justice, 2, 5–7, 10, 17, 45, 51, 56, 60, 71, 87, 126, 169, 171; of humanity, 73, 171; ontological, 17, 45

Einstein, Albert, 7, 17

enslavement, 74, 80, 173, 176

equality, 17, 81, 125, 140, 148, 152–53, 161–66

ethnos, 132, 149–50, 155, 176

evil, 1, 5, 15–16, 22, 24, 26–30, 33–34, 37, 45, 54, 63–64, 68, 70, 71–75, 83, 98, 144, 125–26, 132, 149, 156–57, 169, 171, 177

exploitation, 1, 15, 74, 108, 177

falsity, 1, 13, 15, 28, 30, 45, 144, 171

family, 5–6, 12, 14–15, 40, 49–50, 52–55, 62–63, 66–68, 73, 77, 80, 82–83, 85, 87, 144–45, 155, 158–59, 165, 167, 170–73, 177–78; of humanity, 5–6, 159, 167, 169, 172; global, 158–59, 167

fitness, 22, 24–25, 29–30, 33, 36, 38

Foucault, Michel, 118

globalization, 1, 83–84, 87, 121, 124, 132, 156, 165, 174, 177

good, 1, 5, 8, 11–17, 22–23, 27–30, 32, 41–42, 44–45, 49–57, 61, 63, 66–67, 70–72, 75, 77–78, 93, 97–98, 101–4, 111, 116, 118, 122, 125, 131–32, 139, 142–62, 165–77

Guanzi (<<管子>>), 23, 33, 38

Habermas, Jürgen, 9, 13–14, 41–43, 47, 60–61, 69–70,81, 94, 96, 100–3, 107, 111, 116–17, 119–20, 149–52, 154–55, 160

harmony, 17, 24, 65, 125, 132, 136, 140, 142–43, 173

Hegel, Georg W. F., 2, 10–11, 74, 114, 116, 146, 175

hegemony, 1, 83, 124–25

heretic, the, 24, 28

Horton, John, 98, 102, 105–7

Huai Nan Zi (<<淮南子>>), 22, 24, 33

humanity, 1–36, 49–88, 170–73; crimes against, 54–56, 58, 71, 73–76, 81–83, 101, 123, 157–58, 169, 171, 173; global, 173, 177; universal, 58, 61, 78–79

Hume, David, 146

Huntington, Samuel P., 121–22

identity, 6, 12, 14–15, 56–57, 63, 68–69, 74, 76, 87–88, 145, 150, 155, 165, 170, 176–77; humanity, 6, 12, 14–15, 63, 176

imperialism, 1, 15–16, 84, 123, 125, 167

inclusion, 12, 83–85, 109–10, 120, 150–52, 155–58, 160–73, 177, 180

inhumanity, 2, 16, 35, 72–73, 75, 82, 84, 171, 173

integration, 154–56, 158, 161, 177

inviolability, 61–62, 64–66

James, William, 116, 188

justice, 1–18, 21–22, 28–45, 49–88, 93, 97–99, 117–26, 131–39, 146–54, 156–61, 165–78; corrective, 12, 14–15, 49–50, 52–54, 57, 60, 62, 71, 80–84, 87, 158, 165, 169–70;

daoyi (道义), 26, 28; distributive, 12, 14–15, 49–50, 52–54, 57, 59–60, 62, 80–82, 84–85, 87, 139, 148, 158, 165, 169–70; global, 81, 177–78; normative, 14–17, 49–50, 52–62, 65–71, 74–77, 79–80, 148, 158, 165, 169–70

justification, 10–11, 43, 50, 55, 57, 80, 94–97, 99, 102, 142, 149, 174

Kant, Immanuel, 3, 6, 51, 58, 60–61, 74, 146, 159, 171, 173
Kong Zi Jia Yu (<<孔子家语>>), 34
Kong Zi Zheng Yi (<<孔子正义>>), 22
Korsgaard, Christine M., 6, 51, 56–57, 69

liberalism, 57–58, 148–49
li yi fen shu (理一分殊), 36–37, 40–42, 44
Locke, John, 99, 146–47
loyalty, 13–14, 23, 29, 56, 58, 60–62, 67–68, 74–77, 84, 116–20, 125, 145, 151, 159, 165, 170, 170

Marcuse, Herbert, 94,
Mencius, 6, 22–25, 27–28, 32, 35, 63–65
Mill, John Stuart, 5, 38
morality, the humanitarian, 14–15, 45, 54–55, 69–71, 80, 85–87, 126, 165, 173

Nagel, Thomas, 45, 55, 56, 58–59, 79–82
Newton, Isaac, 7, 9, 172
Nietzsche, Friedrich, 7, 18, 132
nude zheng (虐政), 34–36, 63, 139, 144

objectification, 74
obligation, 2, 5–8, 14–15, 41–42, 44–45, 49–52, 54–61, 66–69, 71, 75, 79–87, 93–94, 96–97, 105, 115, 125, 125–26, 136, 161, 165, 167, 170–73, 176–77

oppression, 34–36, 41–42, 63, 71, 95, 106, 108, 113, 118–20, 124–25, 135–36, 166, 169, 176–77
orthodox, the, 22, 24, 37, 118
outlook, 6, 8, 11, 59, 79–81, 86, 11; cosmopolitan, 6, 8, 11, 59, 79–81, 86; political, 8, 79, 81, 86

Pascal, Blaise, 68, 78
patriotism, constitutional, 151–52, 155
Pericles, 140–42
perversion, 27–30, 45, 70–72, 74
Plato, 7, 9–10, 31, 35, 42, 140–44, 146–47, 163, 173
pluralism, 125, 142
Pogge, Thomas, 59

qing yi (情义), 22
quan (权), 36–42, 47

rape of Nanjing, 2
rationality, 7, 9–12, 31–32, 34, 36, 74, 102, 117, 120, 134, 150–51, 153, 161, 166–68,
Rawls, John, 9, 16, 19, 43, 47, 58, 60–61, 97–98, 148–49, 153, 174
reason, 17, 59, 69, 70, 75, 86, 91, 110
reciprocity, 17, 59, 69, 70, 75, 86, 91, 110
rights, 1, 3, 8, 12, 14–18, 41, 49–57, 61, 64–66, 68–71, 73, 76, 77–85, 93–94, 96, 97, 99, 101, 104, 107, 108, 109, 113, 115, 117–18, 122–24, 132, 134, 136–40, 142-45, 147–53, 156–59, 161–65, 167–70, 172–73, 177
Rorty, Richard, 9, 75–76
Rousseau, Jean-Jacques, 99
Royce, Josiah, 58, 60–62

Sabel, Charles, 59, 82, 157
Scanlon, Thomas, 56–57, 88, 94, 96, 98–100, 107–8, 115, 154

Smith, Carl, 159
solidarity, 4, 14, 60–61, 122, 145, 155, 161, 172
stability, 17, 112–14, 122, 136, 138, 175–76
subjectification, 74
subjugation, 71

terrorism, 1, 15, 17, 77, 83, 95, 98, 101, 106, 167
tolerance, 11–12, 15–17, 41, 63, 93–126, 172; intellectual, 11
toleration, 2, 6, 11–12, 15–17, 41, 84, 93–126, 131, 138–39, 146, 150, 152, 154, 160–61,166, 173, 176–78; global, 173; intellectual, 11
totalitarianism, 15, 17, 42, 106, 119, 124, 135, 166
trust, 22, 32, 62–63, 99, 116, 118, 136, 144, 146, 149, 161–62
truth, 1–5, 8–10, 12–13, 15, 17, 22–24, 26, 28–30, 33, 36, 37–45, 49–54, 64–65, 68, 74, 79, 87, 106, 108–9, 111, 116–20, 124–25, 132, 140, 147, 151, 154–55, 161, 166–67, 169, 171–72, 174, 177

universality, 4, 8, 38, 140, 168–69, 172
utilitarianism, 57–58

value, 2, 8–9, 10, 12–13, 17, 34, 37, 42–44, 50–52, 54, 56-57, 61, 66–69, 71, 73–74, 76–77, 83, 88, 90, 93–98, 101, 106, 108–9, 111–13, 118, 121, 123–25, 131, 134, 136, 139–40, 142, 145, 147–49, 152–53, 155, 160–61, 167, 169, 171, 172, 174; instrumental, 95–96, 112, 131, 147; intrinsic, 17, 56, 61, 67, 95, 112, 147; primary, 112; secondary, 112
virtue, 1, 3, 5–6, 8, 23, 29, 45, 51, 57, 59–62, 70, 83, 93–94, 96, 99, 105–6, 110, 111, 119, 140, 142, 145, 154, 165, 178
Voltaire (François-Maric Arouet), 98, 103, 146

Walzer, Michael, 16, 94–95, 107–8,
"Warsaw Declaration," the, 140
Williams, Bernard, 16, 56, 76, 94
Wolff, Robert P., 125

Xunzi, 22–23, 25–28,

yi bu rong ci (义不容辞), 8, 45
yin zheng (淫政), 34–36, 63, 139, 144

Zeitgeist, 2, 41, 88
Zhuxi, 22–23, 26, 33–34, 36

About the Author

Xunwu Chen, PhD, is an associate professor in the Department of English, Classics, and Philosophy at the University of Texas at San Antonio (UTSA). Dr. Chen received his BA in philosophy from Zhongshan University, Guangzhou, China, after which he taught as a lecturer at Southwestern University of Finance and Economics, Chengdu, China. He received his PhD in philosophy from Fordham University, after which he spent two years in the Department of Eastern Asian Language and Civilization at Harvard University as a postdoctoral research associate. Dr. Chen spent a year at the Eastern Asian Institute of Columbia University and a half-year in the Philosophy Department at New York University as a visiting scholar. He joined the faculty at UTSA in January 1998, first as a visiting assistant professor, and then as an assistant professor, and now an associate professor.

Dr. Chen is the author of *Being and Authenticity* (2004) and several journal articles, including "The Human Voice of Justice" (*Journal of Chinese Philosophy*, 2007), "Moral Reason and Feeling: Confucianism and Contractualism" (*Journal of Chinese Philosophy*, 2002), "A Hermeneutic Reading of Confucianism" (*Journal of Chinese Philosophy*, 2001), "Rationalism and Equalitarianism: The Yin-Yang Dialectic of Chinese Struggle for Democracy" (*Asian Thought and Society*, 2000), and "Conflict and Constellation: The New Trend of Value Conflict in China" (*Journal of Value Inquiry*, 1997). He also has a book in Chinese, *On Habermas* (2007).

From December 2001 to December 2003, Dr. Chen served as the president of the Association of Chinese Philosophers in (North) America. From July

2004 to July 2007, he served as a member of the Committee on the Status of Asian Philosophies and Asian Philosophers of the American Philosophical Association.